Studies in the Economics

of Income Maintenance

# Studies of Government Finance

## TITLES PUBLISHED

*Federal Fiscal Policy in the Postwar Recessions*, by Wilfred Lewis, Jr.

*Federal Tax Treatment of State and Local Securities*, by David J. Ott and Allan H. Meltzer.

*Federal Tax Treatment of Income from Oil and Gas*, by Stephen L. McDonald.

*Federal Tax Treatment of the Family*, by Harold M. Groves.

*The Role of Direct and Indirect Taxes in the Federal Revenue System*, John F. Due, Editor. A Report of the National Bureau of Economic Research and the Brookings Institution (Princeton University Press).

*The Individual Income Tax*, by Richard Goode.

*Federal Tax Treatment of Foreign Income*, by Lawrence B. Krause and Kenneth W. Dam.

*Measuring Benefits of Government Investments*, Robert Dorfman, Editor.

*Federal Budget Policy*, by David J. Ott and Attiat F. Ott.

*Financing State and Local Governments*, by James A. Maxwell.

*Essays in Fiscal Federalism*, Richard A. Musgrave, Editor.

*Economics of the Property Tax*, by Dick Netzer.

*A Capital Budget Statement for the U.S. Government*, by Maynard S. Comiez.

*Foreign Tax Policies and Economic Growth*, E. Gordon Keith, Editor. A Report of the National Bureau of Economic Research and the Brookings Institution (Columbia University Press).

*Defense Purchases and Regional Growth*, by Roger E. Bolton.

*Federal Budget Projections*, by Gerhard Colm and Peter Wagner. A Report of the National Planning Association and the Brookings Institution.

*Corporate Dividend Policy*, by John A. Brittain.

*Federal Estate and Gift Taxes*, by Carl S. Shoup.

*Federal Tax Policy*, by Joseph A. Pechman.

*Economic Behavior of the Affluent*, by Robin Barlow, Harvey E. Brazer, and James N. Morgan.

*Intergovernmental Fiscal Relations in the United States*, by George F. Break.

*Studies in the Economics of Income Maintenance*, Otto Eckstein, Editor.

# Studies in the Economics

# of Income Maintenance

OTTO ECKSTEIN, *Editor*

GREENWOOD PRESS, PUBLISHERS
WESTPORT, CONNECTICUT

**Library of Congress Cataloging in Publication Data**

Eckstein, Otto, ed.
    Studies in the economics of income maintenance.

    Reprint of the ed. published by Brookings Institution,
Washington, in series: Studies of government finance.
    Includes bibliographical references and index.
    1.  Social security--United States--Case studies.
2.  Income maintenance programs--Case studies.
3.  Social security--Case studies.  I.  Title.  II.  Series: Studies of government finance.
    [HD7125.E23  1977]    368.4'008    77-592
    ISBN 0-8371-9488-1

© 1967 by

## THE BROOKINGS INSTITUTION
*1775 Massachusetts Avenue, N.W., Washington, D.C.*

Originally published in 1967 by The Brookings Institution,
Washington

Reprinted with the permission of The Brookings Institution

Reprinted in 1977 by Greenwood Press, Inc.

Library of Congress catalog card number 77-592

ISBN 0-8371-9488-1

Printed in the United States of America

THE BROOKINGS INSTITUTION is an independent organization devoted to nonpartisan research, education, and publication in economics, government, foreign policy, and the social sciences generally. Its principal purposes are to aid in the development of sound public policies and to promote public understanding of issues of national importance.

The Institution was founded December 8, 1927, to merge the activities of the Institute for Government Research, founded in 1916, the Institute of Economics, founded in 1922, and the Robert Brookings Graduate School of Economics and Government, founded in 1924.

The general administration of the Institution is the responsibility of a self-perpetuating Board of Trustees. The trustees are likewise charged with maintaining the independence of the staff and fostering the most favorable conditions for creative research and education. The immediate direction of the policies, program, and staff of the Institution is vested in the President, assisted by the division directors and an advisory council, chosen from the professional staff of the Institution.

In publishing a study, the Institution presents it as a competent treatment of a subject worthy of public consideration. The interpretations and conclusions in such publications are those of the author or authors and do not purport to represent the views of the other staff members, officers, or trustees of the Brookings Institution.

# Foreword

GOVERNMENTAL POLICIES to improve the well-being of low income persons have come under increasing scrutiny in recent years, as the nation's economic growth has increased. The objective of this new interest is to evaluate the effectiveness of current programs and to suggest new approaches that might help to achieve a more rational system of income maintenance.

This volume presents four studies designed to shed light on the determinants and effectiveness of several present income maintenance programs. The first study—consisting of the two chapters by Henry Aaron—compares the level of benefits and the scope of coverage of income maintenance programs in twenty-two industrialized countries, and then investigates the history of adjustments in benefits under this country's Social Security system. The second study, by Charles Warden, Jr., attempts to account for the distribution of the costs of unemployment insurance according to the type of unemployment (seasonal, cyclical, irregular, and long-term) experienced by beneficiaries. The third study, by Lora S. Collins, measures the strength of socioeconomic influences on the level of expenditures of four public assistance and all general assistance programs. The final study, by John W. Dorsey, analyzes the economic adjustments and re-employment problems encountered by a group of industrial workers after the relocation of their plant.

The studies were originally prepared as doctoral dissertations at Harvard University, under the direction of Otto Eckstein, who also wrote the introductory chapter of this volume.

The manuscript was reviewed by a reading committee consisting of Eveline Burns of Columbia University, Louis Shere of Indiana University, Robert Lampman of the University of Wisconsin, and Ida C. Merriam of the Social Security Administration. The authors wish to express their appreciation for the helpful comments of this committee, and for the assistance of Professor Eckstein and others, including Mrs. Merriam, who advised both Henry Aaron and Lora S. Collins; Mrs. Ellen J. Perkins of the Social Security Administration, who also assisted Miss Collins; Edward Barker, Information Officer of the Massachusetts Division of Employment Security, who gave valuable aid to Charles Warden, Jr.; and John Dunlop of Harvard University, Raymond Male, New Jersey Commissioner of Labor and Industry, and David Brown, coordinator of the New Jersey Employment Service's "Mack Project," who assisted John W. Dorsey. The manuscript was edited by Verrick O. French and Charlene Semer. Mrs. Semer also prepared the index.

This project was part of a special program of research and education on taxation and public expenditures, supervised by the National Committee on Government Finance and financed by a special grant from the Ford Foundation.

The views expressed in this book are those of the authors and are not presented as the views of the institutions with which the authors are affiliated, or the views of the National Committee on Government Finance or its Advisory Committee, or the staff members, officers, or trustees of the Brookings Institution, or the Ford Foundation.

Robert D. Calkins
*President*

*November 1966*
*Washington, D.C.*

## Studies of Government Finance

Studies of Government Finance is a special program of research and education in taxation and government expenditures at the federal, state, and local levels. These studies are under the supervision of the National Committee on Government Finance appointed by the trustees of the Brookings Institution, and are supported by a special grant from the Ford Foundation.

# MEMBERS OF THE ADVISORY COMMITTEE

# Contents

*Authors' Tables and Charts*

*Aaron*

OTTO ECKSTEIN*

# Introduction

As MODERN ECONOMIES have advanced, governments have accepted increasing responsibility for maintaining the incomes of people who do not have the ability to earn an adequate income through their own efforts. People beyond the working age, the disabled, the involuntarily unemployed, dependent children and their families, and other people with little or no incomes have received rising amounts of social insurance and public assistance. In 1966, it is estimated that these income maintenance payments will total about $35 billion in the United States, representing 17 percent of all public expenditures, and 4.6 percent of gross national income. With medical insurance for older persons now added to the scope of protection and a larger fraction of the population reaching the retirement age, these expenditures are likely to take a rising share of our gross national income.

The United States has taken two broadly different approaches to income maintenance. On the one hand, there are large programs of social insurance, financed by earmarked payroll taxes with benefits fixed by formula and without any suggestion of "charity." These include the Federal Old-Age, Survivors, and Disability Insurance system and unemployment insurance.

The other approach is public assistance, which is wholly based on need and financed out of general revenues. Public assistance is

* Harvard University.

given on a "case" basis, with each recipient's "need" determined by budget studies of living costs and analyses of his resources. Usually, social workers are assigned to each case to certify the "need" and to give advice to the recipient in an effort to promote his restoration to a productive life where possible, to bring his family in contact with available social services, and to help improve living conditions.

Although both systems effect great redistributions of income and are major instruments of social policy, public assistance has proved to be the more controversial. Social insurance is not a burden on the general funds of the government or on the general (mainly income) tax base. Because of the "earned" nature of the benefits, few people question the propriety of the payments. It has been hoped that the social insurance systems would take over more and more of the task of income maintenance.

The biggest of the social insurance programs—the Federal Old-Age, Survivors, and Disability Insurance System—is national in scope, with the same rules and formulas applying throughout the country. Public assistance programs, on the other hand, are administered by states and localities, although more than half of all of their financing derives from matching grants-in-aid of the federal government. Unemployment insurance is a joint federal-state activity, with the federal government administering tax collections, paying the costs of administration, and setting down some of the rules, but leaving most decisions about levels of benefits, criteria for eligibility, and to some degree the payroll tax rates, to the discretion of the states.

Although the various programs operating in the United States do not possess organizational unity or a common approach, they have, through repeated revisions and extensions, been gradually shaped into a comprehensive set of measures. Today, most of the major categories of inability to earn income are covered by one program or another.

But there still are important gaps in our income maintenance system. Families suffering from chronic unemployment are ineligible for public assistance in many states. There are only limited provisions against loss of earning power due to temporary disability. There are still many individuals and families who receive little help because they do not know how to seek it or who are poor for such reasons as mental illness, alcoholism, or drug addiction. There are also great variations in the intensity of effort with which communities search out the people who need help. Most importantly, there are still millions of people in families headed by workers who have jobs that yield an income too low to lift the family out of poverty.

Our income maintenance systems have other weaknesses. The levels of benefits are frequently inadequate: social insurance benefits have not kept pace with the rise of real incomes in our society; public assistance benefits vary widely among states and among categories of low-income cases. In comparison to the systems of other advanced countries, those in the United States make less provision for the expenses of illness.

The federal government has placed particular emphasis in the last few years on removal of the causes of poverty, through investment in education and training, promotion of equality of opportunity, and job creation through an expansionary economic policy. In the long term, these measures should produce savings to the government in income maintenance payments and, more importantly, they should serve to confine the payments more and more to individuals that the society would agree ought to remain outside the labor force. As this goal is achieved, it will be possible to conduct a fundamental re-examination of our notions of the adequacy of benefit levels.

In the last year, new proposals have been advanced which would represent major breakthroughs in income maintenance. The Medicare Act has important new benefits which provide some insurance against medical outlays for older people, thereby helping to insure the adequacy of their incomes for their other needs. Now new ideas are beginning to stir which hold the promise of future advances in income maintenance. A variety of "negative income tax" proposals have been advanced as a way to replace or supplement public assistance with pure cash payments based on a formula, thus eliminating most of the subjective elements in the current case-by-case approach, and separating all social service inputs from formula-based money. Some of these proposals would operate through the tax system, by giving refunds for unused exemptions. Other proposals would make cash payments to families based on the gap between their incomes and the poverty income standards defined by the government. Such payments could fill the entire gap between actual incomes and the poverty line—a gap of about $12 billion—or they could fill part of the gap for lesser amounts. Plans can be devised with a wide variety of rate schedules, designed to preserve incentives to earn income. This approach is a reorientation of income maintenance programs toward the specific objective of eliminating poverty. It would assure uniform income-related federal payments regardless of the recipient's location or personal characteristics, and would virtually eliminate subjective administrative discretion. The approach could also be used as a supplement to present programs, providing a floor on which states can build their benefit structures in accordance with their local preferences.

Another major new strand of thinking on income maintenance is the greater use of general revenue financing for social insurance. Exclusive reliance on payroll taxes has meant that the tax burden on wage earners and on wage payers has mounted greatly in recent years, even while other taxes have been cut. The beginnings of financing of social insurance out of general revenues occurred in the 1965 Medicare program. The definition of the proper role of general financing will pose a key problem in the next few years.

The present volume does not attempt to present a comprehensive survey of American income maintenance programs or of the alternative approaches. Rather it consists of several analyses of particular aspects of the present major programs. Although the improvement of policies is their ultimate aim, these studies are mainly in the positive tradition of economics rather than the normative. Most of the studies use the standard statistical technique of multiple regression. This method conveniently sorts out quantitative relationships and makes possible statistical testing to determine whether the results could be due to chance. The technique does not reveal final causality, however, and judgment must be exercised in interpreting the results. It will be seen in the studies that several of the most interesting results lend themselves to alternative interpretations.

The book cannot pretend to a unity that it does not possess. The studies share a common focus—each being a statistical analysis of some aspect of the economics of income maintenance. But each author has developed his own formulation of his problem and his own framework and technique of analysis.

The remainder of this introductory chapter presents the major conclusions of the individual studies.

## International Comparison of Income Maintenance Expenditures

The first study by Henry Aaron seeks to explain the differences in the levels of overall income maintenance expenditures in twenty-two advanced countries. He finds systematic relationships among objectively measurable variables which account for many of these differences.

The most important single variable is the age of the programs. Countries such as Germany that began to introduce major programs early spend relatively more than the latecomers, such as the United States. This age factor in part represents permanent philosophical differences in attitudes toward state intervention in economic affairs; the more interventionist countries began social welfare programs early. It also reflects the inherent process through which outlays increase as a pension system matures and more people become eligible, as well as the expansion of programs as benefit levels are gradually raised, a larger fraction of the population is given coverage, and the scope of programs is broadened.

The per capita level of national income also accounts for part of the differences. However, the response of income maintenance expenditures to higher income levels is less than proportionate.

Aaron finds in addition that those countries that rely more heavily on general revenues than on earmarked taxes provide relatively less income maintenance, holding other factors constant, than do countries where the reverse is true. The extent of income redistribution is greater if the expenditures are financed out of general revenues, including a progressive income tax. This condition makes for greater opposition to improvements in the systems. General revenue financing also makes it more difficult to develop the programs because the expenditures have to compete with all other expenditures in the budgeting process, and because political opposition to increases is greater. Thus, in a sense, the choice of method of financing is indirectly also a choice between the level of benefits and the extent of insurance against income loss, as opposed to the degree of income redistribution. These findings give pause as this country enters into general revenue financing for the OASDI system.

There is a negative relationship between the extent of social security expenditures and household savings rates. This can be due to two factors: On the one hand, the existence of public pensions reduces the private need for saving for old age. On the other hand, a strong tradition of private saving may reduce the political pressure for public pensions; for example, a country with a long history of inflation and little private saving is likely to make greater use of public pensions. Aaron's study does not permit us to distinguish between these two hypotheses.

Aaron also makes some structural comparisons of social insurance systems in the twenty-two countries: (1) Of the nine countries that have been using financial reserve systems, only the United States puts the entire reserve into government securities or cash. All the other countries make some provision for channeling these public savings into productive investment outlets. (2) The United States relies most heavily on nonstatutory social security schemes, such as employer-sponsored pensions and group insurance. This is one of the explanations of our lesser use of public programs.

## Forms of Pension Escalation and Lifetime Income Redistribution

In all countries public pensions are revised upward periodically. Given the long-term upward trends of prices and of real incomes, such revision has to be undertaken everywhere. In nine of the countries studied by Aaron, revision has been made automatic; four (Belgium, Denmark, Finland, and Sweden) relate pensions automatically to a price index, while four others (Chile, France, Germany, and the Netherlands) adjust pensions on the basis of changes in the wage level so that pensioners automatically participate in the rise of real incomes of workers.

The American system does not have an automatic feature. Instead, Congress revises the statutory benefit schedules every few years. The magnitude of individual benefits has mainly been tied to the employee's contribution levels in the years before his retirement; particularly in the first decades of the system, relatively few years enter into the determination of benefits.

Aaron has computed the income redistributions associated with this system. Because contributions and benefits are collected over many years, redistribution has to be redefined in lifetime rather than annual terms. He finds that:

(1) At this time virtually all beneficiaries receive more benefits than they paid in on an actuarial basis, even allowing for the depreciation of the dollar. This is because none of the people retiring now have contributed over an entire lifetime and because the contribution rates were substantially lower in the earlier years. As long as total receipts and expenditures of the system are about equal and the total number of people participating in the system increases steadily, the actuarial value of an individual's benefits will, in most instances, exceed the value of his contributions.

(2) The ratio of the present value of benefits to the present value of contributions is greatest for the people at the lower end of the income and benefit scales. However, the absolute amount of excess of benefits over contributions increases with income.

(3) Individuals with a rising pattern of income receive a greater net gain than those whose incomes hit a peak early in their working life and then level off or decline. This occurs because benefits are so heavily tied to the contributions in the late years, while contributions are based on earnings over an entire lifetime. Since unskilled workers reach their peak earlier in their working lives than skilled, professional, or white collar workers, this feature of the present system works to their disadvantage.

(4) The Social Security system is unfavorable to working wives by comparison with women who remain at home. Under the present benefit schedules, it is not at all uncommon for a woman who worked many years for a moderate income to find that her benefits as a wife or widow would be greater on the basis of her husband's entitlement than on the basis of her own contributions. Thus, in effect, she receives nothing for her own contributions. If the system is to be based on the insurance principle that there be some relation between contributions and benefits, there is a strong case for giving extra benefits to women who have contributed over a considerable period of years.

## Costs in Massachusetts Unemployment Compensation

The study by Charles Warden, Jr., uses statistical techniques to classify the costs of the unemployment compensation system according to the types of unemployment which cause them. Confining himself to industry data for Massachusetts in the 1947-58 period, he finds that about one-third of all payments were for seasonal unemployment, most of which is predictable and is incurred by a few industries, particularly construction. Cyclical unemployment accounts for another one-third, irregular unemployment for about 15 percent, and unemployment due to the long-term decline of certain industries for 5 to 10 percent. The remaining 10 to 15 percent could not be identified with any particular one of the four types of unemployment.

The unemployment insurance system has had at least three objectives from its inception: maintenance of employee income; stabilization of purchasing power of the economy; and regularization of company employment practices. The extent of stabilization of total purchasing power has been surprisingly low, with no more than 10 percent of recession-induced declines of wages offset by unemployment benefits. This limited response is chiefly due to the relatively low ratio of benefits to earned wages, to short periods of eligibility, and to incomplete coverage of the work force.

Warden's findings partially explain why the frequently proposed improvements in the duration and levels of benefits have not been carried out. If so much of the outlay is absorbed by routine seasonal and irregular unemployment, a major improvement in the benefits would be expensive. If unemployment insurance is to replace a large fraction of income lost due to cyclical changes or to secular industry declines, yet remain at a moderate cost level, the system must carry out more precisely its original intention: to cope with unemployment caused by developments outside the control of the employee and the employer.

## Determinants of Public Assistance Expenditures

The study by Lora S. Collins analyzes a cross section of state data for the several public assistance programs in the United States. The objective of the study is to see if variations among the states in expenditures, recipient rates, and average payments can be explained by objective economic factors.

Miss Collins' study develops a statistical model of state public assistance expenditures. To be sure, only a fraction of the variation among states can be explained by objective economic and demographic factors. The remainder reflect differences in attitudes among state and local governments, economic factors peculiar to each state which could not be measured fully, and random elements.

Public assistance programs are administered by the states, and each state determines the basic characteristics of its own program. The federal government pays a portion of the cost for each recipient according to statutory formulas. Miss Collins' study analyzes separately the federal and the state-local costs of the program.

Miss Collins finds that public assistance expenditures rise with the income level of the state. Average payments are greater in the wealthier states, and their income elasticities range from 0.81 for Old Age Assistance to 1.05 for Aid to the Permanently and Totally Disabled. On the other hand, recipient rates—that is, the percentage of the relevant population which receives benefits—are higher in the poorer states.

The growth of pensions under Old-Age and Survivors Insurance (OASI) reduces needs for public assistance for the aged. The percentage of the population over age sixty-five receiving OASI benefits is an important explanatory variable for the recipient rate and per capita expenditure of Old Age Assistance (OAA). The same tendency occurs less strongly in the cases of Aid to the Blind (AB) and Aid to the Permanently and Totally Disabled (APTD).

High unemployment rates lead to public assistance expenditures, with the Aid to Families with Dependent Children (AFDC), and AB and OAA programs all showing some influence. The effect is large for AFDC.

While per capita public assistance expenditures rise with the percentage of the population which is nonwhite, this relationship is reversed when explicit allowance is made for differences in average income levels and urbanization. In every public assistance program, the average payment declines as the fraction of the population which is nonwhite increases, if income and urbanization are held constant. The relatively low payments for nonwhites are due to the average lower "needs" computed for nonwhite families, with "needs" possibly reflecting differences in attitude among the states toward the colored population. Recipient rates for the nonwhite population are greater in all of the programs.

Urbanization, which has been widely postulated as an important variable in determining public assistance expenditures, proved to have only a mild influence. Only in the AFDC program were the results statistically significant.

Federal participation in financing the programs proved to exert an equalizing fiscal influence among the states. Because the poorer states have substantially higher recipient rates, and the aid formulas pay a larger share of lower assistance payments, federal expenditures are relatively greater in poor states.

Miss Collins also tested to see if the several programs were politically competitive in their ability to attract state funds. States that were generous in one assistance program proved to be generous in the others. These results bear out some international findings of Aaron: The scope and level of particular income maintenance programs appear to reflect common attitudes of governments toward all of them, rather than competition for a fixed volume of resources.

Miss Collins' empirical findings suggest that the public assistance system is in need of modernization. The great variations in benefit levels and recipient rates are only partly accountable by objective factors that could reflect differences in "needs." Local fiscal capacity and local attitudes clearly play a very large role. To make income maintenance programs more effective instruments in the war on poverty, public assistance must either be generalized and be given some nationwide minimum standards, or else be supplemented or replaced by a more universal plan such as a negative income tax.

## The Mack Case: A Study in Unemployment

John W. Dorsey analyzed the economic adjustments of workers to the relocation of an industrial plant. Because some of the workers received very substantial private and public income maintenance payments, the study was intended, in part, as a means of shedding some light on the economic effects of such payments.

The study was concerned with three broad areas: (1) the willingness of workers to transfer to the new plant; (2) the re-employment experience and problems of workers who did not move; and (3) the financial adjustment of the workers to unemployment, including the effects of the income maintenance payments. The case examined is the closing of the Mack Truck Company's plant in

Plainfield, New Jersey, and its reopening in Hagerstown, Maryland. Dorsey's study is based on intensive interviews of a stratified random sample of former Mack employees in New Jersey and of employees who transferred with the company to Maryland.

The decision Mack employees made when they had to choose between staying in New Jersey and moving to Maryland varied rather consistently with their status and job in the company. Professional employees were able to transfer on very favorable terms and possessed strong company loyalty. A large portion of them went with the company to its new location.

Production workers seemed largely motivated by two sets of factors. Those workers who had been with Mack for a long time felt attached to the company; they liked their jobs and did not want to lose the advantages of long seniority. But most workers also felt strong geographic attachment to their area. They owned their homes; they had children in school or grown children who had settled nearby; they had friends and relatives in the area and were active in civic affairs. When area attachment was combined with the prospect of a substantial wage cut at the new plant in Maryland and, on the other hand, the company's offer of generous separation or retirement benefits, most of them decided not to transfer. For those who did transfer, job attachment outweighed area attachment. The promise of substantial income maintenance payments gave the workers the security of income to sustain their families for some months. This permitted them to make their transfer decisions with less fear of the long period of unemployment which could follow.

Since most of the production and clerical workers did not move to the new plant, there were suddenly nearly 3,000 unemployed workers in the affected area of New Jersey.

The success of the workers in finding new jobs depended on a variety of factors. Younger workers and workers with comparatively high levels of formal education were considerably more successful in finding jobs. In addition, those workers who occupied the position of breadwinner in their families went back to work more quickly than others.

The re-employment of a worker was affected by the general economic condition of the local area in which he lived. Workers who lived in the Plainfield area itself, where unemployment became very high, found it much more difficult to find new jobs than those who lived in areas with lower unemployment rates. Since Mack workers had been accustomed to high wages, many were reluctant to accept jobs at lower rates of pay which involved relatively long commuting distances.

The effect of skill on re-employment was particularly striking. The skilled workers experienced little trouble in finding new jobs; by the tenth month, all of those in the sample were working. The unskilled tended to go on to other unskilled jobs after a period. It was the semi-skilled workers who were least successful in their job search. Their "skills" typically had little transferability to other companies in the area, yet they viewed themselves as skilled labor and thus clung to unrealistic job demands. They suffered the largest reductions in wages when they did go back to work.

There is considerable anecdotal evidence that the high income maintenance payments did in some instances increase the period of unemployment by making workers more particular about the kinds of jobs they would accept. However, statistical analysis did not find any systematic relationship between the length of the unemployment period and the amount of income maintenance payments they received.

About 30 percent of the sample of Mack workers were unemployed for longer than six months, and about 20 percent were still unemployed at the time they were interviewed, nine to ten months after the shutdown. A subsample of workers who had been unemployed for at least six months was given an extended interview about financial adjustment during unemployment.

The unemployed workers had to reduce outlays, but the decline in their consumer spending was substantially less than the decline in their income. They reduced some categories of expenditure, but there was a substantial core of expenditures over which they had little control, such as rent, mortgage payments, taxes, insurance, medical care and items purchased on the installment plan before the layoff. Expenditures on most other types of items, notably outlays for food, were cut, but the evidence indicates that workers made every effort to cling to previously established consumption standards. Income maintenance payments helped them to retain many of their standards of consumption of ordinary, recurrently consumed items. When the payments ran out, a broader category of expenditures was curtailed.

HENRY AARON*

# Social Security:
# International Comparisons

ALL INDUSTRIALIZED and most pre-industrialized countries have social security systems.[1] They make payments to residents in contingencies such as old age, invalidism or death, war injuries, job-related injuries, unemployment, sickness, indigence, or over-sized families. A large variety of methods has developed to meet these

* Council of Economic Advisers.

[1] The term "social security," as used here, includes the systems defined as social security programs in the International Labor Organization's handbook, *The Cost of Social Security 1949-57* (Geneva: 1961). It includes not only the core social security programs universally subsumed under the rubric "social security," such as old age insurance, family allowances, health insurance, and other pensions and direct payments, but also it includes assistance, public relief, public health expenditures, pension programs for civil servants, former members of the armed services, and war victims, and workmen's compensation. Narrower concepts were used by the Organization for European Economic Cooperation (which excluded payments to vendors under health insurance and certain public health expenditures), and by the International Labor Organization in a series formerly published in the International Labor Organization's *Yearbook of Labor Statistics*. Administrative dissimilarities may still lead to the exclusion of certain programs in one country and their inclusion in another, despite functional identity.

The term "social insurance" will denote old age, survivors, disability, health and unemployment insurance. The term "social security" will not be used to denote only old age, survivors and disability insurance as is done in the United States, unless specific mention is made, such as "American Social Security."

contingencies. Programs differ from country to country, and within each country particular risks are dealt with in different ways. Each plan may vary in scope, the manner by which eligibility is acquired, the level and duration of benefits under each program, and the method of finance. The manner in which each country deals with these aspects of social security determines the economic and social impact of its social welfare expenditures.

Although government social security programs differ widely, they are designed to fill similar needs. The goal of this study is to discover whether the level of statutory social security expenditures may have common determinants in spite of the bewildering institutional diversity. Hypotheses about the nature and behavior of these determinants have been tested by relating the level of expenditure on social security and on component programs to various economic and noneconomic factors in twenty-two countries. The countries for which data have been collected are those that devoted 5 percent or more of national income to social security expenditures in the period 1949-57; these include most of the industrialized noncommunist states of the world.[2]

Expenditures under programs not administered by public, semipublic, or autonomous agencies are not included in this study, although workmen's compensation is included even if the carrier is a private insurance company. Since the "division of labor" between social insurance and nonstatutory schemes for dealing with different risks varies greatly between countries, completely acceptable comparisons of the level of protection against these risks would require that all programs, individual and collective be included. To the extent that nonstatutory schemes are ignored, data on social security programs may be less accurate indicators of the level of protection within each nation.[3]

[2] See Appendix Tables A-1 and A-2 for a list of these countries and a general summary of some of the characteristics of their social security programs. The selection of these countries is based on 1957 data. If more recent data had been used, Panama and Malaya would have been added to the sample.

[3] There is some evidence that the general ranking of countries by the proportion of national income devoted to compulsory social welfare expenditures would not seriously misrepresent their relative position. A comparison of statutory and nonstatutory social security programs in eight countries, published by the International Labor Organization, is shown on p. 15.

The data include employer-sponsored plans, group insurance, and friendly so-

## Factors Affecting the Level of Expenditures

Although social security programs in different countries are widely divergent in formulation, the level of social security expenditures appears to be influenced by similar factors regardless of the individual characteristics of any particular program.

### Age of the Program

The age or maturity of the social security system is clearly relevant to a country's expenditures on the program. For some pro-

cieties or mutual benefit societies, but exclude private insurance and direct benefit schemes in which no special fund is created by the employer.

| Country | Year | Expenditures as a Percentage of National Income | | Private Programs as a Percentage of Statutory Schemes | |
|---|---|---|---|---|---|
| | | Private Programs | Statutory Programs | Private Contributions | Private Benefits |
| Australia | 1952 | 0.9 | 7.8 | 13 | 11 |
| Canada | 1953 | 1.4 | 8.2 | 56 | 17 |
| Germany | 1954 | 0.9 | 19.0 | 6 | 5 |
| Netherlands | 1954 | 2.0 | 10.1 | 25 | 20 |
| Sweden | 1954 | 1.4 | 11.4 | 53 | 12 |
| Switzerland | 1954 | 1.4 | 7.6 | 33 | 18 |
| United Kingdom | 1953 | 1.9 | 12.0 | 41 | 16 |
| United States | 1954 | 2.0 | 5.4 | 63 | 34 |

Source: "Cost of Non-Statutory Social Security Schemes," *International Labor Review* (October 1958), pp. 388–403.

The data show that the relative importance of nonstatutory schemes varies from one country to another, and that a substantial negative correlation (approximately —.75) exists between the proportion of national income spent on statutory and nonstatutory programs. In no case, however, do benefits from nonstatutory schemes exceed 2 percent of national income or 35 percent of statutory social security expenditures.

Contribution levels for these programs represent an approximation of their future importance. However, the ratio of benefits to contributions is probably lower than under statutory programs. Private pension plans are usually much more conservatively financed than public pension plans, and reserves tend to be much larger relative to benefit payments or liability. In addition, many workers lose private pension rights when they change jobs.

Nonstatutory pension plans are, and will probably continue to be, relatively unimportant compared to statutory retirement programs. Even in the United States, which relies most heavily on nonstatutory programs, retirement benefit payments under private plans, while expected to increase, will probably never amount to as much as one-fourth of payments under the Social Security program.

grams, such as pensions, eligibility for and participation in benefits
often depend on the length of past covered employment. The expenditure level for these programs automatically increases as they
mature.[4]

In addition to the inherent tendency for some program expenditures to be amplified over time, a pattern of legislative expansion of
the system is typical of many countries. The system may be inaugu-
rated with the enactment of one program; after a few years, the legislature raises benefit levels and adds other programs; within a few
decades, the whole system is revised and liberalized. For example,
Germany initially enacted sickness and maternity insurance in
1883, work injury insurance in 1884, old age and invalidism pensions in 1889. Revision and codification followed in 1911 and unemployment insurance in 1927. Periodic amendments have been
made since then. In the United Kingdom, the basic programs of social insurance date from 1911. They were all revised and liberalized, family allowances were added, and the system was reorganized
in 1945. The National Health Service was added in 1946. In 1935,
the United States Congress enacted the basic social insurance programs, except for survivors, disability, and health insurance. Sur-
vivor benefits were added in 1939, disability benefits in 1954, and
health insurance for the aged in 1965. Coverage and benefits were
liberalized in 1950 and several times since. Portugal's first social
insurance laws, which date from 1919, were inoperative; effective
legislation was passed in 1935 and 1936. Family allowances were
added in 1942. The pattern repeats itself in most other countries.[5]

The positive correlation between the magnitude of social securi-

[4] Expenditures data are converted to United States dollars according to 1957
rates of exchange. Except where otherwise stated, the source of statistics on social
welfare expenditures in countries other than the United States is the International
Labor Organization handbook (referred to hereafter as *ILO Handbook*), *The Cost
of Social Security, 1949-57* (Geneva: 1961). The source for statistics on social
security in the United States is the *Social Security Bulletin* of the U.S. Social Security Administration. It should be noted that the statistics employed in the regressions in this study refer to the year 1957. The study was completed before the
publication of expenditures data for 1960 in the International Labor Organization
handbook published in 1964. In the years since 1957, the countries covered in this
study have amended their social security programs in a number of ways, some of
which are quite basic. Where subsequent developments or data are pertinent to
the findings of this study, they will be mentioned in the text.

[5] In many countries, social insurance programs were considerably liberalized
after the end of World War II.

ty expenditures and the maturity of the system does not, of course, explain the fundamental factors that determined the timing of the enactment of the initial program and, therefore, the age of the system. Why did Japan and Chile enact their first programs in the 1920's, Germany and Austria in the 1880's, the United States and Portugal in the 1930's? It is clear that a variety of forces was at work. The stage of industrialization apparently plays some role. Few underdeveloped countries make extensive social security expenditures; only Panama and Malaya spent as much as 5 percent of national income on social security in 1960. But the stage of economic development alone cannot explain why in the initiation of social security both Portugal and the United States lagged Germany by fifty years.

The political complexion of the governments in power when social security programs are first introduced is usually rather similar. Moderately leftist governments, which come to power on promises of social reform, take the first steps. This would suggest that an old social security program is indicative that the nation decided to settle a relatively large number of economic questions, including that of social welfare, outside the market place.

Since the positive correlation between social security expenditures and the age of the program might be only one of the manifestations of an activist government, total government expenditures on programs other than social security are also considered in order to account for differences in the activity of governments outside the realm of social security.

### Per Capita National Income

The rise in national income over time also contributes to the pressure for liberalization of social security expenditures. The statistics show very clearly that high per capita social security outlays accompany high per capita income. Differences in levels of national income will influence the level of per capita expenditures unless the income elasticity of demand for social insurance is zero. Whether the elasticity is greater or less than one is speculative, however.

The value of income insurance should be greater at low income levels where private saving is difficult. However, the demand for private insurance appears to have high income elasticity, and, by analogy, the demand for public insurance may be similar. Furthermore, the proportion of national income the government can gain through taxation probably increases with income so that financing higher welfare expenditures should be less difficult.

## Rate of Growth of National Income

Not only is the level of national income probably related to social security expenditures in any particular country, but its rate of growth may also be pertinent. The direction of the relationship is difficult to predict, however. Unfavorable expectations about future income levels would aggravate concern over risks to be met out of future incomes. Private saving would be discouraged by relatively stable incomes so that pooled and compulsory savings under social insurance become an attractive alternative. In this situation, large outlays on social security would be associated with low growth rates.

On the other hand, it is also possible that welfare expenditures may increase with rapid growth. At any given level of income, consumption is likely to be lower if incomes are reaching new highs than if they are stable or falling. The government will find it easier to increase the level of taxation where voluntary nonconsumption is relatively large. The government could expand its expenditures, including those for social security, more rapidly than if national income were growing more slowly.

## Household Saving

Some microeconomic theories of saving and much empirical research suggest that people follow a lifetime savings cycle.[6] When a worker first enters the labor force, his income is relatively low and he is likely to have expenses of family formation. During his middle working years his earnings are relatively high and current expenses tend to be lower. Consequently, he can save at a higher rate than before. Still later, his efficiency and current earnings decline and so does his rate of saving. After retirement, he begins to dissave. This theory emphasizes retirement and the expenses attendant to old age

---

[6] See, for example, F. Modigliani and R. E. Brumberg, "Utility Analysis and the Consumption Function: An Interpretation of Cross Section Data," in K. Kurihara (ed.), *Post Keynesian Economics* (Rutgers University Press, 1954), pp. 388-436; and R. F. Harrod, "The Supply of Savings," in *Towards a Dynamic Economics* (Macmillan, 1948), pp. 35-62.

as the motivation for saving, but, without serious modification, the theory can also be applied to saving for protection against current risks, such as sickness or unemployment.

The purpose of social insurance in most countries is to guard against risks not adequately met through private means. High personal savings rates might be expected to reduce the demand for high social welfare expenditures. Conversely, a highly developed system of social insurance may reduce the motivation for larger personal savings.

In a historical sense, household saving predates large-scale welfare programs. If household savings were successful in providing adequate funds, the pressure for government expenditure to meet common social risk should be lower. On the other hand, comprehensive social security programs reduce the residual of risks individuals must meet from their own resources.

In this study, both explanations of the inverse association between private saving and social security expenditures are examined. In addition, personal saving and social security will be regarded as jointly determined, that is, as complementary answers to the same problems.

## Participation in Past Wars

One theory of government expenditures suggests that the temporary fiscal exertions of war accustom taxpayers to higher tax rates, and lead to some permanent expansion of expenditures even after the war ends.[7] The common social welfare programs are not directly influenced by wars. Consequently, except for payments to the victims of war and to veterans, the association of large civilian social welfare outlays with participation in past wars would be evidence in support of this theory.

[7] The suggested impact of wars on postwar expenditures is one form of "the displacement effect" discussed by Alan T. Peacock and Jack Wiseman in *The Growth of Public Expenditures in the United Kingdom* (Princeton University Press, 1961), pp. 24-30. Peacock and Wiseman argue that government expenditures are constrained by revenues which, in turn, can only be expanded sharply "by social disturbances that destroy established conceptions and produce a displacement effect"; *ibid.*, p. 27. Peacock and Wiseman test the hypothesis with time series for government expenditures in the United Kingdom. The text uses cross sectional data to test the same hypothesis.

*The Source of Social Security Funds*

There are few safe generalizations about the incidence of social security taxes.[8] There is virtual unanimity that payroll taxes levied on the employer are largely shifted, but unanimity breaks down over the direction in which they are shifted. To the extent that they are shifted forward in the form of higher prices, they are proportional to consumption expenditures[9] and regressive as far as income is concerned. To the extent that they are shifted backward, they are, of course, taxes on employees' wages. Where taxes on corporate profits and individual income are major sources of general revenues, the greater the proportion of social insurance income derived from general revenues, the more progressive is the social insurance tax structure.

There are several reasons why large support from general revenues might be associated with smaller total social welfare expenditures. In the development of American Social Security, for instance, the growth of expenditures has probably been influenced by removal of the program from annual scrutiny by the appropriations committees of Congress. In general, given progressive tax systems, general revenue financing involves more drastic income redistribution than does financing through earmarked or payroll taxes. Consequently, there is likely to be more vociferous opposition to social insurance financed from general revenues. Eleven countries derive nearly half or more of the revenues of social insurance programs from general revenues.[10] It is notable that the proportion of national income devoted to social security is higher in some of the countries that rely less on general revenues for financing these expenditures.[11]

---

[8] Reference here is made to "differential tax incidence" as defined by Richard A. Musgrave, *The Theory of Public Finance* (McGraw-Hill, 1959), p. 212. This is the change in income distribution that occurs when all adjustments have been made to the substitution of one tax for another so that the level of aggregate demand is not appreciably affected.

[9] I assume that goods purchased by different income classes do not differ systematically in the amount of "covered employment" embodied in them.

[10] Australia, Canada, Denmark, Finland, Iceland, Ireland, New Zealand, Norway, South Africa, Sweden, and the United Kingdom. The same pattern is present in revenues for the years 1959-61 as shown in ILO, *The Cost of Social Security* (Geneva: 1964), pp. 266-71.

[11] For example, France, Germany, Belgium, Austria, and Italy.

## Population

The age distribution of the population and its rate of growth are also related to expenditures on certain social welfare programs. The larger the percentage of the aged, the larger must be the cost of programs for the aged, unless benefit levels are reduced or eligibility is made more difficult. Health expenditures also tend to increase for the aged.

## Statistical Results

The relationship between social security expenditures and the factors discussed in the previous section was analyzed statistically by the use of linear correlation models.[12] The level of expenditures was expressed both on a per capita basis and as a percentage of national income. Using either measure, the relationship between social security outlays and the factors tested appeared to be highly significant.[13]

A high percentage of the variation in expenditure levels among different countries appears to be explained by these factors. This would indicate that common determinants of the level of social security outlays are far more important than administrative or other differences peculiar to each country.

This result is somewhat surprising since social security is an intensely political issue. Differences in political or social conditions between countries might have been expected to influence social security expenditures even more, perhaps, than the quantitative factors examined here. Some of these quantitative variables, however, may also represent differences in political climate; the age of the social security system might be such an instance. It is also possible that the political or social atmosphere might itself be partially determined by the same economic or quantitative factors that influence

[12] See Appendix B for the list of variables used to represent these factors in the statistical analysis.

[13] The statistical results may be, in one sense, "too good." The data cover extremely diverse programs, and the inclusion of expenditures for different programs is not uniform. Some countries meet particular problems with statutory programs, while other countries rely on nonstatutory programs which were not included in this part of the study. Further, with one exception, linear models were used even though relations between the variables may well be nonlinear.

# TABLE 1. Regression Results, Determinants of Per Capita Social Security Expenditures ($E_p$), 1957

(Constant term in billions of U. S. dollars)

| Equation Number | Constant Term | Per Capita National Income $Y_p$ | Per Capita National Income $\log Y_p$ | Regression Coefficients[a] Age of System $D_s$ | Household Saving $S$ | Income Growth Rate $y$ | Past Wars $D_w$ | Other Variables | Coefficients of Determination $R^2$ | Coefficients of Determination $\bar{R}^2$ |
|---|---|---|---|---|---|---|---|---|---|---|
| (1.1) | 28.4980 | | | 19.2480** (5.834) | | | | | .3524** | .2870** |
| (1.2) | 34.8825 | .0717** (.0165) | | | | | | | .4862** | .4355** |
| (1.3) | −28.7588 | .0696** (.0103) | | 18.6410** (3.2449) | | | | | .8100** | .7800** |
| (1.4) | −326.8460 | | 64.1860** (9.668) | | | | | | .6879** | .6567** |
| (1.5) | −314.2455 | | 55.5493** (7.7598) | 12.5221** (3.2545) | | | | | .8246** | .7969** |
| (1.6) | −307.3034 | | 50.1569** (8.8046) | | | | | 7.8951[b] (2.3027) | .8072** | .7767** |
| (1.7) | −298.5091 | | 57.0088** (7.7870) | 13.8205** (3.1276) | −3.0303 (1.3550) | | | | .8722** | .8381** |
| (1.8) | −323.6200 | | 56.0683** (7.3809) | 11.5411** (3.1402) | | | 2.7654 (1.5764) | | .8502** | .8169** |
| (1.9) | −371.0894 | | 63.4979** (8.5384) | 12.3785** (3.0742) | −4.0967* (1.1976) | | | 21.5479[c] (11.8480) | .8518** | .8189** |
| (1.10) | −353.3257 | | 63.1258** (6.8813) | 13.8862** (2.6138) | | 5.9033 (2.1587) | | | .9167** | .8869** |
| (1.11) | −304.2180 | | 56.7279** (7.6211) | 13.3770** (3.0788) | −2.9726 (1.3263) | | 2.1870 (1.6908) | | .8858** | .8450** |
| (1.12) | −361.3121 | | 64.4894** (7.4949) | 14.1277** (2.7189) | −4.3390** (1.3075) | 7.0798* (3.0991) | −1.1256 (2.0734) | | .9185** | .8809** |

Source: See text note 4.

Note: Figures in parentheses are standard errors of the coefficients. * Indicates statistical significance at the 95 percent level. ** Indicates statistical significance at the 99 percent level.

[a] For a more detailed description of variables, see Appendix B.

[b] Variable $P_r$, the percentage of total population over age sixty-five.

[c] Variable $D_c$, a dummy variable for predominantly Catholic countries.

social security expenditures, so that its impact is absorbed in the use of more basic variables. The statistical results do indicate, however, that differences in social security outlays among various countries cannot be attributed solely to political factors.

A statistical warning is also necessary. Since the following results are based on cross-sectional data, great caution must be exercised in drawing conclusions about the future development of programs in a particular country. Such inferences from cross-sectional data would be justified only if it were known that the relationship between the independent and the explanatory variables were identical over time within each country. Otherwise, only time series for particular countries can support predictions about the future development of individual programs. Therefore, the results which follow report static international patterns and draw inferences from them. This evidence suggests certain plausible lines of development for particular programs, but these predictions are presented with considerable diffidence and they should be viewed with caution.

## Per Capita National Income

Per capita national income $(Y_p)$ was tested as a determinant of per capita social security expenditures $(E_p)$ and of social security expenditures as a percentage of national income $(E_v)$. The regression equations involved both per capita income, or its logarithm, alone and with other variables included.

Table 1 shows results for regressions on per capita social security outlays. Per capita income appeared to be an important determinant of these expenditures, and their relationship to the logarithm of per capita income was even closer. This result is not surprising since social security per capita in most of the high income countries was nearly as great as per capita income in the poorest countries.

In contrast, per capita income is consistently insignificant as a determinant of the percentage of national income that is spent on social security $(E_v)$ with a simple correlation coefficient of 0.1 for both untransformed and logarithmic data.[14] The contribution of per

---

[14] Since $E_v = E_p/Y_p$, the results imply a nonlinear relationship between $E_v$ and $Y_p$ of the form $E_v = a + b(1/Y_p)$, where $a$ is the coefficient of $Y_p$ in the regressions reported in the text and $b$ is the constant term. Since $b$ is negative, this result indicates an elasticity of social security with respect to per capita national income of less than 1 since the percentage of national income devoted to social security declines as income rises.

## TABLE 2. Regression Results, Determinants of Social Security Expenditures as a Percentage of National Income (E$_y$), 1957

(Constant term in billions of U. S. dollars)

| Equation Number | Constant Term | Regression Coefficients[a] | | | | | | | Coefficients of Determination | |
|---|---|---|---|---|---|---|---|---|---|---|
| | | Age of System D$_s$ | Household Saving S | General Revenue Financing E$_t$ | Income Growth Rate y | Other Government Expenditures G$_y$ | Past Wars D$_w$ | Other Variables | R$^2$ | R̄$^2$ |
| (2.1) | 3.4598 | 2.2498** (.4287) | | | | | | | .5793** | .5372** |
| (2.2) | 6.3613 | 2.5146* (.4078) | −.3934* (.1820) | | | | | | .7083** | .6536** |
| (2.3) | 3.9737 | 2.6331** (.5247) | | −.4083 (.3306) | | | | | .6106** | .5491** |
| (2.4) | 2.2370 | 2.0679** (.3769) | | | | | .5478* (.1976) | | .7004** | .6532** |
| (2.5) | 2.0678 | 2.3959** (.3615) | | | | | | 3.8452**b (1.2398) | .7207** | .6766** |
| (2.6) | .2079 | | | | | | | 1.2137**c (.3107) | .4327** | .3760** |
| (2.7) | 8.1256 | 3.2112** (.4437) | −.5012** (.1622) | −.6954* (.2706) | | | | | .7975** | .744 ** |
| (2.8) | 4.5210 | 2.6022** (.3607) | −.5363** (.1710) | | .6943* (.2916) | | | | .7883** | .745 ** |
| (2.9) | 2.2188 | 2.5093** (.3809) | −.4388** (.1728) | | | .2120 (.1195) | | | .7589** | .6945** |
| (2.10) | 4.4740 | 2.3953** (.3438) | −.3771* (.1524) | | | | .5499* (.1961) | | .8087** | .758 ** |
| (2.11) | 4.6268 | 2.4963** (.3641) | −.2694 (.1715) | | | | | 3.1122b (1.3798) | .7822** | .7241** |
| (2.12) | 6.3881 | 3.1031** (.4228) | −.5760** (.1589) | −.5247* (.2739) | .4922 (.2886) | | | | .8323** | .7722** |
| (2.13) | 3.7642 | 3.2351** (.3883) | −.5542** (.1437) | −.7239** (.2371) | | .2270* (.0960) | | | .8553** | .8035** |
| (2.14) | 6.1797 | 2.9164** (.4227) | −.4571** (.1474) | −.4904 (.2618) | | | .4154* (.1952) | | .8470** | .7924** |
| (2.15) | 5.8930 | 2.9339** (.4331) | −.5004** (.1658) | −.4600 (.2721) | .2200 (.3516) | | .3223* (.2489) | | .8515** | .783 ** |
| (2.16) | 3.5318 | 3.0290** (.4029) | −.5111** (.1422) | −.5779 (.2516) | | .1704 (.1011) | .2815 (.1999) | | .8745** | .8165** |

Source: See text note 4.

Note: Figures in parentheses are standard errors of the coefficients. * Indicates statistical significance at the 95 percent level. ** Indicates statistical significance at the 99 percent level.

a For a more detailed description of these variables, see Appendix B.

b Variable D$_{Ct}$, a dummy variable for predominantly Catholic countries.

c Variable P$_t$*, the percentage of total population over age sixty-five.

capita income, in either form, remains insignificant even when other variables are included in the equation.

The regression coefficients of both per capita income and its logarithm tend to be negative. This indicates that the elasticity of social security with respect to per capita national income is less than one; that is, that the percentage of national income devoted to social security declines as income rises. The elasticity of per capita expenditures with respect to per capita income is also less than one, estimated as about 0.6, and it remains near that value as other variables are added.[15] This indicates that the demand for social security does not expand as rapidly as per capita income, other things held constant.

## The Age of the Social Security System

The maturity of the system in each of the twenty-two countries is represented in the regression equations as the number of decades since the institution of the first program (variable $D_s$). This variable is the most important of any tested in this study in explaining the percentage of national income devoted to social security. As indicated in Table 2, few of the coefficients of other variables are significant when this variable is not included in the equation. Its coefficient, however, is positive and highly significant regardless of whether other variables are present.

The $D_s$ variable is one of two that may roughly reflect a country's prevailing political attitudes toward economic problems; the other measures the percentage of national income devoted to government programs other than social security (variable $G_v$). When both variables are included in the regressions, the significance of the factor reflecting the age of the program ($D_s$) is unaffected, and the size of its regression coefficients remains nearly constant.[16]

[15] The results are unaffected if the regression is run without the United States. Equation (2.7), applied to data for the remaining twenty-one countries, becomes

$$E_p = -28.4780 + .1757Y + 17.1764 \log Y_p$$
$$R^2 = .8109 \qquad \bar{R}^2 = .7794$$

The elasticity of per capita social security expenditures ($E_p$) with respect to per capita national income ($Y_p$) becomes .6381 (.8280 when $\log Y_p$ is excluded), and is still significantly less than 1.

[16] See equations (2.9), (2.13), (2.16) in Table 2, and (4.8), (4.11), (4.14) in Table 4. The $G_v$ variable was also included in the regressions on per capita social security expenditure. The coefficients were always positive, generally larger than their standard errors, but never significant at the 95 percent level.

## TABLE 3. Regression Results, Determinants of Household Savings (S), 1957

(Constant term in billions of U. S. dollars)

| Equation Number | Constant Term | Age of System $D_s$ | Total Social Security Expenditures $E_y$ | Net Social Security Expenditures $N_y$ | General Revenue Financing $E_t$ | Income Growth Rate $y$ | Average Old Age Benefit[b] | $R^2$ | $\bar{R}^2$ |
|---|---|---|---|---|---|---|---|---|---|
| (3.1) | 9.5157 | 1.8000* (.7857) | −.5743* (.2658) | | | | | .2585 | .119 |
| (3.2) | 9.7323 | 1.9624* (.7941) | | −.6865 (.2916) | | | | .2885 | .1551 |
| (3.3) | 11.2937 | 3.0198** (.8731) | −.7762** (.2512) | | −.8035* (.3469) | | | .4538* | .308* |
| (3.4) | 11.6019 | 3.2497** (.8630) | | −.9217** (.2706) | −.8290** (.3336) | | | .4961** | .3617* |
| (3.5) | 8.3447 | 2.9610** (.7988) | −.8404** (.2319) | | −.5569 (.3405) | .6723* (.3384) | | .5740** | .422* |
| (3.6) | 8.7790 | 3.1552** (.7948) | | .9710** (.2500) | −.5904 (.3304) | .6302 (.3253) | | .6026** | .4606** |
| (3.7) | 9.0572 | 3.0897** (.7490) | | −1.1256** (.2527) | −.6775 (.3157) | .5191 (.3133) | 5.7115 (3.4102) | .6731** | .5222** |

Regression Coefficients[a] / Coefficients of Determination

Source: See text note 4.
Note: Figures in parentheses are standard errors of the coefficients. * Indicates statistical significance at the 95 percent level. ** Indicates statistical significance at the 99 percent level.
[a] For detailed description of variables, see Appendix B.
[b] This variable is the ratio of $A_y$, the percentage of national income spent on payments to the aged, to $P_r$, the percentage of total population over retirement age.

To the extent that the $G_y$ variable accounts for the degree of economic intervention by the government, the relationship of $D_s$ to the level of social security expenditures may be interpreted as the increase in outlays accounted for by the financial maturing of certain programs and by a pattern of legislative expansion of programs over time. Insofar as the $G_y$ variable is not a perfect measure of the tendency for government to solve economic problems outside the market, the coefficient of $D_s$ probably reflects not only technical increases in social security, but also national attitudes toward state intervention in economic affairs.

*Household Saving*

The coefficients of the household savings variable ($S$) are consistently negative. They are also generally highly significant and take on plausible values.[17] According to the regressions shown in Table 2, each additional percent of personal income saved is associated with a reduction of about 0.5 percent in the amount of national income devoted to social security.

While these results are consistent with the hypothesis that higher savings rates reduce the demand for social welfare programs, they are not inconsistent with the inverse hypothesis, that welfare expenditures may reduce the propensity to save. This interpretation is supported by the regression results shown in Table 3, where social security expenditures appear to be a highly significant determinant of household savings.

It is not possible to make a conclusive choice between these hypotheses on the basis of these regressions, and there is apparently no significant direct relationship between saving and social security expenditures.[18] The significance of the relationship appears to de-

[17] Because data on household saving were unavailable from Iceland and Switzerland, and because rampant inflation led to negative savings in Chile, these countries were eliminated from any regression in which household saving was a variable. Thus, of the full sample of twenty-two countries, only nineteen are in these regressions.

In many countries, household savings rates were very low in the years immediately following the end of World War II, years during which populations tried to restore their economies to pre-war levels of prosperity. Household savings rates were abnormally low and in some cases were negative. In the 1950's household savings rates began to climb and reached plateaus during the mid-1950's. The statistics on savings are averages of annual rates after such plateaus were attained.

[18] There was also no significant simple correlation between household saving and each of the variables listed below. None of the following simple correlation coefficients

pend, generally, on the inclusion of the variable representing the age of the system. It is possible that this variable, which indicates the point in time when a country first became sufficiently "security conscious" to enact social security and had the means to do so, may contribute to the explanation of the propensity to save by acting as a proxy for the sociological or economic factors not explicitly included in the regression.

The regressions are consistent with the interpretation that countries could have relatively high propensities to save at the time social insurance is introduced, but that these propensities are reduced somewhat over time by the natural growth in welfare expenditures.[19] They are also consistent with a contrary interpretation, however. It may be argued that social insurance teaches people the advantage of saving as protection against a multiplicity of risks. The longer social insurance is in force, the greater personal saving will be, unless exceptionally large social welfare expenditures currently reduce the need for private saving.

This issue cannot be resolved with cross-sectional data; time series analysis of the impact of social security on savings within a number of countries is necessary to discriminate between these hypotheses.

## General Revenues vs. Earmarked Taxes

The simple correlation between the percentage of national income spent on social security ($E_y$) and the percentage of national in-

---

is significant at the 95 percent level.

| Correlation between household saving and: | R | $R^2$ |
|---|---|---|
| Per capita social security expenditures ($E_p$) | − .1807 | .0327 |
| Social security expenditures as a percent of national income ($E_y$) | − .1236 | .0153 |
| Age of the social security system ($D_s$) | .2051 | .0421 |
| Social security expenditures from general revenues as a percent of national income ($E_t$) | − .0878 | .0077 |
| Rate of growth of national income, 1950–59 ($y$) | .3383 | .1144 |
| Rate of growth of per capita national income ($y_p$) | .2542 | .0646 |
| Percent of national income spent on payments to the aged ($A_y$) | .0305 | .0010 |
| Male life expectancy at birth ($L$) | .0660 | .0043 |
| Percent of total population over retirement age ($P_r$) | − .1767 | .0312 |

[19] John Henry Richardson takes this position in *Economic and Financial Aspects of Social Security* (University of Toronto Press, 1960), p. 61. Richardson notes, however, that "the introduction of social insurance may stimulate greater interest in making provision for old age and other contingencies . . .". Similar inferences can be drawn from the discussion of saving by Simon Kuznets, *Capital in the American Economy* (Princeton University Press, 1961), pp. 100-03.

come absorbed by general revenue taxation for social security outlays ($E_t$) is rather low ($r^2 = .09$). Table 3 shows, however, that once some allowance is made for the age of the system ($D_s$) and household saving ($S$), correlation between the use of general revenues and social security outlays is somewhat greater and clearly negative.[20] The coefficient of $E_t$ averages about —.55. This would indicate that, other things equal, countries spend less on social security in proportion to their national income if they rely to a relatively greater extent on general revenues rather than payroll taxes to finance these expenditures.

## Participation in Past Wars

The hypothesis that past involvement in wars leads to increased social security expenditures is also supported by the regression results, but the evidence is considerably weaker. Regressions were run on expenditures net of benefits to victims of war in order to isolate social security outlays that were not directly related to war. These are shown in Tables 5 and 6. Participation in past wars is accounted for in the regressions by a dummy variable ($D_w$) which assumed maximum values for Austria, France, Germany, Italy, Japan,[21] and the United Kingdom; zero values were assigned for Portugal, Sweden, Chile, Iceland, and Switzerland; the remaining countries had intermediate positive values.

Coefficients of the war participation variable were always positive, but generally not significant, when total social security was measured as a percent of national income. When it was measured in dollars per capita, coefficients of $D_w$ were again positive unless the variable representing the growth of national income was present ($y$). The netting out of benefits to war victims reduced the value of the coefficients without exception.

The results indicate that heavy participation in past wars does increase total social security expenditures, in large part, apparently because of payments to war victims. There is little evidence for the thesis that the wartime expansion of government expenditures results in permanent increases in other social security programs. This

[20] The partial correlation between $E_y$ and $E_t$ when $D_s$ and $S$ are present is $r = -.55$, and $r^2 = .31$.

[21] Japan posed something of a problem, because it is the only country in the sample which reimbursed war victims by lump sum payments, mostly paid soon after the war. As a result, there are no continuing Japanese veterans' programs.

# TABLE 4. Regression Results, Determinants of Per Capita Social Security Expenditures Net of Benefits to War Victims ($N_P$), 1957

(Constant term in billions of U.S. dollars)

| Equation Number | Constant Term | Per Capita National Income | | Age of System $D_s$ | Household Saving $S$ | Income Growth Rate $y$ | Past Wars $D_w$ | Coefficients of Determination | |
|---|---|---|---|---|---|---|---|---|---|
| | | $Y_p$ | $\log Y_p$ | | | | | $R^2$ | $\bar{R}^2$ |
| (4.1) | 25.2576 | | | 18.3376** (5.2708) | | | | .3770** | .3147** |
| (4.2) | 17.0988 | .0643** (.0156) | | | | | | .4609** | .4070** |
| (4.3) | −297.2281 | | 58.7179** (9.0355) | | | | | .6786** | .6465** |
| (4.4) | −288.6049 | | 50.4731** (7.0785) | 11.8635** (3.0116) | | | 1.0928 (1.5119) | .8376** | .8015** |
| (4.5) | −300.7865 | | 54.6070** (6.6883) | 13.9229** (2.5405) | −3.9174* (1.1640) | 4.4986 (2.0981) | | .9066** | .8732** |
| (4.6) | −260.7808 | | 49.8585** (7.2472) | 13.7355** (2.9278) | −3.0869 (1.2612) | | .0677 (1.6080) | .8774** | .8337** |
| (4.7) | −320.6126 | | 57.9921** (6.8135) | 14.5222** (2.4717) | −4.5188** (1.1886) | 7.4193* (2.8173) | −2.7944 (1.8851) | .9201** | .8832** |

Regression Coefficients[a]

Source: See text note 4.
Note: Figures in parentheses are standard errors of the coefficients. * Indicates statistical significance at the 95 percent level. ** Indicates statistical significance at the 99 percent level.
[a] For a more detailed description of variables, see Appendix B.

**TABLE 5. Regression Results, Determinants of Social Security Expenditures Net of Benefits to War Victims as a Percentage of National Income ($N_y$), 1957**

*(Constant term in billions of U. S. dollars)*

| Equation Number | Constant Term | Regression Coefficients[A] Age of System $D_s$ | Household Saving $S$ | General Revenue Financing $E_t$ | Income Growth Rate $y$ | Other Government Expenditures $G_y$ | Past Wars $D_w$ | Other Variables | Coefficients of Determination $R^2$ | $\bar{R}^2$ |
|---|---|---|---|---|---|---|---|---|---|---|
| (5.1) | 3.3952 | 2.1052** (.3657) | | | | | | | .6236** | .5860** |
| (5.2) | 5.9831 | 2.3613* (.3566) | −.3747* (.1592) | | | | | | .7372** | .6879** |
| (5.3) | 3.8904 | 2.4745** (.4427) | | −.3934 (.2789) | | | | | .6593** | .6055** |
| (5.4) | 2.6489 | 1.9942** (.3518) | | | | | .3343 (.1845) | | .6791** | .6284** |
| (5.5) | 0.6113 | | | | | | | 1.1077**b (.2777) | .4431** | .3874** |
| (5.6) | 7.5952 | 2.9987** (.3801) | −.4733** (.1389) | −.6354* (.2318) | | | | | .8249** | .7782** |
| (5.7) | 4.4147 | 2.4359** (.3184) | −.4966** (.1510) | | .5917* (.2574) | | | | .8056** | .7538** |
| (5.8) | 2.2562 | 2.3565** (.3328) | −.4156* (.1502) | | | .1907 (.1039) | | | .7854** | .7282** |
| (5.9) | 4.6846 | 2.2791** (.3293) | −.3636* (.1460) | | | | .3783 (.1878) | | .7931** | .7380** |
| (5.10) | 6.182 | 2.9099** (.3658) | −.5342** (.1375) | −.4966 (.2370) | .4004 (.2497) | | | | .8520** | .7992** |
| (5.11) | 3.6676 | 3.0194** (.3256) | .5210** (.1204) | .6611** (.1988) | | .2044* (.0804) | | | .8801** | .8373** |
| (5.12) | 6.4896 | 2.8306** (.3936) | −.4482 (.1372) | −.5190 (.2438) | | | .2361 (.1817) | | .8437** | .7879** |
| (5.13) | 6.0050 | 2.8555** (.3951) | −.5099** (.1513) | −.4758 (.2482) | .3129 (.3207) | | .1036 (.2271) | | .8544** | .7872** |
| (5.14) | 3.5936 | 2.9538** (.3592) | −.5073** (.1268) | −.6146* (.2243) | | .1864 (.0901) | .0896 (.1782) | | .8824** | .8282** |

Source: See text 4.

Note: Figures in parentheses are standard errors of the coefficients. * Indicates statistical significance at the 95 percent level. ** Indicates statistical significance at the 99 percent level.

a For a more detailed description of these variables, see Appendix B.

b Variable $P_r$,* the percentage of total population over age sixty-five.

31

is apparent from the insignificant coefficients of the war participation variable when payments to war victims are netted out. Even the small positive values of these coefficients are doubtful because certain social security costs imposed by wars may be met from ordinary programs, such as disability or health insurance.

## Demographic Variables

Several demographic variables were tested. Of these, the rate of growth of population ($p$), the logarithm of population density (log $P$), life expectancy ($L$), and retirement age under social insurance ($R$) did not add significantly to correlation coefficients when other variables were present, and regression coefficients were insignificant. Both the percent of population over the social insurance retirement age ($P_r$) and the percent of population over age sixty-five ($P_r^*$) are significantly correlated with social security outlays ($E_y$).[22] However, these variables do not improve the regression fit when the variable representing the age of the program is present.

The statistical results indicate that none of the demographic characteristics tested explain the level of social security expenditures. This result is surprising and requires some explanation.

First, to some extent there may be a trade-off between the proportion of the population covered by social insurance and the level of benefits. For instance, a large aged population may imply low per capita benefits when other factors, such as the extent of coverage, are held constant.

Secondly, it is striking that the age of program variable ($D_s$) deprives the population variables of statistical significance, when the simple correlations between social security outlays ($E_y$) and the percentage of population over sixty-five ($P_r^*$) or retirement age ($P_r$) are so high. This fact, and the high correlation between $D_s$ and $P_r$ ($r^2 = .4601$), suggests that the aging of the population may be one

[22] Simple correlation coefficients between $E_y$ and the demographic variables were:

| Variable | R | R² |
|---|---|---|
| Population growth rate ($p$) | $-.3970$ | .1576 |
| Logarithm of population density (log $P$) | .4106 | .1686 |
| Male life expectancy ($L$) | .2013 | .0405 |
| Retirement age ($R$) | $-.1703$ | .0289 |
| Percentage of population over retirement age ($P_r$) | .5827** | .3395** |
| Percentage of population over age 65 ($P_r^*$) | .6578** | .4327** |

** Indicates statistical significance at the 99 percent level.

of the forces that helps explain the timing of the initiation and subsequent growth of social security in various countries.

### Rate of Economic Growth

Coefficients of $y$, the rate of economic growth, are all positive, but are generally not significant. It was previously estimated that the elasticity of social security expenditures with respect to per capita income is less than unity. In view of the positive coefficients of $y$, this suggests that the supply of funds for social welfare programs is relatively abundant in more rapidly growing countries, after allowance is made for the other variables with which social security is correlated.

## Estimates of Social Security Outlays

The most important determinants of social security expenditures of those factors tested in this study were per capita national income ($Y_p$ or log $Y_p$), the age of the social security system ($D_p$), and household saving ($S$). Together, these variables explain 87 percent of the variation in per capita social security outlays and 74 percent of the variation in the percentage of national income devoted to social security. The signs of the coefficients of these variables are consistent with their hypothesized effect on social expenditures. The coefficients of other variables tested were occasionally significant, but not as consistently so and not at as high a level of significance.

The variation in social security outlays not accounted for by variables included in this study did not appear to be systematic and did not follow any discernible pattern. For example, expenditures estimated by Equation (4.7) are within $15, or 20 percent, of actual expenditures for eighteen of the nineteen countries included. The exception was France, where outlays were greater than estimated. This was probably because of extraordinarily large family allowances. Estimates based on Equation (5.14) were higher than observed expenditures for nine of the nineteen countries and, except for South Africa and the United States, the estimates differed from actual expenditures by less than 25 percent of the actual value. In the two exceptional countries, estimates also exceeded actual outlays.

For the United States, estimates generally tended to be some-

# TABLE 6. Regression Results, Determinants of Social Security Expenditures on the Aged as a Percentage of National Income ($A_y$), 1957

(Constant term in billions of U.S. dollars)

| Equation Number | Constant Term | Age of System $D_a$ | Household Saving $S$ | General Revenue Financing $E_t$ | Income Growth Rate $y$ | Other Government Expenditures $G_y$ | Population Over 65 $P_r*$ | Other Variables | Regression Coefficient[a] — $R^2$ | $\bar{R}^2$ |
|---|---|---|---|---|---|---|---|---|---|---|
| (6.1) | .4030 | 1.1530** (.2221) | | | | | | | .5740** | .5314** |
| (6.2) | 2.3860 | | | | | | | .7718[b] | .3302** | .265** |
| (6.3) | −.9944 | | | | | | .5929** (.1660) | | .3896** | .3285** |
| (6.4) | −.6443 | .9421 (.3018) | | | | | .1940 (.1884) | | .5965** | .5328** |
| (6.5) | −1.1380 | | | | | | .4515* (.1622) | .5320[b] (.2289) | .5244** | .4492** |
| (6.6) | .9778 | 1.2112** (.2568) | −.0897 (.1146) | | | | | | .5820** | .503** |
| (6.7) | .8343 | 1.4746** (.2535) | | −.3427* (−.597) | | | | | .6571** | .6025** |
| (6.8) | .8833 | 1.1465** (.2080) | | | .3144 (.1611) | | | | .6452** | .5891** |
| (6.9) | −.1161 | 1.0758** (.2078) | | | | | | .2326[c] (.1090) | .6563** | .6021** |
| (6.10) | .2045 | .9675** (.2024) | | | | | | 1.2992[d] (.4613) | .6995** | .6520** |
| (6.11) | 2.0127 | 1.6024** (.2874) | −.1529 (.1051) | −.4079 (.1753) | .4486* (.1818) | | | | .6929** | .611** |
| (6.12) | −.2133 | 1.2678** (.2248) | −.1820 (.1066) | | | | | | .7028** | .624** |
| (6.13) | −.1271 | 1.3869** (.2611) | | −.2537 (.1744) | .2077 (.1729) | | | | .6825** | .598** |
| (6.14) | .3336 | 1.3497** (.2512) | | −.2755 (.1565) | | | | .1864[c] (.1067) | .7068** | .6416** |
| (6.15) | −4.4891 | | | | .5745** (.1511) | | .5475** (.1311) | .5105*[b] (.1792) | .7250** | .6638** |
| (6.16) | .8249 | 1.5458** (.2706) | −.2041 (.1017) | −.2912 (.1753) | .3365 (.1847) | | | | .7517** | .661** |
| (6.17) | −1.1777 | .6371** (.2373) | −.1917* (.0878) | −.4288* (.1449) | | .1660* (.0586) | | | .8047** | .7325** |
| (6.18) | −1.2899 | 1.5376** (.2532) | −.1709 (.0893) | −.3583 (.1581) | | .1387 (.0635) | | .1359[d] (.1256) | .8208** | .738** |
| (6.19) | −1.3658 | 1.5922** (.2393) | −.2148** (.0897) | −.3594* (.1547) | .1909 (.1752) | .1407* (.0627) | | | .8211** | .7385** |

Source: See text note 4.

Note: Figures in parentheses are standard errors of the coefficients. * Indicates statistical significance at the 95 percent level. ** Indicates statistical significance at the 99 percent level.

[a] For a more detailed description of variables, see Appendix B.

[b] Variable $D_{au}$, decades since old age insurance was introduced.

[c] Variable $D_{au}$, participation in past wars.

what above actual expenditures in the best-fitting equations. Excluding benefits to war victims, actual social welfare expenditures in the United States in 1956-57 were $103.7 per capita, or 4.9 percent of national income. Estimates of these figures, based on Equations (4.7) and (5.13), were $113.3 and 6.2 percent, respectively.

There is no apparent pattern in these deviations of estimates from observed data. They probably arise from a combination of special national characteristics and inexact statistical specification. For example, the great reliance on nonstatutory programs in the United States, the dual society in South Africa, and the large family allowances in France are the result of unique political circumstances that shaped the character of social security programs in these countries. On the statistical side, nonlinearities in the relationships could easily account for some portion of the remaining unexplained variance, since only per capita income and population density were tested in logarithmic form.          1964361

## Expenditures on Specific Programs

The factors that influence social welfare expenditures as a whole should also influence expenditures for component programs. The strength of this influence may vary among particular programs, however. The factors that appeared to be important determinants of the level of total expenditures were also tested as determinants of the percentage of national income spent on programs for the aged, on health programs, on family allowances, and on benefits for war victims.[23]

### Expenditures on the Aged

Expenditures on the aged form the largest single category of social security outlays. They account, on the average, for about 40 percent of the total. The same variables that are statistically significant in explaining the level of all welfare expenditures are also significant in explaining the level of outlays for the aged. As shown in Table 6, the signs of the coefficients of these variables do not change, but significance levels and correlation coefficients are lower.

[23] Although expenditures on unemployment insurance, workmen's compensation, and general assistance were included in total expenditures, their determinants have not been tested separately here.

These results are not surprising since old age benefits are a large proportion of total social security in most countries. Further, hypotheses about the relationships governing social security expenditures in general apply with equal force to old age benefits. Thus, the maturity of the system, household savings, general revenue financing, growth of national income, and the level of other government expenditures are all relevant to the level of benefits for these programs.

A more unexpected result was that the age of the social security system in general appeared to be consistently more closely related to old age benefits than the age of the old age insurance program itself. This suggests that the social insurance legislative cycle permits expenditures on later programs to "catch up" with the level of benefits for initial programs. It also suggests that public acceptance of the social security principle depends on the whole gamut of programs. This suggestion is supported by the result that ordinary government expenditures, the variable $G_y$ representing the relative economic importance of government, have positive and significant coefficients which do not decrease the explanatory value of the age of the social security system ($D_s$).

As Table 6 indicates, results for other variables were less consistent. The simple correlation between percentage of the population over sixty-five ($P^*_r$) and expenditures on the aged is highly significant, but, in this case, the regression coefficient loses significance with the inclusion of $D_s$. Participation in past wars was not a significant factor in any of the regressions in which it was included. The coefficients of the war variable are alternately positive and negative and always insignificant.

These results are generally supported by an alternate approach to explaining expenditures on old age benefits. Insofar as the cost of social security programs for the aged is determined by the number of persons over retirement age and the level of individual benefits, the factors that determine these elements should be important influences on the overall outlay on old age benefits. The choice of retirement age under old age pensions, at any given level of benefits, determines the cost of the program. The level of old age benefits itself, however, appears to be influenced by the number of persons of retirement age, as well as per capita national income and age of the social security system.

**TABLE 7. Regression Results, Determinants of the Retirement Age under Social Insurance (R), 1957**

*(Constant term in years)*

| Equation Number | Constant Term | Regression Coefficients[a] | | Coefficients of Determination | |
|---|---|---|---|---|---|
| | | Past Wars $D_w$ | Per Capita National Income (log) Log $Y_p$ | $R^2$ | $\bar{R}^2$ |
| (7.1) | 66.9436 | −.7168** (.2032) | | .3835** | .3218** |
| (7.2) | 53.9697 | −.7222** (.1817) | 1.9687* (.8348) | .5231** | .4478** |

Source: See text note 4.
Note: Figures in parentheses are standard errors of the coefficients. * Indicates statistical significance at the 95 percent level. ** Indicates statistical significance at the 99 percent level.
[a] For a more detailed description of variables, see Appendix B.

The highly significant negative correlation between the variable representing participation in wars $(D_w)$ and the retirement age, shown in Table 7, is unexpected in the light of the failure of this variable to significantly influence the level of old age expenditures. It does suggest, however, that one aftermath of war may be a reduction in the ability or willingness of a nation's working force to put in long working lives.

The reason for the positive coefficient relating retirement age to per capita income is more obscure. The initial indication would be that the income elasticity of demand for leisure is negative. It is more likely, however, that longer working lives and higher per capita incomes are joint effects of national attitudes toward work.

The liberality of old age benefits[24] is associated with the same variables in the same way as the general level of social security expenditures $(E_y)$. Table 8 shows that the variable representing the age of the system $(D_s)$ has highly significant positive coefficients, as does the variable indicating the percentage of the total population over retirement age $(P_r)$.

These results suggest a trade-off between the number of retired persons and benefit levels. Countries seem forced to choose between early retirement under social insurance and high benefit levels. This

[24] This variable is the ratio of $A_y$, the percentage of national income spent on payments to the aged, to $P_r$, the percentage of the population over retirement age.

**TABLE 8. Regression Results, Determinants of Old Age Benefit Levels, 1957**

*(Constant term in billions of U. S. dollars)*

| Equation Number | Constant Term | Age of System $D_s$ | Population Over Retirement Age $P_r$ | Other Government Expenditures $G_y$ | Household Savings $S$ | Other Variables | Coefficients of Determination | |
|---|---|---|---|---|---|---|---|---|
| | | | | | | | $R^2$ | $\overline{R}^2$ |
| (8.1) | .4589 | .1121** (.0268) | -.0394** (.0114) | | | | .5246** | .449 ** |
| (8.2) | .2901 | .1043 (.0265) | -.0379** (.0111) | .0088 (.0059) | | | .5769** | .4829** |
| (8.3) | .1237 | .1082** (.0216) | -.0256** (.0096) | .0229** (.0065) | | -.0047ᵇ (.0069) | .7541** | .6680** |
| (8.4) | .0788 | .1098** (.0217) | -.0274** (.0099) | .0219 (.0060) | -.0076 (.0090) | | .7582** | .6720** |
| (8.5) | .2126 | .1144** (.0229) | -.0281** (.0101) | .0237** (.0066) | -.0081 (.0092) | -.0052ᵇ (.0070) | .7679** | .672 ** |

Source: See text note 4.

Note: Figures in parentheses are standard errors of the coefficients. ** Indicates statistical significance at the 99 percent level.

ᵃ For detailed descriptions of variables, see Appendix B.

ᵇ Variable L, male life expectancy at birth.

finding is supported by the association of long life expectancy ($L$) with lower benefits on the average. There is some implication, however, that interventionist governments tend to provide relatively larger benefits for their aged population in that the level of regular government expenditures ($G_v$) is positively and significantly correlated with old age benefits.[25]

## Expenditures on Other Programs

HEALTH INSURANCE. The results are not so clear in the case of expenditures on health programs. The age of the general system ($D_s$) again has more explanatory value than its specific counterpart $D_h$. This reaffirms that later programs are likely to catch up with earlier ones, and that popular attitudes toward each program are shaped by experience with all of them. Highly significant simple correlations with the proportion of aged population ($P_r$*) and with reliance on general revenues ($E_t$) appear in Equations (9.3) and (9.4) shown in Table 9, but statistical significance vanishes when $D_s$ is included in the regressions.

There appears to be no significant relationship between health expenditures and participation in past wars. However, there is a significant negative relationship between health outlays and payments to war victims ($W_v$). It is possible that this reflects varying solutions to the medical problems resulting from wars. In some countries, these are met through direct payments to war victims and, in others, through health insurance. It may indicate, however, that the level

[25] This conclusion may be qualified, however, by the comparison of per capita expenditures on the aged to per capita national income shown in Column 7 of Appendix Table A-1. In most countries, the ratio of per capita old age benefits to per capita national income was very low, but the variation from country to country was quite wide. In Germany, for instance, when all payments to the aged are accounted for, per capita benefits appeared to exceed per capita national income for the country at large. The United States ranked sixteenth in the sample of twenty-two countries. Pensions in many of the countries often described as "welfare states" were surprisingly small in comparison to some others.

These statistics on payments to the aged include benefits from social insurance and noncontributory programs, but they do not necessarily reflect the economic condition of the aged accurately. There are many other possible sources of current income for persons over retirement age, such as wages, savings, relatives, or nonstatutory programs. The extent to which these sources are available and utilized to supplement or supplant pension benefits determines, in part, the adequacy of standards of living for the aged.

**TABLE 9. Regression Results, Determinants of Social Security Expenditures on Health as a Percentage of National Income ($H_y$), 1957[a]**

(Constant term in billions of U.S. dollars)

| Equation Number | Constant Term | Regression Coefficients[b] | | | | | Coefficients of Determination | |
|---|---|---|---|---|---|---|---|---|
| | | Age of System $D_s$ | General Revenue Financing $E_g$ | Past Wars $D_w$ | Payments to War Victims $W_y$ | Other | $R^2$ | $\bar{R}^2$ |
| (9.1) | .8208 | .5608** (.0957) | | | | | .6320** | .5952** |
| (9.2) | 1.8419 | | .2576** (.0810) | | | .3800**c (.0838) | .5072** | .4585** |
| (9.3) | 1.6276 | (.0810) | | | | | .3360** | .2700** |
| (9.4) | .5130 | | | | | .2482**d (.0813) | .3177** | .2495** |
| (9.5) | .7266 | .4905** (.1186) | .0749 (.0749) | | | | .6505** | .5955** |
| (9.6) | .7133 | .5392** (.1334) | | | | .0199d (.0833) | .6331** | .5752** |
| (9.7) | .8555 | .5227** (.1243) | .0576 (.0775) | -.0480 (.0528) | | | .6659** | .592 ** |
| (9.8) | .7300 | .5447** (.1174) | .0817 (.0739) | .0491 (.0724) | -.5594 (.3037) | | .7215** | .6395** |
| (9.9) | .8271 | .6407** (.0944) | | | -.4664* (.2148) | | .7192** | .6725** |
| (9.10) | .7874 | .6408** (.0961) | | .0690 (.1139) | -.7329 (.4915) | | .7252** | .6605** |

Source: See text note 4.
Note: Figures in parentheses are standard errors of the coefficients. * Indicates statistical significance at the 95 percent level. ** Indicates statistical significance at the 99 percent level.
[a] Equations (9.9) and (9.10) do not include Japan because of the special way Japan reimbursed war victims.
[b] For a more detailed description of variables, see Appendix B.
[c] Variable $D_h$, the number of decades since the introduction of health insurance.
[d] Variable $P_r*$, the percentage of total population over age sixty-five.

## TABLE 10. Regression Results, Determinants of Family Allowances as a Percentage of National Income (F_y), 1957

*(Constant term in billions of U. S. dollars)*

| Equation Number | Constant Term | Regression Coefficients[a] | | | Coefficients of Determination | |
|---|---|---|---|---|---|---|
| | | Age of Program $D_f$ | Catholic Country $D_c$ | Income Growth Rate $y$ | $R^2$ | $\bar{R}^2$ |
| (10.1) | 1.0295 | 1.7215** (.4394) | | | .4343** | .377 ** |
| (10.2) | 1.1118 | | 2.0482** (.6232) | | .3507** | .2858** |
| (10.3) | .7819 | 1.4017** (.3859) | 1.5370** (.5110) | | .6168** | .5563** |
| (10.4) | 1.5359 | 1.3959** (.3665) | 1.6247** (.4878) | −.1854 (.1059) | .6725** | .5998** |

Source: See text note 4.
Note: Figures in parentheses are standard errors of the coefficients. ** Indicates statistical significance at the 99 percent level.
[a] For a more detailed description of variables, see Appendix B.

of payments to war victims is a more sensitive indicator of the consequences of war than is the variable representing participation in war. Coefficients of the level of ordinary government expenditures ($G_v$) are not statistically significant in any of these regressions.

FAMILY ALLOWANCES. Less than 15 percent of social welfare expenditures, on the average, are for family allowances. They are most highly developed in France, Chile, Italy and Belgium, although at least 1 percent of national income is spent on these programs in fourteen of the twenty-two countries included in this study.[26]

Two of the variables included in Table 10 explain over 60 percent of the variation in family allowances. These were the age of the family allowance program ($D_f$) and a variable indicating whether a country is predominantly Catholic ($D_c$). Coefficients of both variables are highly significant.

In contrast to earlier results, the age of the social security system ($D_s$) did not have significant coefficients. The demographic variables also did not add significantly to the coefficient of determina-

[26] The United States, Iceland, Switzerland, and Japan spent nothing on family allowances. Germany, Norway, South Africa and the United Kingdom all spent less than one percent of national income on family allowances.

tion; neither the rate of growth of population nor population density bore any statistically significant relation to family allowances.

BENEFITS TO WAR VICTIMS. Benefit levels for these programs were, in general, unrelated to the factors that influence expenditures on other social security programs. Participation in past wars $(D_w)$ explained over half the variance, but other variables, including per capita income and the age of the system, proved to be insignificant.

## Total Personal Security Expenditures

Total expenditures on the risks covered by social welfare programs are the sum of social security expenditures and privately financed expenditures for purposes that complement social security. While household savings[27] are not the same as privately financed security expenditures, it is assumed here that these private expenditures are at least proportional to household savings. Total personal security expenditures $(E_s)$ may then be approximated by adding government social security expenditures net of benefits to war victims $(N_v)$ to some multiple of household saving $(S)$. That is,

$$E_s = N_v + aS$$

where $a$ has a value ranging between 0.5 and 0.9.

Equations (11.1) through (11.4) report the results of regressions on $E_s$ when $a = 0.6$.[28] The coefficient of variable $D_s$, the age of the system, is not markedly larger in those equations than it is for regressions of these variables on social security expenditures $(N_v)$ or on household savings $(S)$. The simple and partial correlations between $E_s$ and $D_s$, however, are markedly higher than those between $D_s$ and $N_v$ or between $D_s$ and $S$. This improved fit suggests that especially large social security outlays are balanced by smaller household sav-

---

[27] Statistics on household savings measure net additions rather than the stock of household savings.

[28] Correlation coefficients were higher when $a = .6$ than when $a$ assumed other values, but the differences were not large. For example, in equation (11.4), the coefficients of determination, adjusted for degrees of freedom, were as follows:

| $a$ | $\bar{R}^2$ |
|-----|-----|
| 0.5 | .8515 |
| 0.6 | .8604 |
| 0.7 | .8556 |
| 0.8 | .8390 |
| 0.9 | .8180 |

**TABLE 11. Regression Results, Determinants of Total Public and Private Personal Security Expenditures ($E_s$), 1957**

(*Constant term in billions of U. S. dollars*)

| Equation Number | Constant Term | Regression Coefficients[a] | | | | Coefficients of Determination | |
|---|---|---|---|---|---|---|---|
| | | Age of System $D_s$ | General Revenue Financing $E_t$ | Income Growth Rate $y$ | Other Government Expenditures $G_y$ | $R^2$ | $\bar{R}^2$ |
| (11.1) | 7.6731 | 2.4654** (.3582) | | | | .7359** | .7049** |
| (11.2) | 8.6074 | 3.1041** (.3587) | −.6854** (.2227) | | | .8341** | .8031** |
| (11.3) | 4.1393 | 3.0829** (.3037) | −.6907** (.1885) | | .2115* (.0781) | .8886** | .8589** |
| (11.4) | 3.7173 | 2.9993** (.3119) | −.5878* (.2105) | .2471 (.2298) | .1757 (.0845) | .8971** | .8604** |

Source: See text note 4.
Note: Figures in parentheses are standard errors of the coefficients. * Indicates statistical significance at the 95 percent level. ** Indicates statistical significance at the 99 percent level.
[a] For a more detailed description of variables, see Appendix B.

ings. The fact that the coefficient of $D_s$ is about the same whether $N_y$ or $E_s$ is dependent[29] points in the same direction.

The regression results also suggest that some countries are more security conscious than others. For instance, large outlays on the aged relative to per capita national income are positively associated with savings, even though the analysis indicates that personal saving and social security are supplementary. The positive value of the coefficient of $D_s$ in the regressions on total government and private personal security expenditures indicates that this national security consciousness is probably related to the age of the governmental social security system.

Although these findings do not explain how social security and household saving have influenced one another over time, they may have some implications with regard to the treatment of social security funds. To the extent that social welfare expenditures reduce the propensity to save, an increase in the level of social security expenditures will reduce the quantity of private savings available for investment purposes and conflict with a national goal of encouraging economic growth. This effect might be offset, however, by ac-

[29] Compare equations (5.14) and (11.4).

cumulating social insurance reserves and actively using these reserve funds to increase capital formation.[30]

## Summary and Conclusions

Most of the variation in the level of social security outlays in various countries is related to quantifiable variables. The regressions suggest that the length of time a country has had a social security system is the most important single determinant of its cost. There is a negative relationship between social security and household saving. Apparently, more of the one reduces the stimulus for the other, but the causal direction of the relationship can not be established with these data. Surprisingly, demographic variables do not show any systematic relationship to social security expenditures. The income elasticity of social security with respect to national income is apparently less than one, indicating that very wealthy countries spend proportionately less on social security.

Compared to social security in other industrial countries, the United States system is new and modest. It is also relatively narrow. Its limited health insurance program is in its infancy, and it completely eschews family allowances; both are programs which most other countries have adopted. The level of benefits for the aged relative to per capita income is lower in the United States than in most other developed countries. The importance of the age of the system indicated by these regressions, however, suggests that both the risks covered by social insurance programs and the relative size of benefits will expand as the United States program matures.

[30] In 1960, Sweden extensively revised its social insurance system. The possible conflict between saving and social insurance expenditures was given as a motive for reserve accumulation. "The decision to build up a huge fund was promoted by the need for making up for the decrease in private savings and state pension funds which may result from the adoption of the new pension system." Ernst Michanek, "Sweden's New National Pension Insurance," *Bulletin of the International Social Security Association* (September 1960), pp. 422-23.

# APPENDIX A

# Summary of National Social Security Systems

**TABLE A-1. Some Characteristics of Social Security Programs in Twenty-two Countries, 1957**

(Dollar amounts in millions of U. S. dollars)

| Country | Per Capita National Income (1956–57) | Population Over Retirement Age (Percent) | Retirement Age Under Social Security[a] | Pension Test | Automatic Adjustment of Pensions[b] | Ratio to Per Capita National Income | |
|---|---|---|---|---|---|---|---|
| | | | | | | Maximum Taxable Wages | Old Age Benefits |
| Australia | $1,058 | 10.5 | 65/60 | Means | No | 7 times | .29 |
| Austria | 541 | 14.6 | 65/60 | Income | No | 4 times | .60 |
| Belgium | 920 | 14.3 | 65/60 | Income | Prices[f] | 2 times | .38 |
| Canada | 1,458 | 4.8 | 70 | Retirement | No | 2 times | .48 |
| Chile | 321 | 4.0 | 65 | Income | Wages | No ceiling | .75 |
| Denmark | 872 | 10.5 | 67/62 | Retirement | Prices | No ceiling | .38 |
| Finland | 901 | 6.9 | 65 | Income | Prices | No ceiling | .64 |
| France | 846 | 16.9 | 60 | No | Wages | 2 times | .44 |
| Germany | 742 | 10.1 | 65 | No | Wages | 3.5 times | 1.09 |
| Iceland | 1,416 | 6.4 | 67 | No | No | Lump sum | .80 |
| Ireland | 451 | 6.7 | 70 | Income | No | Lump sum | .91 |
| Italy | 404 | 14.7 | 60/55 | No | No | 1.8 times | .27 |
| Japan | 252 | 11.0 | 60/55 | No | Yes | 6 times | .16 |
| Netherlands | 690 | 8.4 | 65 | Retirement | Wages | 3.5 times | .60 |
| New Zealand | 1,110 | 9.2 | 65[c] | No | No | No ceiling | .50 |
| Norway | 941 | 6.5 | 70 | No | No | g | .58 |
| Portugal | 197 | 7.3 | 65 | No | No | 8.5 times | .16 |
| South Africa | 336 | 8.0 | 65/60 | No | No | h | .19 |
| Sweden | 1,267 | 9.3 | 67 | No | Prices | 2.3 times | .55 |
| Switzerland | 1,223 | 10.8 | 65/63 | No | No | 3 times | .40 |
| United Kingdom | 954 | 14.2 | 65/60 | Means | No | Lump sum | .28 |
| United States | 2,101 | 8.6 | 65[d] | { Retirement Income[e] | No | 2.3 times | .36 |

Source: See text note 4.

[a] When two figures appear, the first refers to men and the second to women.

[b] "Yes" indicates that provision for automatic adjustment exists, but details are unspecified.

[c] Pensions are payable at age sixty if the beneficiary passes a means test.

[d] Full pensions are awarded at age sixty-five, but reduced pensions are available at sixty-two.

[e] The "income" test applies only to earnings received from employment covered by social security (not to dividends or interest, for example).

[f] Miners' pensions are tied to the level of miners' wages.

[g] Norway divides eligible workers into wage classes. Workers in each wage class must pay a graduated lump sum tax.

[h] Workers are required to contribute to unemployment insurance only; the sums are trivial. Public employees and railway and harbor employees contribute to their own pension funds.

**TABLE A-2.** Social Security Expenditures and Revenues in 1957 as a Percentage of National Income (1956–57) in Twenty-two Countries

| Country | Social Security Expenditures | | Sources of Social Security Revenues | | | |
|---|---|---|---|---|---|---|
| | Total | On the Aged | Taxes on Workers | Taxes on Employers | General Revenues and Special Taxes | Interest and Other Sources |
| Australia | 9.1 | 3.1 | .7[c] | 7.1 | 1.1 | .2 |
| Austria | 17.6 | 8.8 | 4.2 | 3.2 | 9.3 | .7 |
| Belgium | 16.3 | 5.4 | 3.1 | 4.6 | 7.3 | 1.3 |
| Canada | 8.7 | 2.3 | .9 | 5.8 | 1.5 | .5 |
| Chile | 9.7 | 3.0 | 1.9 | 3.2 | 4.0 | .8 |
| Denmark | 12.0 | 4.0 | 1.4 | 9.2 | 1.2 | .1 |
| Finland | 12.0 | 4.4 | .7 | 6.5 | 4.0 | .7 |
| France | 18.9 | 7.5[a] | 2.8 | 4.2 | 11.3 | .6 |
| Germany | 20.8 | 11.0 | 4.8 | 6.2 | 8.3 | 1.5 |
| Iceland | 7.9 | 5.1[a] | 1.8 | 4.3 | 1.2 | .5 |
| Ireland | 11.5 | 6.1 | .6 | 8.4 | 2.4 | .1 |
| Italy | 15.2 | 4.4 | 1.4 | 2.6 | 10.1 | 1.2 |
| Japan | 5.8 | 1.8 | 1.4 | 1.4 | 2.6 | .4 |
| Netherlands | 12.3 | 5.0 | 4.9 | 1.7 | 4.9 | .7 |
| New Zealand | 13.0 | 4.6 | 6.5 | 6.0 | .5 | .1 |
| Norway | 10.1 | 3.8 | 3.2 | 4.4 | 2.1 | .2 |
| Portugal | 6.5 | 2.2[b] | .8 | 1.4 | 2.9 | 1.4 |
| South Africa | 4.5 | 1.5 | .5 | 2.8 | .7 | .5 |
| Sweden | 12.9 | 5.1 | 1.9 | 9.3 | 1.5 | .1 |
| Switzerland | 8.7 | 4.3 | 2.8 | 2.5 | 2.0 | 1.3 |
| United Kingdom | 12.1 | 4.5 | 2.2 | 7.2 | 2.0 | .7 |
| United States | 6.0 | 3.1 | 1.4 | 2.2 | 2.2 | .2 |

Source: See text note 4.
[a] Revisions of original figures in which public health expenditures were included.
[b] Revisions of original figures in which unemployment insurance was included.
[c] Only public employees are required to contribute to social insurance in Australia.

# APPENDIX B

# Variables and Sources

THE FOLLOWING VARIABLES were tested for significance during the course of this study. Since the discussion in the text was generally confined to those variables that did appear to be significantly related to social security, some variables are included in the list below that were not mentioned explicitly in the text. The figures in parentheses refer to the sources listed on page 48.

$A_b$ = Average social security benefits of all kinds for the aged. $A_b = A_y/P_r$.

$A_t$ = Expenditures on the aged from general revenues as a percentage of national income (1) (2).

$A_y$ = Percent of national income spent on payments to the aged (1) (2).

$D_a$ = Dummy variable indicating the number of decades since old age insurance was introduced (3).

$D_c$ = Dummy variable for predominantly Catholic country—1; for non-Catholic country—0.

$D_f$ = Dummy variable indicating the number of decades since family allowances were introduced (3).

$D_h$ = Dummy variable indicating the number of decades since health insurance was introduced (3).

$D_s$ = Dummy variable indicating the number of decades since the first social security program was introduced (3).

$D_w$ = Dummy variable indicating participation in past wars.

$E_g$ = Social security expenditures as a percentage of total government expenditures. $E_g = E_y/G_y$.

$E_p$ = Social security expenditures per capita in 1956–57, measured in U.S. dollars at the current exchange rate (1).

$E_t$ = Expenditures on social security out of general revenues as a percentage of national income (1) (2).

$E_y$ = Social security expenditures as a percentage of national income in 1956–57 (1) (2).

47

$E_y{}^*$ = Percent of national income spent on social security payments to the aged, on health insurance, and on family allowances (1) (2).

$E_y{}^{**}$ = Percent of national income spent on programs other than for the aged (1) (2).

$F_y$ = Percent of national income spent on family allowances (1) (2).

$G_y$ = Government expenditures other than welfare as a percentage of national income in 1956–57 (1) (2).

$H_y$ = Percent of national income spent on health through social security (1) (2).

$L$ = Male life expectancy at birth (4).

$M_y$ = Percent of national income spent on miscellaneous social security programs (1) (2).

$N_p$ = Social security expenditures per capita in 1956–57 net of benefits to war victims. $N_p = E_p(1 - W_y/E_y)$.

$N_y$ = Social security expenditures net of benefits to war victims as a percentage of national income. $N_y = E_y - W_y$.

$p$ = Rate of population growth, 1959–60 (4).

Log $P$ = Logarithm of population density (5).

$P_r$ = Percent of total population over retirement age (3) (4).

$P_r{}^*$ = Percent of total population over age 65 (4).

$R$ = Retirement age under social insurance (3).

$S$ = Household saving as a percentage of personal expenditures plus savings (2).

$W_y$ = Percent of national income spent on payments to war victims (1) (2).

$y$ = Rate of growth of national income, 1950–59 (5).

$y_p$ = Rate of growth of per capita national income, 1950–59 (5).

$Y_p$ = National income per capita in 1956–57 (4).

Log $Y_p$ = The logarithm of per capita national income in 1956–57.

Sources:

(1) International Labor Office, *The Cost of Social Security*. Geneva, annual, 1949–57.

(2) The United Nations, *Yearbook of National Accounts Statistics*. Lake Success: 1959.

(3) United States Social Security Administration, *Social Security Programs Throughout the World*. Washington, 1961.

(4) The United Nations, *Demographic Yearbook*. Lake Success, annual, 1949–57.

(5) The United Nations, *Statistical Yearbook*. Lake Success, annual, 1949–57.

HENRY AARON*

# Benefits Under the American
# Social Security System

To MOST AMERICANS, "Social Security" means Old-Age, Survivors, and Disability Insurance (OASDI). While social welfare programs, broadly defined, affected many more persons and dispensed $66.5 billion in benefits in 1963, OASDI is the most pervasive single program. In 1964, for instance, a portion of every paycheck of every worker in covered employment was deducted for OASDI, and almost 20 million persons, including 74.5 percent of the population over age sixty-five, received more than $16 billion in benefits under this program.

This chapter is concerned with two aspects of the American Social Security system. The first is the technique for adjusting benefit levels. The method of legislative adjustment, based on projected cost estimates, is briefly compared with methods used by other countries; the cost estimates, themselves, are then evaluated with respect to major economic objectives, such as growth. Secondly, the income transfers, both over time and among individuals, that result from the American benefit formula will be analyzed; in particular, the equity of the redistributive effects of the Social Security system among different groups of workers will be considered by comparing contribution and benefit levels.

* Council of Economic Advisers.

## Adjustment of Social Insurance Levels

Inflation and growth of real wages create pressures for adjustments in the levels of social security taxes and benefits. The factors that produce pressures for amendment of the system, by adding a new program, for instance, are more complex and primarily political in nature. In several countries, changes in pension levels can be made more or less automatically. In the United States, adjustments in the benefit formula, like changes in the system, must be made by Congress.

The process of adjusting pension levels in the United States seems quite cumbersome in comparison with automatic adjustment systems. Changes in pension levels are rarely coordinated with changes in living costs and real wages. One of the aims of the Congress in adjusting pensions, as well as in amending the system, however, is to keep benefit costs and contributions in actuarial balance. To do this, it relies on estimates of future expenditures and revenues prepared by the Division of the Actuary of the Social Security Administration. A review of the estimating methods used indicates that the technique itself may influence the adjustment of the system.

### Automatic Adjustment of Pension Levels

Relatively moderate price inflation can quickly erode the value of even a generous pension, and growth in real wages, even in the absence of inflation, can cause dissatisfaction over given pension levels. Consequently, all social insurance systems have been amended often.

Eight of the twenty-two countries considered in the previous chapter have established administrative machinery by which these adjustments can be made more or less automatically.[1] Three indexes were used as bases to which automatic adjustment is tied: the consumer price index, the average wage, and the minimum wage.

Adjustment according to the consumer price index is the most

[1] See Armand Kayser, "Adjustment of Old Age Pensions to Fluctuations in Economic Conditions," *Bulletin of the International Social Security Association* (March-April 1962), pp. 19-96, for a full discussion of this machinery; or Daniel Gerig, "Automatic Cost of Living Adjustments of Pensions in Foreign Countries," *Social Security Bulletin* (March 1960), p. 13.

In addition to the eight countries discussed here, Japan has provided for automatic adjustment by law, but administrative provisions have not been worked out.

modest approach of the three. The social insurance laws of Belgium, Denmark, Finland, and Sweden related pensions automatically to the price level so that the real value of pensions is constant. Pensions currently being paid were simply raised or lowered according to price movements. Contributions of those who have not yet retired were, in effect, multiplied by the reciprocal of the consumer price index in order to assure comparability in benefit computation of contributions made in different years. In some cases, the movement of the index must exceed a certain percentage before any adjustment is made. This method does not maintain parity between pensions and real wages. Even strict adherence to this approach permits pensions to decline relative to a rising standard of living.

Changes in the wage level automatically triggered adjustment of pensions in Chile, France, Germany, and the Netherlands.[2] The exact provisions varied from place to place and, in some cases, from industry to industry. But, in general, under these arrangements contributions made in different years with different wage levels were comparable to each other. They also raised the real value of pensions as per capita income increased.

The German system is illustrative. Contributions equal 14 percent of wages up to a ceiling which is adjusted annually. Individual benefits, however, are not computed from previous money contributions, but from the ratio of a worker's earnings to average earnings in covered employment in each year. The average of these ratios and the length of his working life determine what percentage of the base pension the worker will receive when he retires. The base pension is a percentage of the average wage level in all covered employment in the previous three years; the legislature fixes the average wage level each year on the basis of statistics compiled by the Federal Statistical Office. Pensions already in effect may also be modified by the legislature in response to changes in the average wage level used in the formula.

The German benefit formula automatically adjusts new pensions to reflect changes in prices and in earning levels up until the time of retirement. Unless the legislature wishes to modify the structure of the pension system or the income of the pensioner rela-

---

[2] In a few other countries pensions were a fixed percentage of a legally established minimum wage and an increase in this minimum wage automatically raised pensions to the same degree.

tive to that of the rest of the population, the law is virtually self-regulating.[3]

### Adjustment of Benefits in the United States

In the United States, while adjustments in the benefit formula must be made by Congress, newly awarded benefits may rise without legislative action because average covered earnings of those

**TABLE 1. Social Security Benefit Adjustments in the United States, 1940-64**

(Index 1950=100)

| Year | Consumer Price Index | Average Gross Real Wages In Manufacturing | Index of Average Monthly Benefits | | | |
| | | | In Current Payment Status at End of Year | | Awarded During Year | |
| | | | Money | Real | Money | Real |
|---|---|---|---|---|---|---|
| 1940 | 58.2 | 52.6 | 51.5 | 88.5 | 68.3 | 117.4 |
| 1945 | 74.8 | 105.5 | 55.1 | 73.6 | 75.5 | 100.9 |
| 1950 | 100.0 | 100.0 | 100.0 | 100.0 | 100.0[a] | 100.0[a] |
| 1955 | 111.3 | 123.7 | 141.1 | 126.7 | 209.8 | 188.5 |
| 1958 | 120.2 | 113.0 | 151.3 | 125.8 | 224.0 | 186.4 |
| 1960 | 123.0 | 126.1 | 168.6 | 137.1 | 245.9 | 199.9 |
| 1962 | 124.8 | 131.4 | 173.4 | 139.4 | 237.1 | 190.0 |
| 1963 | 127.3 | 134.1 | 175.3 | 137.7 | 241.6 | 189.8 |
| 1964 | 129.0 | 137.4 | 176.4 | 136.8 | 241.3 | 187.1 |

Sources: U. S. Department of Commerce and Social Security Administration.
[a] Under the 1950 amendments. Under the 1939 benefits, the average benefit was 12.7 percent lower.

reaching retirement age increase. However, the *average* benefit level in any period is a weighted average of newly awarded benefits and of benefits already being paid at the beginning of the period.

A comparison of changes in benefits with changes in consumer prices and manufacturing real wages is shown in Table 1. Newly awarded benefits rose more rapidly than average real wages in manufacturing over the period 1940-64. This was the result of liberalization of the benefit formula, increases in the contribution

[3] For a general description of social insurance in Germany, see Theodore Blank, "Situation and Problems of Social Security in the Federal Republic of Germany," *Bulletin of the International Social Security Administration* (June 1960), pp. 261-69.

ceiling, and the fact that benefits were tied to the length of time in covered employment. On the other hand, the real value of benefits during retirement fell nearly 50 percent between 1940 and 1950. In 1950, previously awarded benefits were increased to their original purchasing power. Subsequently, amendments have raised the real value of previously awarded benefits about one-third as much as the increase in real per capita income.

## Social Security Cost Estimates

When Congress wishes to change benefit formulas or add new social insurance programs to the system, its primary source of statistical information is a set of cost estimates prepared by the Division of the Actuary of the Social Security Administration. These estimates make it possible to compare costs of programs that provide different kinds or amounts of benefits at different times, and to determine how high taxes must be in different years to pay for these programs. By focusing on long-run as well as short-run costs, the estimates enable the policy maker to consider the full price of the programs he advocates. The estimates also enable officials concerned with short-run economic policy to evaluate the fiscal impact of social insurance at each point in time. These two purposes call for estimates with different attributes.

For the first purpose, a meticulously accurate "forecast" of the dollar amount of benefits, revenues, and changes in the trust funds is unnecessary. What is needed is a set of estimates which are done consistently and which accord nontrivial weight to future events. Subsequent amendments, however unlikely they may be, seem to be irrelevant to estimates of benefits and revenues under one specific program. Moreover, since the Social Security Act and all subsequent amendments relate both benefits and contributions to covered earnings, the estimates need only show benefits and costs as percentages of covered earnings. Absolute dollar figures are of minor interest.

For the second purpose, however, the relative figures are little help, and the absolute dollar figures are useful only if they give an approximately correct idea of the level of expenditures and revenues and of the increase or decrease in the trust funds. If estimates indicate a program is actuarially sound, but also show that it will produce intolerable economic effects, the question of actuarial soundness becomes irrelevant, for the program will be changed. For the second purpose, then, accuracy of dollar estimates is crucial insofar as they affect *economic* policy; for the first purpose, accuracy of relative figures is crucial insofar as they affect *political* deliberations.

The cost estimates involve projections of many variables ranging from population and labor force participation rates to the numbers of parents over age sixty-five who outlive OASDI insured children and of dependents of disabled workers.[4] The actuary makes two estimates for each variable. One entails high costs or produces low revenues. The other entails low costs or produces high revenues. All of the projections of the first type are grouped together, yielding a "high cost estimate"; all of those of the second type are grouped together yielding a "low cost estimate." The arithmetic average of these two results, called the "intermediate cost estimate," is used in legislative work on Social Security.

Wages and prices are held constant in all of these estimates. Population growth is the only economic variable for which increases are predicted and it is the uncertainty of the population forecasts that explains most of the difference between the estimates.[5] These estimates are, therefore, not meant to be forecasts of actual expenditure, revenue, and trust fund developments.

In addition to the regular cost estimates, special studies of costs have also been made. For example, to estimate costs and revenues under more realistic economic assumptions, calculations were made which allowed for the growth of money wages, but no change in the contribution ceilings.[6] All other variables took on the same values as under the intermediate cost estimate. Another estimate assumed that the contribution ceiling would be raised so that the ratio of taxable wages to total wages in covered employment remains the same, and that the benefit formula would be amended so that the ratio of benefits to taxable wages remains the same as in some base year.

[4] For a full list of these variables, see U.S. Social Security Administration, *Actuarial Study Number 49* (May 1959), pp. 5-6.

[5] U.S. Social Security Administration, Annual Report, *The Federal Old-Age and Survivors Insurance and Disability Insurance Trust Funds, Fiscal Year 1964* (1963), p. 53. (Referred to hereafter as the *1964 Annual Report.*)

[6] U.S. Social Security Administration, Division of the Actuary, *Actuarial Study Number 53* (August 1961), and Division of Program Research, *Economic Assumptions Underlying the Medium-Range Projections of the Federal Old-Age and Survivors Insurance and Disability Insurance Trust Funds, 1966-1975* (August 1961).

## The Time Horizon of the Estimates

The choice of how far into the future cost estimates are projected affects the size of benefits that a given set of taxes appears actuarially adequate to finance. Until 1965, estimates were projected in perpetuity. That is, expenditures and revenues were computed partly from projected demographic data based on the current population; beyond a certain future point, eighty-five to ninety years hence, the demographic situation *then prevailing* was assumed to continue indefinitely.

In 1965, in response to urgings of the Advisory Council on Social Security,[7] the horizon used in the estimates was changed. Cost estimates now extend seventy-five years into the future and then terminate. Recomputation in 1964 of the status of the 1961 Act altered the actuarial status of the OASDI funds from a deficit of .24 percent of covered payroll when the estimates are carried to infinity, to a surplus of .01 percent of covered payroll when the seventy-five-year horizon is used.

Clearly, as this example shows, the choice of the horizon for estimates is of great significance in judging the adequacy of supporting taxes. On the other hand, the choice of the horizon has no effect on the usefulness of estimates in shaping economic policy. It is actual expenditures and revenues in the near future, not percentages of covered payroll, that describe the immediate impact of the Social Security system on the economy.

## Earnings Assumptions

The 1965 intermediate cost estimate is based on the assumption that "earning rates of covered workers by age and sex will continue over the next 75 years at the levels experienced in 1963."[8] It is also pointed out, however, that if it were assumed that earnings are increased while benefits are assumed to remain at current levels, then

[7] *The Status of the Social Security Program and Recommendations for Its Improvement,* Report of the Advisory Council on Social Security (1965), pp. 16-17. (Referred to hereafter as *Advisory Council.*)

[8] *Actuarial Cost Estimates and Summary of Provisions of the Old-Age, Survivors, and Disability Insurance System as Modified by the Social Security Amendments of 1965,* House Committee on Ways and Means. 89 Cong. 1 sess. (July 30, 1965), p. 71. (Referred to hereafter as *1965 Cost Estimates.*)

"cost relative to payroll would, of course, be lower."[9] In other words, if wages rise, the actuarial balance or imbalance of the estimates would be accurate only if benefits and the contribution ceiling are increased along with rising wages. The dollar amount of benefits and contributions would be greater, of course.

The explicit failure to include the assumption of increasing earnings in estimates used for legislative planning is odd since projections of participation rates, birth rates, and many other variables central to the cost estimates are specified. Future earnings could be estimated with at least as much confidence since real wages can be expected to rise over the long run at a rate not far from the secular historical trend of about 3 percent per year.

The intermediate cost estimates also ignore possible future amendments to the benefit formula. In view of the virtual certainty that earnings will increase, the assumption that benefit levels will not rise implies that relative benefits decrease. The intermediate cost estimates are accurate for planning purposes only if Congress annually raises benefits, both newly awarded and in current payment status, by exactly the same amount as the increase in covered earnings. If the contribution ceiling were also raised annually along with earnings, benefit levels would have to be raised still more to maintain the same cost-revenue ratio.

The same effect could be secured much more simply by a pension adjustment scheme similar to that used in Germany. Unlike the German scheme, however, pensions already awarded would have to be raised along with the increase in covered earnings. If Congress intends to raise pensions by a smaller amount than would be provided by automatic adjustment, then the Social Security system is now over-financed. If Congress intends to raise pensions by a larger amount than would be provided by automatic adjustment, then the Social Security system is now under-financed. Once again, the choice of assumptions about how Congress will respond to future increase in covered earnings affects the level of benefits which any set of taxes appears adequate to finance. In view of the high probability that earnings will increase, the intermediate cost estimates involve implicit assumptions about how Congress will respond. Since these assumptions have an important bearing on the tax rate schedule necessary to

[9] *Ibid.,* p. 7.

finance a given set of benefits, they are politically significant and should be examined.

## Reserve Accumulation and Trust Fund Management

Current contributions under Old-Age, Survivors, and Disability Insurance create a specific future liability for the program. There are two approaches to financing these liabilities. The current level of taxation may be set so as to accumulate a reserve against the estimated future liability incurred, or it may be set at a level sufficient to meet only the current costs of the program.

In general, only contingency reserves have been accumulated for nonpension programs. Reserve accumulation has been avoided because of political fears that the trust fund might be spent on unde-

**TABLE 2. A Comparison of the Size, Growth, and Use of Social Security Trust Funds in Nine Countries, Selected Years, 1937-63**

| Country | Percentage of National Income, 1952–56[a] | | Approximate Percentage of Trust Funds Held in Cash Plus Government Securities[b] | |
|---|---|---|---|---|
| | Trust Funds | Annual Additions to Trust Funds | International Labor Organization Estimates[c] | Independent Estimates[d] |
| Switzerland | 20 | 4.6 | 40 (1950–53) | 15 (1960) |
| Chile[e] | 13 | 2.2 | 50 (1950–52) | |
| Portugal[e] | . . . | 2.1 | . . . | 68 (1958) |
| Germany | 4 | 1.0 | 80 (1950–53) | |
| Iceland[f] | 6 | 1.0 | 50 (1950–53) | |
| Finland | 10 | 1.0[g] | 77 (1950–54) | 8 (1955–61) |
| Netherlands | 9 | 1.0 | 80 (1950–53) | 12 (1957–59) |
| Austria | 3 | 0.8 | 80 (1950–53) | 70 (1956–60) |
| United States | 10 | 0.7[h] | 100 (1950–53) | 100 (1937–63) |

[a] Source, International Labor Organization, *Social Security Handbook.*
[b] Numbers in parentheses refer to the years for which the estimates were made.
[c] Source, International Labor Organization, *Yearbook of Labor Statistics, 1951–55.*
[d] Sources, for Austria, Switzerland, and Finland, private correspondence; for the Netherlands, *Sociale Zekerheid in Nederland, 1948–59,* pp. 89–104; for the United States, *Annual Statistical Supplement to the Social Security Bulletin* (1960), pp. 8–9; for Portugal, *Estatistica da Organizacao Corporativa e Providencia Social* (1958).
[e] Numbers derived indirectly by multiplying the surplus as a percent of social security expenditures by expenditures as a percent of national income.
[f] The meaning of a trust fund is not clear since central and local governments meet over 50 percent of the cost of pensions.
[g] Finland officially abandoned the reserve principle in 1957, but the fund continued to increase at the rate of about 0.7 percent of national income per year during the period 1957–61.
[h] There was no fund accumulation in the United States from 1957 to 1961. Figures do not include state and local government pension programs under which accumulation proceeded at the annual rate of about $1.5 billion during the late 1950's.

sirable projects or because of concern that the real value of reserves might be undermined by inflation or currency devaluation.

Only the nine countries shown in Table 2 accumulated reserves during the years shown. In the United States, although each set of amendments to the Social Security Act has projected reserve accumulation in future years, in practice reserve accumulation has virtually stopped. Under the 1965 amendments, for example, rapid reserve accumulation is scheduled to begin in 1969, when over $4.3 billion will be added to the Trust Funds.[10] Since 1956, however, Congress has amended Social Security laws before such rapid accumulation could begin. In fact, the OASDI Trust Funds were smaller in 1965 than they were in 1956, before the addition of Disability Insurance. The management of fiscal policy has been an important factor in this divergence of policy and practice.

The United States is the only country with a declared policy of reserve accumulation that holds its reserves only in government securities. To the extent that reserves are not held in this form, countries may to some degree promote capital formation directly through their policies of reserve investment. Independent estimates of the proportion of reserves held in government securities or cash, shown in Table 2, suggest that in many countries a large portion of the funds is used for capital formation.

*Significance for Cost Estimates*

The future actuarial balance of the Social Security system in the United States will be affected by the policy toward reserve accumulation because interest earned on the trust funds can supplement payroll taxes needed to support a given level of benefits. When the law calls for tax rates that will lead to reserve accumulation, the apparent cost of a set of benefits depends on the accumulation projected and the interest rate. Thus, to the extent that ultimate contribution rates influence decisions about how much Social Security the country can afford, the interest rate used in cost estimates is important.

The Trust Funds are invested in government securities. These may be ordinary government issues or special obligations issued exclusive-

---

[10] Statements of the 1965 Advisory Council strongly urge that rapid reserve accumulation not be allowed to occur. *Advisory Council,* pp. 18-20.

ly to the Trust Funds. At the time they are issued, special obligations must bear interest at a rate equal to the average market yield at the end of the preceding month on all interest-bearing marketable obligations of the United States not due or callable for at least four years after that date. The average interest rate earned by securities in the OASDI Trust Funds in 1964 was 3.13 percent.[11] For purposes of the cost estimates, an interest rate of 3.75 percent is used for the low cost estimate, 3.25 percent in the high cost estimate, and 3.50 percent in the intermediate cost estimate. These rates are all below the average on new government obligations which were being paid at the middle of 1965—about 4.125 percent.[12]

The choice of the interest rate used in the cost estimates matters little for fiscal policy purposes. The estimates of interest earnings on the Trust Funds all involve a slow transition from rates being paid currently to the future rate of 3.25 percent, 3.50 percent, or 3.75 percent. Even if the expectations of future rates err widely, the interest earnings of the Trust Funds are unlikely to deviate from the estimates by as much as $100 million in the year or two after estimates are made.

On the other hand, the interest rate may have important effects on the way in which the Social Security program is designed. The intermediate cost estimates of OASDI programs passed by Congress have all projected the accumulation of large reserves sometime in the future. Under the 1965 amendments, for example, rapid reserve accumulation is scheduled to begin in 1969, when over $4.3 billion will be added to the Trust Funds (OASDI, DI, and Medical Insurance). Since 1956, Congress has amended Social Security before such rapid accumulation has begun. As a result of these amendments, in fact, there has been slight decumulation of the Trust Funds since 1956. Statements of the 1965 Advisory Council strongly urge that rapid reserve accumulation not be allowed to occur. However, since legislative planning is based on cost estimates which ignore future amendments and since the estimates project large reserves for the future, interest earnings bulk large in the cost estimates. As in the case

[11] *1965 Cost Estimates*, p. 12. The rate on the OASI Trust Fund is lower than that on the DI Trust Fund because the OASI Fund contains relatively more special issues of the 1940's and early 1950's when interest rates were lower than they have been recently, while the DI Fund contains only issues dating from 1954, when Disability Insurance was introduced.

[12] *1965 Cost Estimates*, p. 12.

of the time horizon of the estimates, the choice of the interest rate to be used in the cost estimate affects the level and scope of benefits which Social Security taxes appear adequate to support.

According to the 1964 trustees' report,[13] for example, if a 4 percent interest rate instead of the 3.5 percent rate had been used, "the combined actuarial deficit [of .24 percent of taxable payroll] of both [OASI and DI] would have been virtually eliminated." In general, the higher the interest rate used, the larger the benefits that any set of Social Security taxes can support. If Congress continues to forestall reserve accumulation, the level of payroll taxes necessary to cover current benefits will be affected very little by the actual interest rate. But when the law calls for future reserve accumulation, the apparent cost of a set of benefits does depend on the interest rate. Thus, to the extent that ultimate contribution rates influence Congressional decisions about how much social security the country can afford, the interest rate used in cost estimates is important. The rationale for using a rate of 3.5 percent in the cost estimates is not clear. That rate is greater than the average rate actually earned by the Funds; it is less than the rate on long-term government bonds; it in no way reflects what a trustee, not legally constrained to invest in securities of the federal government, could earn. It is not clear why the interest rate used in the cost estimates should be less than the rate the government would have to pay other lenders to accept debt of similar maturity, and it is at least arguable that the rate used in the estimates should be equal to what unconstrained management by private trustees could earn. This does not imply that the Trust Funds should necessarily be invested in nongovernmental securities, it merely suggests that the rate of interest used in the cost estimates be reexamined.

*Conclusion*

In the United States, where there is no provision for automatic adjustment of pension levels, changes in Social Security benefits are brought about through legislation. One of the major considerations of Congress in changing levels of benefits and contributions, as in amending the system itself, is the actuarial balance of the system. This determination is based upon estimates of future costs of

---

[13] *1964 Annual Report*, p. 53.

benefits compared with anticipated contributions. The technique used in making these estimates significantly affects the apparent cost of benefits. Three aspects of the estimating technique appeared to have a systematic influence. These are the planning horizon, the interest rate, and the earnings assumption. Recent changes in the planning horizon have reduced the weight of possibly unfavorable, but certainly very distant, demographic trends. It is suggested, however, that the interest rate and earnings assumptions should also be reexamined.

## Income Transfers Under Social Security

At the personal level, social security compels employees covered by the system and most self-employed persons to defer receiving a portion of their earnings until after retirement. Thus, it requires the reallocation of income and expenditure over time, resulting, in effect, in "lifetime income redistribution."[14] The temporal redistribution of each individual's income may also, on a collective level, result in income transfers among various groups of workers. The development of quantitative information about these transfers provides some basis for judgments about the horizontal and vertical equity of such redistribution. Are all income classes or wage groups treated alike? Are there administrative inconsistencies? Do people pay more or less for this insurance than it is actually worth? The benefit formulas, themselves, provide some information.

### The OASDI Benefit Formula

Under the American benefit formula, retirement benefits for most workers are based on wages earned after 1950.[15] A period of not less than five years in which earnings were lowest is dropped

---

[14] Redistribution more usually refers to the changes caused by government taxation and expenditures in the disposable income of persons or groups at any point in time. Redistribution in this sense will be ignored here. For a review and critique of previous studies of the degree to which social security, both in the United States and in other countries, redistributes income in this sense, see my unpublished doctoral dissertation, "Social Security in an Expanding Economy" (Harvard University, 1963).

[15] A special benefit formula is used if a higher benefit results when wages earned before 1950 are included.

before the average wage is computed. The primary insurance amount, computed from this average wage, serves as the basis for determining most benefits.

Eligibility for all except disability benefits is acquired when a worker has earned at least $100 from covered employment in one quarter for every four between 1950 (or the year in which the worker turned twenty-one, if later) and the time he (she) reaches sixty-five (sixty-two). Disability benefits also require work in covered employment in at least five of the last ten years. Eligibility for some survivor benefits, however, can be obtained in as little as eighteen months. A typical worker reaching age sixty-five in 1965 need have worked only fifteen quarters in covered employment in order to receive benefits, and the benefit formula would apply to his average monthly wage computed on the basis of his earnings in the ten years since 1950 in which his earnings were highest.

Periodically since 1950, Congress has expanded coverage, included new risks, relaxed qualifications, or increased contribution ceilings or benefit levels. In every case, however, the benefit formula has been progressive. In the 1965 amendments, for example, the pension for a worker retiring at sixty-five is equal to 62.97 percent of the first $110 of his average monthly wage, plus 22.9 percent of the next $290, plus 21.4 percent of the next $150. Since benefits are related to wages rather than contributions, and most often to wages earned just before retirement, the benefit formula alone cannot show whether beneficiaries have made contributions that would have entitled them to greater or smaller benefits under private insurance.

## Contribution and Benefit Levels

Some critics of OASDI have observed that future contribution rates will rise so high that workers will be able to purchase more insurance privately at these rates than they will receive under Social Security.[16] This will occur, it is argued, because contribution rates have been below the level premium cost (LPC) of benefits[17] and be-

---

[16] An exact comparison is impossible, however, because no private insurer provides insurance equivalent to that offered by OASDI.

[17] The Chief Actuary of the Social Security Administration determines the actuarial imbalance of the system by calculating the tax rate which will yield a revenue stream with present value equal to that of benefits which are projected. That tax is the level premium cost (LPC) of benefits. Similarly, he calculates a single

cause many people have received benefits after brief coverage. The resulting actuarial liability will have to be met by taxes above the LPC of benefits. It may be argued that a worker who, together with his employer, makes contributions of 9.7 percent of taxable payroll (the maximum OASDI contribution rate, scheduled to be reached in 1973) for his entire working life will receive a smaller pension than he could purchase privately with the same payment.

This conclusion holds if there is no growth in real wages, and if no amendments to the current law are made, and if the worker, in the absence of Social Security, would receive additional wages equal to the employer contribution. However, if real wages and the ceiling on taxable earnings grow annually 2 percent or more, and if benefit rates are increased at the same rate, almost everyone under the Social Security law will continue to get at least as much insurance as he and his employer are paying for; those at the lower end of the scale will continue to get considerably more. If the burden of the employer tax is not shifted but falls at least in part on the employer, then the chance that the worker will pay more for insurance than he receives in benefits becomes even more remote.

The incidence of Social Security taxes, the relationship of contributions and benefits, and the distributive equity of the system are significant issues for public policy. Some of the questions they raise, however, may be resolved by analyzing the redistributive effects of Social Security.

*Vertical Redistribution: Hypothetical Wage Histories*

The question of whether the Social Security formula resulted in an equitable distribution of benefits was approached through a comparison of the cumulative value of contributions and benefits, measured at the beginning of retirement, for different industries and at different income levels. Whether the mechanics of the formula lead to inequities is first tested by abstracting from actual wage conditions.

The degree of inequity is measured by comparison of the dis-

---

tax rate which will yield revenue with the same present value as the graduated tax schedule written into the law. This rate is the level premium equivalent (LPE) of the tax schedule. According to opinions expressed by Congressional committees on pending legislation and embodied as rules of thumb in Trustees' reports, the system is actuarially sound if the LPC and the LPE differ by no more than 0.3 percent of taxable payroll.

crepancies between the annuity that would be actuarially justified by contributions accumulated at hypothetical wage levels up to the time of retirement and actual benefits that would be received under Social Security at these wage levels. Average wages in selected industries for the period 1937-62 were deflated using the consumer price index in order to equalize the purchasing power of dollars received in different years. In addition, arbitrary wage patterns were developed in which the money wage for each year had a constant real value in 1947-49 dollars of from $500 to $15,000. Then the OASDI contributions at current rates for each of these years were calculated under two assumptions about the shifting of the burden of contributions. These contributions were accumulated at 3 percent and at 6 percent interest, and, from this total, an actuarially justified annuity (AJA) was calculated.[18] The AJA was compared with the actual basic pension to which each wage history would entitle its recipient by computing, first, the ratio of the actual Social Security pension to the AJA, and second, the difference between the pension and the AJA. Finally, the value of other Social Security benefits was added to the actual pension, and the ratio of total benefits to the AJA and the difference between them was computed.

It is assumed that the last year of active employment is 1961 and that pensions begin in 1962; Social Security tax payments began in 1937. It is also assumed that the taxes were completely shifted backward, that is, that the burden of both the employee and the employer contributions fell on the worker. The calculation may be represented symbolically as

$$A_j = \sum_{k=1937}^{1961} \left[ \frac{W_{jk}}{P_k} r_k (1+i)^{1962-k} \right] \frac{1}{Z^i}$$

where $A_j$ is the actuarially justified annuity for the $j^{th}$ wage pattern, $W_{jk}$ is the money wage in the $j^{th}$ industry in the $k^{th}$ year, $P_k$ is the consumer price index for the $k^{th}$ year (1954 = 100), $r_k$ is the combined employee and employer contribution rate in the $k^{th}$ year, $i$ is the assumed interest rate (3 percent or 6 percent) and $1/z^i$ is the annuity until death which $1 will buy at the age of sixty-five, given the particular interest rate, $i$.[19]

[18] The term "actuarial" is not used in its customary sense. Actuaries generally ignore price changes because insurance contracts are not written in terms of constant dollars. In dealing with the relation between sacrifices which tax payments entail and the utility which benefits yield, price changes must be considered, particularly where the insurer is the government.

[19] Alternative assumptions about the incidence of OASDI taxes were also used,

This method of calculation ignores the possibility that the insured may die before age sixty-five. This would reduce total contributions and forestall pension payments, and would also open up the possibility of other dependency allowances. These results present a retrospective picture, comparing the status of workers

**TABLE 3. Relationship of Basic Pension to Total Pension by Income Class, 1960 Law**[a]

| Income Class | Basic Pension as Percentage of Total Benefit |
|---|---|
| $ 648 | 44.2 |
| 1,200 | 48.8 |
| 2,400 | 48.0 |
| 3,600 | 47.9 |
| 4,800 | 48.4 |

Source: John P. Jones and Marice C. Hart, *Analysis of Benefits: OASDI Program: 1960 Amendments,* U. S. Social Security Administration, Actuarial Study No. 50, pp. 50–54.

[a] The percentages relate to a man with a wife and two children who begins work at age twenty and retires at age sixty-five. These figures do not show the relationship between the actuarial cost of the basic pension and total benefits which have been or will be paid to workers who retired in 1962, who worked less than forty-five years in covered employment, who did not enjoy disability benefits for most of that time, who dropped out most years in computing benefits, and so forth.

who have lived to age sixty-five, and do not necessarily indicate the prospective value of OASDI to a younger person.

The results of this calculation are compared with actual benefit payments at hypothetical income levels. Comparisons were made with the basic pension alone, and with total OASDI benefits. Although the basic pension is less than half of total benefits, the use of one or the other made little difference for these comparisons. Table 3 indicates that the reason for this was that benefits to wives, children, and other relatives are roughly the same for all income classes. Scaling the actual pension upwards to include other benefits, therefore, does not affect the conclusions about income differences.

Chart 1, derived from these calculations, shows clearly that if

---

but did not alter the results substantially. The equation for these calculations was of the type below.

In this example it is assumed that two-thirds of the employer's burden is shifted forward in the form of higher prices, and the burden of one-third of the employer's tax plus all of the employee's tax falls on the worker. The equation then becomes

$$A_j = \sum_{k=1937}^{1961} \left[ \frac{2W_{jk}}{3P_k} \left( r_k + \frac{C_{jk}E_k}{C_k} \right) (1 + i)^{1962-k} \right] \frac{1}{Z^i}.$$

where $C_{jk}$ is the assumed average propensity to consume of the $j^{th}$ wage pattern in the $k^{th}$ year, $E_k$ is the total nationwide employer contribution under OASDI, $C_k$ is the level of personal consumption in the $k^{th}$ year, and the other symbols are as stated above.

# CHART 1. Hypothetical Subsidy in OASDI Pension Benefits at Selected Wage Levels [a]

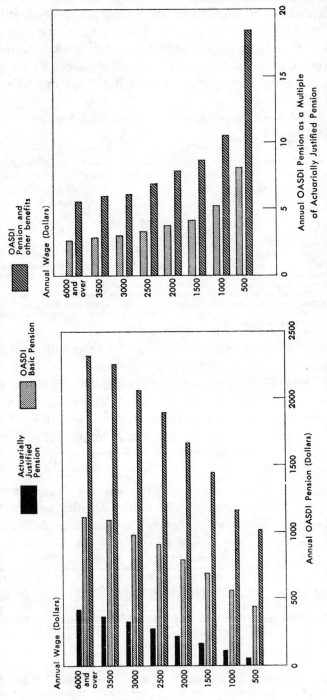

[a] Hypothetical pension is based on an assumption of a 3 percent interest rate on contributions equalling those of both employer and employee under OASDI. The burden of the employee tax is assumed to be borne by the employee; the burden of the employer tax is assumed to be shifted back fully to the employee.

66

the general time shape of wage histories is similar, the OASDI benefit computation procedures yield roughly progressive results, regardless of whether contributions are shifted. That is, the Social Security system of 1962 gave relatively more benefits per dollar of Social Security tax to the lower-paid worker. The benefit formula produces this result unless wages in the lower brackets decline relative to high wages.

A subsidy for all income levels occurs because no one had paid Social Security taxes for a full working life and because the contribution rate was less than the actuarial rate necessary to keep the system self-sustaining over the long run. The subsidy to workers with maximum covered earnings was larger in absolute amount than that received by workers with smaller incomes, but the subsidy increased proportionately less than did covered earnings.[20]

## *Lifetime Vertical Redistribution: Actual Wage Histories*

Actual wage histories show a similar pattern.[21] However, because of differences in timing of income, the same pension can result for different industries despite differences in contributions. The average coal miner and the average electric, light, and gas worker would receive the same pension, although the contributions of the latter were somewhat greater on a present value basis. However, both receive benefits worth at least $750 per year more than their contributions justify.

The relative subsidy received by workers in the various industries is closely related to differences in relative wages among these industries. The benefits subsidy of workers in retailing, for example, is relatively larger than that of workers in higher income industries, although the converse is true of the absolute subsidy. While this result follows from the operation of the benefit formula at different

[20] This subsidy in social insurance is not confined to the American program. Similar calculations, which did not include price adjustments, showed that the capital value of the fund that a British worker would have accumulated between 1926 and 1954 was about one-twentieth the capital value of the pension he was receiving. *Report of the Committee on the Economic and Financial Problems of the Provision for Old Age,* Sir Thomas Phillips, Chairman, Cmd. 9333 (London: 1954). It is probable that a similar pattern would appear in the social insurance systems of most, if not all, other countries.

[21] These results are based on the assumption that the full incidence of Social Security taxes was borne by employees. Different assumptions about the shifting of the tax were used, but the conclusions were substantially the same as those based on the assumption of full backward shifting.

**TABLE 4. Hypothetical Subsidy in OASDI Pension Benefits, Based on Wage Patterns for Various Industries**

*(Annual pensions in 1947–49 dollars)*

| Industry | (1) Actuarially Justified Pension[a] | (2) Actual Basic Pension | (3) Pension Plus Other Benefits | Absolute Subsidy Col. (2)– Col. (1) | Absolute Subsidy Col. (3)– Col. (1) | Relative Subsidy Col. (2) ÷ Col. (1) | Relative Subsidy Col. (3) ÷ Col. (1) |
|---|---|---|---|---|---|---|---|
| Retail Trade | $260.30 | $ 948.12 | $1,975.25 | $687.82 | $1,714.95 | 3.65 | 7.59 |
| Non-Durable Goods | 300.83 | 1,041.00 | 2,168.75 | 740.17 | 1,867.92 | 3.46 | 7.21 |
| Manufacturing | 336.63 | 1,106.16 | 2,304.50 | 769.53 | 1,967.87 | 3.29 | 6.84 |
| Bituminous Coal Mining | 343.13 | 1,115.40 | 2,323.75 | 772.27 | 1,980.62 | 3.25 | 6.77 |
| Wholesale Trade | 345.23 | 1,115.40 | 2,323.75 | 770.17 | 1,978.52 | 3.23 | 6.73 |
| Durable Goods | 352.73 | 1,115.40 | 2,323.75 | 762.67 | 1,971.02 | 3.16 | 6.59 |
| Construction | 360.79 | 1,115.40 | 2,323.75 | 754.61 | 1,962.96 | 3.09 | 6.44 |
| Electricity, Light, and Gas | 363.17 | 1,115.40 | 2,323.75 | 752.23 | 1,960.58 | 3.07 | 6.40 |
| Average taxable OASDI wage | 208.00 | 827.88 | 1,723.50 | 619.88 | 1,515.50 | 3.98 | 8.29 |
| Average total OASDI earnings | 261.74 | 948.12 | 1,975.25 | 686.38 | 1,713.51 | 3.62 | 7.55 |

[a] Calculation of the actuarially justified pension is based on the assumption of a 3 percent interest rate; contributions are assumed to equal those of both employer and employee under Social Security.

68

income levels, it would not have occurred if the relative level of average wages in different industries had changed substantially.

As shown in Table 4, the actual wage histories show that there are some minor inconsistencies in distribution of pension benefits, but that substantial subsidies were received by all groups. These subsidies would be still greater with the inclusion of other benefits.

In general, the relationship between benefits and contributions at different income levels is not constant. However, it appears to be "equitable" in the sense that benefits are progressively related to contributions.

## Horizontal Inequities

Minor horizontal inequities appeared in the industry comparison of benefits and contributions because the time shape of the wage history of specific groups varied slightly, particularly in coverage under Social Security. It is probable that more serious horizontal inequities occur when the time shapes of wage histories differ more sharply.

In the case of individual workers, of course, wage histories do differ widely. In addition to variations in covered employment and covered wages, certain types of employment and employees are treated differently under present Social Security formulas. This can cause major inequities in the sense that workers who have made identical contributions do not receive the same benefits.

DIFFERENCES IN COVERAGE DATES. The first source of inequity is the inevitable result of partial coverage of OASDI in its early years. Latecomers to coverage receive a windfall. This source of inequity may be quite serious today, since eligibility may rest on contributions made over four years or twenty-five years. However, almost all workers are now covered either by OASDI or by comparable retirement plans. In the future virtually universal coverage will cause this source of inequity to become less important.

THE IMPORTANCE OF RECENT WAGE LEVELS. The second source of inequity arises because recent wage levels influence benefit levels far more than wage levels in the past. Since 1950, benefits have been awarded largely on the basis of earnings since 1950. The emphasis was placed on recent earnings because prices and real incomes have increased substantially, and because coverage has been extended to new industries.

The result is that for most workers, earnings in early working years are irrelevant in computing benefits even though they were the basis for Social Security tax payments. Large earnings and the consequent high taxes in the pre-1950 period do not necessarily guarantee a large pension. At the present time, the immaturity of the OASDI system swamps this inequity by paying each beneficiary a larger pension than his OASDI taxes could have purchased. However, as contribution rates rise,[22] and as most workers come to spend the bulk of their working lives in covered employment, the overpayment of benefits will decrease sharply.

The redistribution effect may be illustrated by comparing the experience of an average employee in manufacturing who, with few interruptions, has experienced increases in real as well as money wages throughout the years since 1937, with an employee who has received a constant real wage of $3,500 since 1937. Upon retirement in 1962, the former would have received a basic pension about 5 percent higher than the latter although the value of contributions made by the latter was greater by 11 percent (using a 3 percent interest rate) or 19 percent (using a 6 percent interest rate) than the value of contributions of the former. This redistribution is equal to 15 percent (at 3 percent interest) or 21 percent (at 6 percent) of the pension, or about $165 per year.

When taxes are higher than they are today and the system is older, the subsidy of immaturity may not obscure such an inequity. Stated simply, if workers pay taxes throughout their working lives, but wages earned just before retirement determine pensions, the virtual certainty of inequity exists. Moreover, such inequities are, in fact, generated systematically among workers whose time profiles of earnings differ.

Recipients of relatively increasing incomes are favored by the current method of adjusting benefits to recent wages. One source of discrimination is the occupational difference in earnings histories. Skilled and professional workers, for instance, usually earn relatively low wages in early years while skills are being acquired; their wages increase, more or less steadily, until they retire. Wages of semiskilled or unskilled workers reach an early peak, typically when the worker is in his late thirties or early forties, and then decline. As a result, skilled workers tend to fare better at retirement.

[22] Rates are scheduled to rise eventually above the actuarial rate in order to pay the existing actuarial liability.

Present benefit computation methods also tend to favor workers in growing industries. A common, although not universal, characteristic of declining industries is that wages fall, or rise less rapidly, than do wages in more rapidly growing sectors. Unemployment rates in such industries are also higher. The result is reduced average earnings for employees in these industries and, later on, reduced pensions.

THE FORMULA FOR SELF-EMPLOYED PERSONS. A third possible source of inequity is the fact that the total contributions made by self-employed persons are only three-fourths as large as total contributions made on behalf of the employed worker. The direction of the inequity depends on whether and how the employer's share of the total contribution is shifted.

If it is assumed that the burden of the employer tax is not shifted, then a self-employed worker pays in half again as much as an employed worker at the same income level. If more than half of the employer contribution is shifted backwards, however, the inequity is in the other direction. If some portion of the employer contribution is shifted forward, the real burden of OASDI will be distributed among purchasers of goods produced by industries covered by OASDI. In view of the uncertainty about the incidence of the employer tax, it is impossible to state precisely how the contribution of the self-employed should compare in order to assure horizontal equity.

THE TREATMENT OF WORKING WIVES. Contributions made by working wives add little or nothing to the family pension which is based, in most cases, on the husband's wage history. Working wives with low average wages may receive no benefits whatsoever in return for the OASDI taxes they paid.

For example, if a worker retires with an average monthly wage of $300 and dies within a few years, his widow will receive survivor benefits larger than the pension to which she would have been entitled in her own right unless she had worked and received an average wage of more than $240 per month.

Even in the absence of the death of the husband, the working wife may suffer inequity. A married worker retiring at age sixty-five with a $400 average monthly wage, whose wife never worked, will receive a larger pension than would two single workers retiring at age sixty-five, one with a $400 average monthly wage and the other with a $120 monthly wage. If the second of these two workers is assumed instead to be the working wife of the first, the inequity becomes clear.

In most cases, working wives, unless they earned nearly as much as their husbands, fare no better under the Social Security benefit system than nonworking wives. The contribution of the working wife to the family pension may be zero even though she has paid OASDI taxes, and even though the family's total benefits are far below the current (1965) OASDI maximum of $368. A possible solution would be to calculate the pension of workers other than the head of household by a different schedule and add the resulting amounts to the family pension. This approach would permit a compromise between basing benefits on needs and on contributions. A policy of holding payments to one family below a certain level may well be socially desirable or at least politically prudent, but whether a uniform ceiling on total payments to one household should be retained is an open question.

## Conclusion

The American Social Security system gives higher benefits per contribution dollar to workers with low incomes than to workers with high incomes. However, the benefit formula is so constructed that two workers who have made equal contributions may receive widely different pensions. This occurs because the formula, in effect, ignores earnings of most workers in all years except those just before retirement.

Since the system has not been in effect long enough to have collected contributions over the entire working life of most workers, current beneficiaries receive a pension larger than their contributions would justify. This pension "gift" has largely swamped the inequities inherent in the benefit formula. In time, however, as the system becomes more mature, these inequities will become more apparent.

The special treatment of certain groups of workers also raises important questions about present methods of benefit computation. The working wife, as an individual, does not receive Social Security benefits in accordance with the contributions she has made. The contributions made on behalf of self-employed persons, however, are proportionately less than those for employees.

CHARLES WARDEN, JR. *

# Unemployment Compensation:
# The Massachusetts Experience

AFTER THIRTY YEARS under the Unemployment Compensation law, there remains considerable doubt about the purpose of unemployment insurance. The distinction between its rather limited objectives and those of welfare programs and distressed areas programs is not clear. The intended functions of the unemployment compensation program are difficult to identify, and the relationships between these functions and the mechanism by which they are implemented have become confused.

This is a study of the results of the unemployment compensation program in a single state, Massachusetts. While the postwar economic history of Massachusetts does not reflect the experience of other states with full accuracy, Massachusetts has a wide range of economic activities—as varied as any state in the nation—and, therefore, it serves as an interesting case study. The relationship between benefit payments and the several different causes of unemployment in Massachusetts can be used as a basis for observing how well the current system of unemployment compensation has responded to the intentions of the legislation.

Using Massachusetts data for the postwar period, monthly unemployment patterns for various industry groups were related to

* Council of Economic Advisers.

benefit payments by segregating, statistically, the major types of unemployment—cyclical, seasonal, irregular, and trend. It was found
that roughly a third of the unemployment benefits paid were in response to cyclical unemployment, about a third to seasonal unemployment, and the remainder to a combination of irregular and
trend causes of unemployment.

These findings have implications for some broader issues. What
objectives does the system serve today? How does the unemployment
compensation program affect resource allocation? What is the countercyclical potential of the system? Is the program viable in the long
run? The results suggest some possible improvements to make the
system more responsive to the objective of the Unemployment Compensation Law.

## The Purpose of Unemployment Insurance

The unemployment compensation system in the United States
originated as part of the Social Security Act of 1935. The 1935 report of the House Ways and Means Committee gives one general
statement of the purpose of the program:

The essential idea in unemployment compensation, more commonly but
less accurately called "unemployment insurance" is the accumulation of
reserves in times of employment from which partial compensation may
be paid to workers who become unemployed and are unable to find other
work. Unemployment insurance cannot give complete and unlimited
compensation to all who are unemployed. Any attempt to make it do so
confuses unemployment insurance with relief, which it is designed to replace in large part. It can give compensation only for a limited period and
for a percentage of the wage loss.[1]

The statements and writings that surrounded the enactment of
the law and the early years of its administration identify three fundamental purposes of the program: employment stabilization for
firms, aggregate income maintenance in the economy in general, and
insurance against personal income loss for individual workers. In a
single act of legislation, these purposes added up to a broad program of income maintenance by which it was hoped to offset the
impact of business declines. When considered as separate functions,

[1] House Report No. 615, 74 Cong. 1 sess. (1935), p. 7.

however, these goals reveal a variety of supporting reasons and sometimes conflicting rationales.

For example, John R. Commons, one of the earliest writers on this subject, emphasized that such a program would help to stabilize employment within each firm. His experiences with the Wisconsin system of workmen's compensation suggested that variable taxes would encourage employers to stabilize their employment schedules.[2] This was also cited as a goal by President Roosevelt in his message to the Congress recommending the bill:

An unemployment compensation system should be constructed in such a way as to afford practical aid and incentive toward the larger purpose of employment stabilization. This can be helped by the intelligent planning of both public and private employment.[3]

Later, the Committee on Economic Security, appointed by President Roosevelt, stressed the need for personal income insurance against the hazard of wage loss during recessions:

The hazard of involuntary unemployment is one of the most serious and disastrous of the many risks which confront wage earners in an industrial society. Industry moves through alternating periods of prosperity and depression which introduce serious employment risks; workers, because of conditions entirely beyond their control and largely beyond the control of the men and institutions which employ them, are from time to time deprived of all sources of income.[4]

In 1937 the Social Security Board published a small pamphlet that reemphasized that unemployment compensation was designed for "unpredictable unemployment":

Unemployment compensation is a method of safeguarding individuals against distress for a short period of time after they become unemployed. It is designed to compensate only employable persons who are able and willing to work and who are unemployed *through no fault of their own* (emphasis added). Instead of making the individual get along on a steadily descending level of living until he has exhausted the last shred of his savings, credit, and the generosity of his relatives and friends, thus reach-

[2] Harry Malisoff, "The Emergence of Unemployment Compensation," *Political Science Quarterly,* Vol. 54 (June 1939), p. 242.
[3] U. S. Committee on Economic Security, *Message of the President Recommending Legislation on Economic Security,* H. Doc. 81 (1935), p. vi.
[4] Committee on Economic Security, *Social Security in America,* Publication No. 20 (1937), p. 3.

ing a point of destitution at which he is eligible for relief, unemployment compensation sets aside contributions during periods of employment and provides the individual with benefits as a legal right when he becomes unemployed. During the periods of prosperity a fund is built up, to be available for the payment of benefits in the periods when industry fails to maintain employment.

Unemployment compensation is not a system under which every unemployed person is assured of benefits for any and all unemployed time. It provides protection primarily for the persons who normally are steadily employed.[5]

The spirit of all three goals was captured by Franklin Delano Roosevelt when, as Governor of New York, he stated:

> The dole method of relief for unemployment is not only repugnant to all sound principles of social economics, but is contrary to every principle of American citizenship and of sound government. American labor seeks no charity, but only a chance to work for its living. The relief which the workers of the State should be able to anticipate, when engulfed in a period of industrial depression, should be one of insurance . . .[6]

Later, as President of the United States, he marked both aggregate income maintenance and personal income insurance as goals:

> The law will flatten out the peaks and valleys of deflation and of inflation. It is, in short, a law that will take care of human needs and at the same time provide for the United States an economic structure of vastly greater economic soundness.[7]

In 1935, Arthur Altmeyer, Chairman of the Technical Board on Economic Security, described the role of unemployment insurance in the following way:

> There is considerable misunderstanding as to what unemployment insurance can be expected to do in solving the problem of unemployment. Unemployment insurance will not furnish jobs for idle workers, nor will it eliminate unemployment. The primary function of unemployment insurance is to distribute more equitably the economic risk of unemployment. . . . in this respect [it] is analogous to fire insurance. . . .

---

    [5] U.S. Social Security Board, *Unemployment Compensation, What and Why?*, Publication No. 14 (1937), p. 7.

    [6] Message to the New York State Legislature, March 25, 1931; *The Public Papers and Addresses of Franklin D. Roosevelt* (Random House, 1938), Vol. 1, p. 456.

    [7] Statement on signing the Social Security Act, Aug. 14, 1935; *ibid.*, Vol. 4, p. 324.

Thus, it is possible that few of us carry enough life insurance to protect fully our dependents in case of death, but certainly no one would advocate abandoning the institution of life insurance for that reason.[8]

# The Inconsistency of the Goals

The three purposes for which Congress passed Title III of the Social Security Act of 1935 were clearly aggregate income maintenance, personal income insurance, and industrial employment stabilization.[9] During the quarter century that has intervened, however, administrators have retreated from sharp definition of the law's purpose. The program has become conceived as ". . . a program for the orderly accumulation of funds for use in the payment of benefits, as a matter of right, for unemployment which is beyond the control of the individual worker."[10]

One reason for the more general approach to the law may be that the specific goals of unemployment insurance are not entirely consistent. In operation, the contradictions seem to limit the potential effectiveness of the program. This can be demonstrated by examining each of the goals in isolation.

*Aggregate Income Maintenance*

The system of unemployment compensation functions as an automatic stabilizer, designed to pay benefits to unemployed workers in recessions and tax employers during industrial expansions. In periods of employment contraction, unemployed workers receive benefits that sustain aggregate purchasing power. This, in turn, limits the decline of aggregate demand and employment. During periods of industrial expansion, the hiring of new employees increases the taxable wage base and yields more unemployment tax revenues. This acts to dampen the expansion. The stabilization function of unemployment compensation might be extended by providing for cyclical adjustment of benefits to shrink the size of payments to individuals during boom periods and increase the amount of compen-

[8] Harry Hopkins and others, *Toward Economic Security,* President's Committee on Economic Security (1935), pp. 11-12.

[9] These were recently redefined by Richard Lester in *The Economics of Unemployment Compensation* (Princeton University Press, 1962), p. 14.

[10] Walter Galenson, *A Report of Unemployment Compensation Benefit Costs in Massachusetts* (Division of Employment Security, 1950), p. 8.

sation checks in downturns, as was the proposal of Galbraith in *The Affluent Society*.[11]

The stabilization function is not the sole purpose for which unemployment compensation was designed, however. Varying payments might increase the anticyclical potential of the program, but they would probably be in conflict with the insurance of personal income.

## Personal Income Insurance

The role of the program in insuring personal income does not easily tolerate the countercyclically variable payments that would increase the program's effectiveness in maintaining aggregate income. The personal motivation for insuring against fixed income loss requires that the amount of compensation be fixed. Individual income protection presupposes payments that do not vary for unpredictable reasons. The analogy is found in the private insurance principle of pooling personal risk. A small contribution for each employee provides certain protection for the few who may become unemployed as a result of the hazards of industrial change. From this point of view, variable benefit rates would not be consistent with the insurance goal.

The insurance function of the program is also undermined if it is used to provide protection against predictable or quasi-predictable unemployment, such as regular seasonal layoffs. When unemployment is regular and predictable, the risk-pooling principle no longer applies because there is little uncertainty involved. In this case, the subsidy principle is more applicable, with year-round workers subsidizing the periodic unemployment of others.

When unemployment arises from prolonged regional depression or when the worker is unemployable because age, illness, or skill obsolescence has put him out of the usual market, there develops a further ambiguity between an insurance role and a broader welfare form of income maintenance based on some sort of a needs test. Most observers agree that unemployment insurance is not relief and recognize that "it is a right of the worker, not a gift from the government. It is expected that benefit differentials will be maintained

[11] J. K. Galbraith, *The Affluent Society* (Houghton Mifflin Co., 1958), pp. 292-307.

contrary to equal benefits expected in a welfare program."[12] The distinction between relief and unemployment insurance was stated directly by Arthur Altmeyer, then Chairman of the Social Security Board, in hearings before the Senate Finance Committee:

The purpose of unemployment compensation is to provide some minimum protection when those persons who are ordinarily employed become unemployed. It is not relief nor is it intended to meet all unemployment under all conditions. The prime objective of unemployment compensation is to provide benefits to persons who become unemployed in normal times due to the ordinary changes in business conditions and also to provide the first line of defense during periods of unusual unemployment and severe business depression.[13]

A distortion of the insurance principle may also occur if workers misinterpret their "right" to benefit payments. The right to payments is limited to the occurrence of the contingency insured against. Since there is a lingering belief that workers themselves have made the contributions, however, the right to payments is sometimes interpreted in the same sense as a right to make withdrawals from a savings account. Even though most states have never collected employee contributions,[14] the belief that workers participate directly probably encourages the collection of benefits when unemployment is not involuntary. This may be the foundation of many abuses of the program, such as the case of retiring workers who purposely exhaust unemployment benefits before beginning Social Security benefits.

In summary, if the unemployment compensation program is to function as insurance, at least three conditions must prevail. First, it cannot be used as a welfare fund for the relief of structurally unemployed workers. Second, the fund must be treated as a contingency fund, not as an investment holding; that is, a worker may have an

[12] Cf. Douglas Brown, "The American Philosophy of Social Insurance," *Social Science Review*, Vol. 30, No. 1 (March 1956), pp. 1-3; and Joseph Becker, "Twenty-five Years of Unemployment Insurance," *Political Science Quarterly*, Vol. 75, No. 4 (December 1960), p. 483; he particularly stresses the fact that twenty-one states specifically exclude the able-bodied unemployed from general assistance.

[13] *Hearings on H.R. 6635*, Senate Finance Committee, 76 Cong. 1 sess. (1939), p. 24.

[14] Alabama, Alaska, California, Indiana, Kentucky, Louisiana, Massachusetts, New Hampshire, New Jersey, and Rhode Island have collected employee contributions, but by 1964 only Alabama, Alaska, and New Jersey still did so.

insurance claim, but may not exercise an equity claim. Third, any specific instance of the insured event must be unpredictable. If subgroups of workers have different probabilities of loss, premium differentials may be called for, but the necessary condition of chance occurrence may not be violated without the eventual destruction of the insurance approach. For this reason, seasonal unemployment cannot logically be included under the program since it is largely predictable.

### Industrial Employment Stabilization

The third role of the program, employment stabilization at the firm level, grew out of the views of the Wisconsin group in the President's Committee for Economic Security. They had seen differential taxes under the Wisconsin Workmen's Compensation Law induce employers to implement better workshop safety practices. Similarly, they argued, taxes that vary with the extent of worker layoff should encourage employers to smooth out irregular employment patterns.[15]

An explanation of the notion of variable taxes as an instrument to encourage the regularization of employment at the firm level was given by the 1935 Senate Finance Committee's report on the Social Security bill:

. . . we propose, as a further amendment, a provision that the Federal Government shall recognize credits in the form of lower contribution rates which may be granted by the states to employers who have stabilized their employment. . . . In his message dealing with the subject of social security, the President urged that unemployment compensation should be set up under conditions which will tend toward the regularization of employment. All unemployment cannot be prevented by any employers, but many employers can do much more than they have done in the past to regularize employment. Everyone will agree that it is much better to prevent unemployment than to compensate it.[16]

Taxing employers differentially was rationalized in two ways. First, the variable tax makes unemployment costly to the employer. The employer with the more stable employment pattern gains an

[15] Paul H. Douglas, *Social Security in the United States* (McGraw-Hill, 1936), p. 13ff.
[16] *Senate Report No. 628,* 74 Cong. 1 sess. (1935), p. 14.

advantage from lower taxes, encouraging the others to stabilize their employment. Second, unemployment costs are related to the product that generated the unemployment as a cost of production. For example, consumers of highly fashionable women's shoes having seasonal production schedules and high unemployment would pay for this luxury, because the costs of seasonally laid-off workers would be passed on to the consumer. Presumably, all similar employers have the same problem and there is no inter-firm advantage.

Experience rating, the procedure whereby an employer's unemployment insurance tax liability is related to the amount of benefits drawn by his unemployed workers, was developed in the hope of inducing firms to stabilize their employment patterns. The employer's tax payments are accumulated in his account with the state's general fund, and benefit payments to laid-off workers are debited against this account. If, on annual review, the size of the account shrinks relative to a norm appropriate to the size of the company's labor force, the tax rates are increased. If benefit payments exhaust the employer's account, benefits are drawn from the fund's general reserves. A firm with an unfavorable lay-off pattern might have to pay as much as 2.5 to 3.0 percent tax on the first $3,600 of the employee's wages, and, in some states, tax rates may go over 4.5 percent for the first $4,800 in wages. Experience rating was the hallmark of the "American Plan" and was expected to buttress each of the three goals of the Law.

The implication of this procedure is that the employer is responsible for the unemployment and should bear the cost of the worker's benefits. Employer responsibility, however, may be of different character according to whether the layoff is cyclical, secular, irregular, or seasonal. The effectiveness of experience rating in encouraging remedial employment practices depends on the category of unemployment.

Cyclical unemployment is generally associated with a broad business decline. Most industries respond together and the decline in one firm can often be the result of a cutback in the activity of another firm. These repercussions of changes in aggregate demand are complex. It is rarely possible to pinpoint the blame for job loss in a given industry, and the resulting unemployment cannot be associated narrowly with any particular employer. Calculation of tax rates by experience rating in order to penalize employers for cyclical unemployment does not meet the source of the trouble, and employers cannot make a corrective response.

The cause behind secular decline in employment is more readily seen, but the remedial influence of discriminatory taxation is equally doubtful. In a case of secular decline, the number of available jobs shrinks, and the labor force must turn elsewhere for work. If this is associated with a secular decline in demand for the product, the employer is in no position to bear an increased tax burden to cover unemployment costs. If an employer abandons an area to relocate elsewhere, he also abandons that portion of his work force that stays behind. No change in tax rate can effect his employment of these workers. If the cause of layoff is technological, the employer might be asked to bear part of the cost of the unemployment, and might be expected to adapt his technical devices only after including such costs in his calculations. It is doubtful, however, that he would forego the technological improvements in order to improve his employment record.

These examples of secular decline are not characterized by employment instability which could be corrected through tax incentives to employers. Only in the case of employment induced by automation is the employer in an optional position with regard to layoffs. Even in this case, lump sum quit-pay or retraining is more directly responsive to the problem.

Frictional unemployment presents another problem. This type of unemployment includes workers between jobs for some transitory reason. In this case, employer responsibility for the unemployment depends on whether or not the worker left voluntarily. If the layoff was involuntary and not for cause, the employer is responsible and can be expected to pay the costs of the benefits. Then, sharply rising unemployment taxes may stimulate the employer to follow reasonable work practices.

The fourth category of unemployment, seasonal layoff, deserves particularly careful attention. Two types of seasonality can be distinguished. One is associated directly with the weather. The second derives its seasonal pattern from conditions reflecting social customs, such as festival days, spring and fall fashions, and educational activities. For the most part, unemployment associated with weather-caused seasonality cannot be easily affected at the employer's discretion. The seasonal pattern based on custom is more amenable to modification. A good example is the adoption of multiproduct lines by the shoe manufacturers in Massachusetts in order to smooth out their seasonal employment pattern.[17]

Regardless of the source of the seasonality, the pattern is generally predictable. This means that both the employer and the worker may contract out of this seasonal burden if they choose, and that both involuntarily contract for the periods of unemployment if they elect to stay with the seasonal work. Seasonal unemployment is not usually a chance occurrence so it cannot be classified as involuntary unemployment except during depressed periods when interindustry mobility is very low. Seasonal unemployment is a job characteristic to be reflected in wage rates rather than a hazard requiring insurance protection. The employer and the workers, aware of the seasonal pattern of employment, must be prepared to bear the cost of working in such an industry. The employer should be able to pass on to the consumer the cost of this unemployment by charging higher prices so that the consumer is forced to choose either the higher-cost seasonal item or the lower-cost nonseasonal item. It is doubtful that, in the usual case, a discriminatory tax burden would actually cause employers to adjust their employment patterns. Variations in unemployment insurance taxes are only a minor consideration in the determination of total cost and in the evaulation of uncertainty surrounding production decisions.

Experience rating appears to be an appropriate employer incentive in the case of some irregular and seasonal types of unemployment. For secular and cyclical unemployment it is at best uncertain and more likely quite inappropriate.[18]

---

[17] After a careful study by the trade association and the Division of Employment Security, production of fashionable shoes was phased into the "bread-and-butter" lines which were produced off-season and held in inventory. The trade association demonstrated that savings from unemployment taxes could widen profit margins substantially. This high sensitivity of profits to such minor changes in costs was largely the result of the industry's depressed condition, highly competitive market, and small firm organization. Yet, the trade association economist admitted that the employers, individually, would not have responded to this incentive without the association's leadership.

[18] There is a strong administrative argument in favor of experience rating insofar as it encourages employers to police the program to prevent worker abuse. This argument is usually the first and most forcefully advanced by the officials in charge of the program, although it was not mentioned by the formulators of the Law. An

## The Relative Cost of Unemployment Benefits

The proportion of benefit costs that can be traced to the several types of unemployment would be indicative of the extent to which the unemployment compensation program is being utilized for the purposes for which it was designed. In this study, the relationship between benefit costs and various causes of unemployment was studied empirically using data on unemployment compensation expenditures in Massachusetts since World War II.

### The Benefit-Cause Model

Monthly employment data for various industry groups which in the aggregate represent total Massachusetts industry[19] were used to construct a system of variables reflecting changes in seasonal, cyclical, irregular, and trend employment. The employment variables were used in a simple cross-section regression model to explain differences in annual benefit payments.[20] The model took the form

$$B_j = a + sS_j + cC_j + iI_j + tT_j$$

where, for any industry $j$, $B$ represents benefits per worker. Indexes of employment variation are represented as $S$ for seasonal, $C$ for cyclical, $I$ for irregular, and $T$ for trend causes.

The equation states that unemployment benefits are a function of variations in employment rather than unemployment. The implicit assumption is that unemployment is the mirror of employment. This is not strictly accurate, of course, since job mobility,

---

additional argument against experience rating involves the perverse financing pattern which develops from recalculating tax rates every year to reflect the past year's benefit pay-out record. Prolonged periods of high unemployment will cause annually increased tax rates to cover the fund drawn-down. Of course, this is when business needs diminished tax rates to stimulate lagging activity. In boom times conversely, when business needs a dampener and can afford to accumulate funds for bad times, tax rates tend to fall with each succeeding good year.

[19] The industrial breakdown used was the U.S. Census Standard Industrial Classification two-digit industries.

[20] Ideally, it would have been desirable to compare, say, monthly benefit payments and monthly unemployment for individual industries and then to infer the relationship between seasonal unemployment and seasonally paid benefits, cyclical unemployment and the cyclical benefits, and so on. Unfortunately, the records of the Bureau of Employment Security do not give parallel monthly data series on unemployment and benefits.

moonlighting, and temporary employment are reasons why persons leaving a particular job do not necessarily become unemployed. Trend changes in the labor force also weaken the correlation between employment and unemployment. However, the assumption proved to be serviceable under the circumstances.

The data for the explanatory variables, $S$, $C$, $I$, and $T$, were generated in two steps. First, the single time series of each industry's monthly employment was broken into four component time series measuring seasonal, cyclical, irregular, and trend employment for each month.[21]

The underlying assumption was that total employment was the result of combining the four separate types of employment. The second step was to find an index of variation for each series. For the seasonal, cyclical, and irregular employment series this was done by measuring the standard error of estimate of each series and then dividing it by the average level of employment in the industry in order to remove the effect of differences in industry size. For the trend employment series the index of variation was derived by dividing the slope of the trend by the mean employment of the industry, retaining the algebraic sign of the slope coefficient in order to indicate a negative or positive trend.[22] The benefits-per-worker variable is simply the ratio of the total benefits for each industry to the average level of employment for each industry during the 1947-58 period.

The model was then fitted by least squares to a cross section of twenty-seven two-digit industry groups in the State of Massachusetts for the period 1947-58.[23] This sample covered construction; sixteen manufacturing industries; transportation, communication, and public utilities; six selected wholesale and retail trade groups; insur-

[21] The method for the time series decomposition was similar to that developed by the U. S. Bureau of the Census. For details of this procedure see Julius Shiskin, *Electronic Computers and Business Indicators*, Occasional Paper 57 (National Bureau of Economic Research, 1957).

[22] The actual arithmetic of these steps was done on a computer and, in fact, programmed a bit differently. For example, an interim step toward producing a time series of seasonal employment produces a series of seasonal residuals from a trend-cycle-irregular employment series. The simple standard deviation of these residuals is identical to the standard error of the estimate of the subsequent seasonal employment series. Similar short-cuts were used for the other series.

[23] The period was cut off at 1958 because it was not possible to bridge the break in the series introduced when the 1958 changes in the SIC reassigned enterprises between industry groups.

ance, banking, and real estate; and two service categories—personal services and business services.[24]

The results of the statistical analysis suggested that the $700 million of benefits paid during 1947 to 1958 were roughly allocated as follows: one-third for seasonal unemployment, one-third for cyclical unemployment, between five and ten percent for secular employment decline, and about fifteen percent for irregular unemployment causes.[25] The remaining ten or fifteen percent could not be identified with any particular one of the four types of unemployment.[26]

## The High-Benefit Industries

Four industries—construction, textiles, apparel, and leather—received $365 million, or over 50 percent of all the benefits, and had the highest level of benefits per worker. A special attempt was made to construct monthly benefit data for these industries that could be correlated with monthly fluctuations in the employment components. Data were established for a later period covering from January 1958 to September 1962, and a regression equation of the following form was used:

$$B = a + bTC + cS + dI + eT' + fT''.$$

[24] By SIC code number these industries were 15-17, 20, 22, 23, 25, 26, 27, 28, 30, 31, 32, 33, 34, 35, 36, 37, 38, 40-9, 50, 52, 54, 55, 57, 59, 60-69, 72, and 73, respectively.

[25] The computations produced the following regression equations:

$$B = 241 + .094S + .036C - .84T$$
$$(88.9)\,(.021) \quad (.019) \quad (.19)$$
$$R^2 = .71$$
$$B = 230 + .089S + .026C - .82T + .075I$$
$$(91.6)\,(.022) \quad (.025) \quad (.20) \quad (.11)$$
$$R^2 = .72$$

Introducing the irregular variable, $I$, in the second equation reduced the significance of the cyclical variable because the two were partially collinear ($r = .66$). This collinearity was not a result of the decomposition method, which in fact guarantees orthogonality. Rather, cyclically sensitive industries also seem to have irregular lay-off patterns as well.

[26] A simple test that served to help corroborate part of this finding was to decompose the series for aggregate, statewide benefits into seasonal, cyclical, irregular, and trend components. This exercise showed that fully one-third of all the benefits payments were paid seasonally. Of course, because benefits were paid seasonally does not prove they were paid to persons unemployed for seasonal reasons, though this was in fact what the cross-section regression had suggested.

$B$ represents the number of benefit checks for the third week of each month; $TC$, $S$, and $I$ represent the number of employees in the trend-cycle, seasonal, and irregular components, respectively; and $T'$ and $T''$ represent the time equivalents to the linear and quadratic trend terms, respectively.[27]

The table below shows the percentage of the variation in benefits that was attributable to the various types of unemployment in these industries.[28] These results show that, in three of these four

### Type of Unemployment

| Industry | Seasonal | Irregular | Trend-cycle |
|---|---|---|---|
| Construction | 89.6 | 1.2 | 9.2 |
| Textiles | 14.6 | 1.0 | 84.6 |
| Apparel | 45.7 | 0.7 | 53.6 |
| Leather | 30.2 | 1.6 | 68.2 |

[27] The linear and quadratic time dummies ($T'$ and $T''$) were introduced to take the trend out of the trend-cycle term, leaving the cycle only. In fact, of course, the trend and cycle may not be interpreted independently over such a short time span. Consequently, the results were recombined in the table summarizing the percent of variance attributable to specific types of unemployment.

[28] The table below summarizes the regression results.

| | Construction | Textiles | Apparel | Leather |
|---|---|---|---|---|
| $R^2$ | .97 | .90 | .70 | .64 |
| *Beta Weights* | | | | |
| Seasonal | −.94 | − .38 | −.67 | −.56 |
| Trend-cycle | −.18 | −1.33 | −.56 | −.95 |
| Irregular | −.11 | − .10 | −.08 | −.14 |
| Linear trend | .14 | −2.95 | .61 | −.98 |
| Quadratic trend | | 1.3 | .87 | |
| *Partial Correlation with Benefits* | | | | |
| Seasonal | −.98 | − .77 | −.78 | −.68 |
| Trend-cycle | −.62 | − .87 | −.63 | −.64 |
| Irregular | −.50 | − .29 | −.15 | −.22 |
| Linear trend | .52 | − .89 | .22 | −.65 |
| Quadratic trend | | .71 | −.30 | |

These results were interpreted in terms of variances around the mean. This avoids an immediate concern about the constant, and it employs a set of parameters different from that of the previous cross-section regression to reflect the relative roles of the separate employment components. The explained variance is the sum of separate variances and covariances weighted by the associated squares or cross products of the slope coefficients. In this particular problem, the covariance term disappears because the process of time series decomposition guarantees orthogonality of the seasonal, irregular, and trend-cycle components within any given industry. The percentages of variance attributable to the seasonal and irregular components were calculated and the residual attributed to a combination of trend, cycle, and error.

industries, a large percentage of the benefit charges is associated
with seasonal unemployment. In the construction industry, almost
90 percent of benefit claims seems to have resulted from seasonal
unemployment. In the textile industry, the dominant reason for the
payment of benefits is a combination of secular and cyclical decline.
*A priori* knowledge of this industry's exodus from New England to
the South suggests that trend employment decline was, in fact, a
very important cause of benefits. These results are interesting because they pertain to the four industries that accounted for over
half of all the benefit payments and because they support the findings
of the cross-section study of all industries.[29]

*Findings*

In summary, therefore, the findings of the cross-section study,
supported by the special analysis of the four heavy-benefit industries, suggest about one-third of the benefit charges between
1947-58 was caused by seasonal unemployment, roughly another
third of the benefit charges were related to cyclical unemployment,
between five and ten percent was for secular employment decline,
about fifteen percent was for irregular unemployment, and the remaining percentage was unexplained. These results are important
because they suggest that as little as one-third of the expenditures
for unemployment insurance benefits in Massachusetts arose in response to the goal of aggregate income maintenance during business decline. Another one-third of all benefits was to cover irregular
and secular unemployment, responding to the personal income insurance goal of the law. The other third of the benefits, associated
with seasonal unemployment, seems least likely to have met the purposes of the law. Of the total, therefore, roughly two-thirds were

[29] Caution is required in interpreting these results. First, being an analysis of
the variance around the mean, the method does not permit a direct explanation of
the level of total benefit checks. Rather, it accounts for monthly changes in the
level of benefits. Since the number of benefit checks never drops to zero there is
a remaining unexplained base. Of the maximum number of benefit checks, this
base is about ten percent for construction, twenty percent for textiles, thirty percent for apparel, and thirty percent for leather products. Second, the dependent
variable, benefit checks, does not reflect dollars of benefits directly and must be
weighted by the dollar value of the average check. The average check is different
for each industry and for each month. For the fiscal year 1961 the average check
for these four industries was as follows: construction $45.16; textiles $39.16;
apparel $38.63; leather $38.18. However, these refinements should not alter significantly the major findings of the analysis.

paid out for unemployment arising independently of business cycle fluctuations.

## The Industrial Distribution of Benefits

The experience rating procedure was instituted to make employers bear the cost of their own unemployment. Ideally, the larger the number of workers placed into the pool of the unemployed (as measured by the company's account with the fund), the higher the company's tax rate. If such a system operated as designed, each employer would contribute, over the long run, a sum roughly equivalent to the amount claimed in benefits by his laid-off workers.

The differential tax rates are subject to a ceiling rate, imposed to protect cyclically sensitive industries from bearing the brunt of a general business slump. The result of this modification of the experience rating system has been the development of an interfirm subsidy.[30] Insofar as workers in relatively unstable firms draw benefits in an amount that would justify tax contributions in excess of the ceiling rate, some of the labor costs of the unstable firms are shifted to more stable ones.

The extent and direction of the subsidy among industries in Massachusetts can be seen in Chart 1 which compares total benefits and total contributions for selected industry groups for the period 1947 to 1961. Most industries contributed and withdrew approximately the same amount. But four industries—construction, textiles, apparel, and leather—overdrew their contributions by $226 million. A few others—mainly transportation, communications and public utilities, wholesale trade, and banking, real estate, and insurance—contributed greatly in excess of their claim load to make up the difference.

Chart 2 shows the industrial distribution of employment and of benefits for major industry groups for 1961. The chart indicates the wide disparity among industries in benefit drain. Construction, for

[30] Earlier works dealing with the problem of unemployment compensation subsidy are P. W. Cartwright, "Unemployment Compensation and the Allocation of Resources," in M. Abramovitz and *The Allocation of Economic Resources* (Stanford University Press, 1959), pp. 65-81; and James O'Connor's two articles, "Seasonal Unemployment and Insurance," *The American Economic Review* (June 1962), pp. 460-71, and "Anticipated Employment Instability and Labor Market Equilibrium," *Quarterly Journal of Economics* (February 1961), pp. 128-32.

## CHART 1. Industrial Distribution of Unemployment Benefits and Contributions, Massachusetts, 1947–61

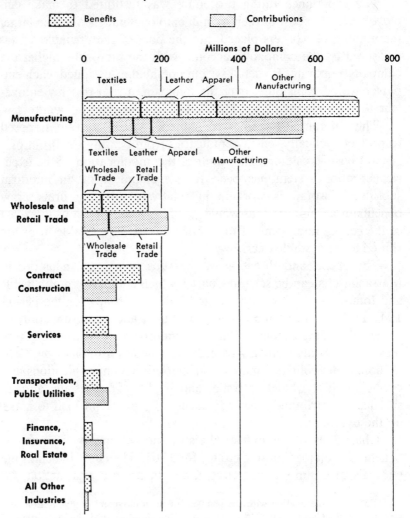

Source: Commonwealth of Massachusetts, Division of Employment Security, *Director's Reports*, 1947 to 1961.

example, with 5.5 percent of covered employment, received 17 percent of the total benefits. In contrast, finance, insurance, and real estate, with 6.5 percent of employment, received only 2.2 percent of the benefits. The difference largely reflects the greater employment volatility in some industries.

An employer's tax rate is increased when unemployment benefits exceed contributions so that his reserve balance is drawn down. The maximum tax rate is reached when the employer's reserve balance reaches a negative 3 percent level. Benefits for the unemployed workers are still paid, of course, and these are "solvency" charges against the general funds accumulated from the excess contributions of other employers. The Division of Employment Security found that, in 1959, four industries caused 75 percent of the solvency charges. The construction industry, which included 11.9 percent of all employers and 6.6 percent of taxable wages, received 32 percent; apparel, with 3.7 percent of taxable wages, generated another 19.3 percent; textiles and leather, with 8.0 percent of taxable wages, caused 15.4 percent of the solvency charges. In the year ending September 1961, employers in these four industries received 65 percent of the solvency charges. The problem is apparently not limited to a small group of employers. In 1959, 31 percent of construction employers, 22 percent of textile employers, 40 percent of apparel manufacturers, and 26 percent of all leather manufacturers had balances in excess of a negative three percent.

Table 1 shows how tax rates vary, in general, with the benefits-contributions position of industries. In 1956, while the tax rates of the four heavy-benefit industries were all comparatively high, indicating that their reserve accounts were at a low level, none of them reached the 2.7 percent maximum employer tax. In 1957, however, the general benefit drain was much greater, and the increase was particularly marked for these volatile industries. Without a tax ceiling, these employers would have faced tax rates well beyond the maximum under the law.

The subsidy effects of this tax ceiling influence wages, labor distribution, and market prices. Assuming a non-seasonal supply of labor, wages for similar occupations should be higher in a seasonal industry than in a non-seasonal industry in order to guarantee comparable annual incomes. If workers prefer real income in the form of leisure, or if there is mobility between jobs with opposing season-

# CHART 2. Industrial Distribution of Unemployment Benefits and of Employment, Massachusetts, 1961

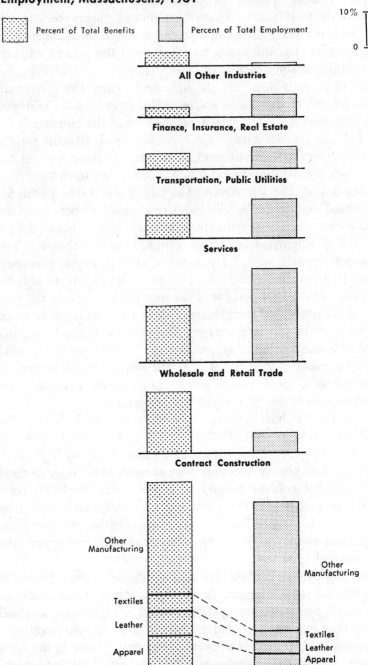

Source: Commonwealth of Massachusetts, Division of Employment Security, *Director's Report*, 1961.

**TABLE 1.** Unemployment Benefits as a Percentage of Contributions and
Average Tax Rates by Industry Group, Massachusetts, 1956 and 1957

| Industry | Unemployment Benefits (Percent of Contributions) | | Average Tax Rate | |
|---|---|---|---|---|
| | 1956 | 1957 | 1956 | 1957 |
| All industries | 65.0 | 119.6 | 1.7 | 1.5 |
| Manufacturing | 73.3 | 137.7 | 1.8 | 1.6 |
| Textile mill products | 101.8 | 244.1 | 2.3 | 2.1 |
| Apparel and related products | 147.6 | 234.4 | 2.5 | 2.4 |
| Leather and leather products | 145.8 | 186.7 | 2.3 | 2.2 |
| Contract construction | 92.4 | 191.1 | 2.4 | 2.3 |
| Transportation and public utilities | 41.1 | 81.3 | 1.4 | 1.2 |
| Wholesale and retail trade | 46.4 | 76.7 | 1.5 | 1.4 |
| Finance, insurance and real estate | 25.5 | 36.6 | 1.2 | 1.1 |
| Services | 44.8 | 63.9 | 1.6 | 1.6 |

Source: Commonwealth of Massachusetts, Division of Employment Security, *Director's Report*, 1956 and 1957.

al patterns, the differential in wages between the seasonal and non-seasonal jobs should lessen, if not disappear. Unemployment benefits that augment the annual income of a seasonal worker will also permit a smaller wage differential. An experience rating system without a tax ceiling, requiring employers to cover all the benefits to employees, would increase employees' effective annual income—earned wages plus benefits—and redistribute wages over the year, with no interfirm subsidy.

When workers in certain industries regularly receive unemployment benefits as a supplement to wages, earned wage rates in these industries can be lower. As a result, the cost of labor is less than it "should be" for unstable employers and relatively higher for stable employers, producing a distortion in normal wage rates. Market prices reflect this wage distortion. If all firms in the stable industry are similarly overtaxed, their cost curves will shift upward in a similar manner. The extent to which this increase in cost is divided between the consumer in higher prices and the entrepreneur in lower profits depends on market elasticities. It is probable, however, that prices of benefit-subsidized items become relatively lower and those of subsidizing items relatively higher.

The distortion of wages also implies a secondary effect on the distribution of labor and capital. Relatively cheaper labor costs encourage the unstable employer to be more labor intensive than he would be if faced with the full costs of his labor input. Conversely, labor will become relatively more expensive for the stable employer and encourage him to shift away from labor-intensive methods. The paradoxical result is that the system encourages the use of labor in unstable jobs and discourages its use by stable employers. It also means that marginal employers can continue to operate with irregular production under reduced labor costs, when bearing the full costs of their own labor might force them out of business. This is the case for some textile mills and shoe factories in New England.

## Implications of the Findings

The findings that a large proportion of the unemployment for which benefits are paid is seasonal in nature and that benefits in some industries regularly exceed their contributions suggest that all of the stated purposes of the Unemployment Compensation Law cannot be satisfied simultaneously under the present system. Furthermore, the drain on reserve funds for these reasons imposes a serious threat to the continuance of the program at all in its present form.

The goal of maintaining aggregate income—the countercyclical role—was fundamental to the rationale of the Law. However, experience under the recent federal programs to extend benefits temporarily for the long-term unemployed shows that state funds are not prepared to handle the impact of cyclical benefit claims. Richard Lester found that no more than one-third of total wage loss during the 1958 recession was compensated by benefit payments.[31] And, through a parallel line of reasoning, Ida Merriam found that only 25 percent of the aggregate wage loss was compensated during the first stages of the downturn of 1954.[32] The evidence for Massachusetts

[31] Richard A. Lester, *The Economics of Unemployment Compensation* (Princeton University Press, 1962); also "The Economic Significance of Unemployment Compensation, 1948-1959," *Review of Economics and Statistics*, Vol. 42, No. 4 (November 1960).

[32] Ida C. Merriam, "Social Security Programs and Economic Stability," *Policies to Combat Depression* (Princeton University Press for the National Bureau of Economic Research, 1956), p. 207.

for the downturn of 1957 shows that $112 million were paid in benefits during fiscal year 1958 (covering the twelve months of the decline in the 1958 recession), but the net impact—total benefits less total contributions—was only $38 million, or about 0.7 percent of total covered wages during that period. It is clear that unemployment compensation in Massachusetts, as in the rest of the country, has not been a large offsetting factor during the early stages of a recession.

Two of the major reasons for this failure are that adequately large reserves are not accumulated during periods of prosperity, and that a large portion of reserves is siphoned off in benefits paid to workers unemployed for seasonal and structural reasons.

The experience of Massachusetts illustrates the consequences of underaccumulation of funds. In 1955, a period of unquestioned prosperity, employment contributions in Massachusetts totaled almost $70 million, while total benefit payments were about $51 million. During this period, the fund should have been accumulating reserves rapidly. Instead, Massachusetts' net addition to reserves was only $19 million, or about 30 percent of that year's total contributions. Had the fund been able to accumulate the greater part of contributions during the prosperous years of 1955 and 1956, either by reducing benefits or raising tax rates, additional reserves of $60 to $70 million would have been available for unemployment benefits during the recession of 1958. This would have covered about 60 percent of total benefits actually dispersed during that recession, an amount equal to twice the net reduction in the fund from June 1957 to June 1958.

The finding of this study that only one-third of the benefits distributed between 1947 and 1962 went for cyclical unemployment indicates another reason why unemployment insurance has not been important as a countercyclical device. In Massachusetts, benefit payments in fiscal 1958, a decidedly depressed year, increased by $51 million, or by only 45 percent, over fiscal 1957, a reasonably prosperous year. In other words, almost 55 percent of the benefits during July 1957 to June 1958 would probably have been disbursed without the occurrence of a recession. The results of this study suggest some important modifications in present procedure are necessary to improve the performance of the unemployment compensation program. Two problems seem most serious: the system does not respond robustly to maintain income (and purchasing power) in the face of a general business decline, and the present ex perience rating procedure encourages a shift in labor costs from habitually unstable industries to stable industries. The major source of trouble is that the macro-economic and the micro-economic objectives of the law are written and administered in such a way as to inhibit the realization of either objective.

A benefit and contribution system, preserving the notion of experience rating, could be devised so as to distinguish between aggregate objectives and objectives relating to firm behavior and employee insurance. Specifically, there might be two funds in place of the present dual-purpose fund. One fund would operate independently of business cycle considerations. Benefits could be keyed to previous income experience and reserved for workers with an attachment to a specific labor force. Experience rating would be used to invoke clear penalty tax rates to discourage unstable individual firm behavior, but the tax rates would not reflect the swing of general business conditions. The other fund would receive constant rate contributions or be financed out of general government revenues, and would be designed to provide benefits at the onset of general business decline. These cyclical benefits could be used to augment other benefit checks, to lengthen the duration of benefit availability, or perhaps to supplement the incomes of some persons not covered by the regular insurance system.

LORA S. COLLINS*

# Public Assistance Expenditures in the United States

PUBLIC ASSISTANCE is the general term for a group of federally assisted programs which provide aid to needy persons in certain categories: Old Age Assistance (OAA) for those aged sixty-five and over; Aid to Dependent Children (ADC) for children under eighteen deprived of one or both parents and, when necessary, for a needy adult relative; Aid to the Blind (AB) with age limits varying among the states; and Aid to the Permanently and Totally Disabled (APTD) for persons aged eighteen and over. Federal aid for public assistance originated with the Social Security Act of 1935, which authorized federal grants-in-aid based on state and local government expenditures for the programs. The establishment of the programs depends on state implementation.[1]

* Federal Reserve Bank of New York.

[1] The 1935 legislation authorized the first three programs; APTD was added in 1950. Because it is not dealt with in this study, Medical Assistance for the Aged (MAA) is omitted from the list. MAA, which became operative in October 1960, differs in purpose and content from the older programs; its sole object is to pay medical costs for "medically indigent" but otherwise self-sufficient persons aged sixty-five and over. MAA is commonly called the Kerr-Mills program. Another recent development not treated in this study is the "unemployed parent" component of ADC. Since May 1961, states have been permitted to establish a subprogram within ADC for families in need due to the unemployment (rather than the death, disability, or absence) of a parent. The 1962 public assistance

97

## Introduction and Summary

Total expenditure in fiscal year 1964 for assistance payments in these four programs was $4.1 billion, of which the federal government paid 61.1 percent. In late 1964, some 6.7 million persons were receiving assistance under them.

In addition to federally aided public assistance, various state and local programs provide "general assistance" for needy persons not eligible for public assistance. The general assistance programs are financed and controlled entirely by state or local governments and vary widely in scope and benefits. Annual general assistance expenditures fluctuate in response to economic conditions; in fiscal 1964, they amounted to $375 million.

Table 1 shows the trends in various public assistance and general assistance program variables since 1940.

Although assistance expenditures are large, as Table 1 indicates, little is known about their determinants.[2] This study attempts to identify empirically some quantitative determinants of assistance expenditure levels in 1960. The analysis is cross-sectional, and uses each state as an observation. The basic objective was to ascertain

---

amendments extended this authorization for at least five years and also changed the name of ADC to Aid to Families with Dependent Children.

[2] A model hypothesizing income, urbanization, and density as determinants was fitted to welfare spending, as well as to spending on a number of other state-local government functions, in two previous studies: Solomon Fabricant, *The Trend of Government Activity in the United States Since 1900* (National Bureau of Economic Research, 1952), Chap. 6; and Glenn W. Fisher, "Determinants of State and Local Government Expenditures: A Preliminary Analysis," *National Tax Journal,* Vol. 14 (December 1961). Relationships between these three determinant variables and per capita expenditures were also investigated, but not by means of muiltple correlation analysis, by: Lucy Edelberg and others, "Public Expenditures and Economic Structure in the United States," *Social Research* (February 1936); and Jozef Berolzheimer, "Influences Shaping Expenditure for Operation of State and Local Governments," *Bulletin of the National Tax Association* (March, April, and May 1947). Results of a cross-sectional analysis of assistance expenditures in Iowa counties, with some results for a cross section of states, were reported in: Karl A. Fox and Donald E. Boles, *Welfare and Highway Functions of Iowa Counties: A Quantitative Analysis* (1961). One other study dealt with general assistance only, investigating the demand of individuals for general assistance payments as a special case of the demand for leisure: C. T. Brehm and T. R. Saving, "The Demand for General Assistance Payments," *American Economic Review* (December 1964).

whether significant relationships can in fact be found between per capita assistance spending and certain economic and demographic variables. The results show that such relationships do exist, but that the relative importance of the hypothesized determinants and their statistical significance differ substantially among the assistance programs.

The study deals both with the total expenditure in each program and separately with the federal and state-local expenditure components of each, because expenditures at different levels of government are determined by somewhat different factors. Federal expenditures are determined by an open-end grant formula and occur only as a result of state-local expenditures. The expenditures of states and localities are combined because every state has its own arrangements for the state-local sharing of assistance costs.

The study also analyzes the determinants of the two factors that most directly govern expenditure levels: (1) recipient rates (proportions of the relevant population groups which receive each type of assistance); and (2) average monthly payments to recipients. These analyses shed more light on the determinants of expenditures than do the models which were fitted directly to expenditures. In general, the results for recipient rates and average payments are statistically more significant than the results for per capita expenditures.

Each of the four public assistance programs is analyzed separately. Additional results are reported for the combined expenditures for all four programs, for the overall public assistance recipient rate, and for administrative expenditures of the programs. General assistance is considered briefly, simply to indicate the extent to which it differs from public assistance.

The analyses reported in this study utilize 1960 data. However, some results were also obtained for 1950 and 1940, and comparisons among these years indicate that there has been a fairly high degree of stability over time in the patterns of determinants of the assistance program variables.

The dependent variables of the regression analyses are: total, federal, and state-local expenditures per capita for each public assistance program and for the four combined; the recipient rate for each program and for the four combined; the average monthly payment per recipient in each program; the average monthly administrative expenditure per case in each public assistance program; and,

**TABLE 1. Changes in the Level of Public Assistance and General Assistance Programs in the United States, Selected Years, 1940–64[a]**

| Program and Year[b] | Total Expenditures[c] (Millions of Dollars) | Federal Share (Percent) | Per Capita Expenditure[d] (In Dollars) | Recipient Rate[e] (Varies; see note) | Average Assistance Payment[f] (In Dollars) |
|---|---|---|---|---|---|
| Old Age Assistance | | | | | |
| 1940 | 472.0 | 49.8 | 3.58 | 220 | 19.96 |
| 1950 | 1,483.4 | 53.9 | 9.84 | 226 | 43.82 |
| 1960 | 1,917.7 | 58.5 | 10.69 | 140 | 69.31 |
| 1964 | 2,027.0 | 65.1 | 10.66 | 120 | 79.48 |
| Aid to Dependent Children | | | | | |
| 1940 | 128.6 | 40.5 | 1.20 | 24.6 | 32.24 |
| 1950 | 552.0 | 46.1 | 3.67 | 34.6 | 77.07 |
| 1960 | 1,045.3 | 59.5 | 5.83 | 36.2 | 110.84 |
| 1964 | 1,528.1 | 57.6 | 8.04 | 42.6 | 141.44 |
| Aid to the Blind | | | | | |
| 1940 | 13.3 | 47.2 | 0.13 | 0.473 | 23.45 |
| 1950 | 44.4 | 51.0 | 0.33 | 0.511 | 47.50 |
| 1960 | 93.8 | 48.1 | 0.52 | 0.602 | 72.57 |
| 1964 | 96.5 | 48.4 | 0.51 | 0.501 | 85.28 |
| Aid to the Permanently and Totally Disabled | | | | | |
| 1940 | — | — | — | — | — |
| 1950 | — | — | — | — | — |
| 1960 | 284.1 | 56.0 | 1.64 | 3.82 | 65.57 |
| 1964 | 440.4 | 57.4 | 2.32 | 4.66 | 81.61 |

**Combined Public Assistance Programs**

| | | | | | |
|---|---|---|---|---|---|
| 1940 | 613.9 | 47.8 | 4.66 | 21.5 | — |
| 1950 | 2,079.8 | 51.8 | 13.80 | 29.8 | — |
| 1960 | 3,340.9 | 58.3 | 18.63 | 32.4 | — |
| 1964 | 4,092.0 | 61.1 | 21.52 | 35.2 | — |

**General Assistance Programs**

| | | | | | |
|---|---|---|---|---|---|
| 1940 | 392.8 | — | 2.98 | 17.12 | 23.85 |
| 1950 | 349.9 | — | 2.32 | 5.68 | 46.84 |
| 1960 | 421.7 | — | 2.39 | 3.96 | 68.75 |
| 1964 | 375.0 | — | 2.02 | 3.26 | 64.69 |

Source: U. S. Bureau of the Census and U. S. Social Security Administration.

a Alaska and Hawaii are included only in 1960 and 1964; Puerto Rico, Guam, and the Virgin Islands are excluded throughout. Data exclude expenditures for Medical Assistance to the Aged (MAA, or "Kerr-Mills"), which amounted to $5.7 million in 1960 and $382.6 million in fiscal 1964. In Puerto Rico, Guam, and the Virgin Islands, in fiscal 1964, expenditures for the four public assistance programs combined were $16.2 million; for the MAA program, $1 million; and for general assistance, $0.2 million.

b Fiscal year data are used for expenditures in 1964 and for the federal share of expenditures in all years; other expenditure data are for calendar years.

c Total expenditures are net of any recoveries made during the year.

d Per capita expenditures for each program are national averages and are calculated excluding the populations of those states not operating the program or (in the case of general assistance programs) not reporting data. Population data for 1940, 1950, and 1960 are from the decennial censuses; for fiscal 1964, the estimated population on January 1, 1964 was used.

e Recipient rates are expressed as follows:
OAA:  Recipients per 1,000 persons aged 65 and over.
ADC:  Child recipients per 1,000 persons under age 18.
AB:  Recipients per 1,000 total population.
APTD:  Recipients per 1,000 persons aged 18 to 64.
Four public assistance programs combined: Total recipients, including adults in ADC, per 1,000 total population.
General assistance: Cases (not persons) per 1,000 persons aged 18 to 64.
For 1940, 1950, and 1960, recipient rates were determined by calculating the average number of recipients per month during the year divided by the appropriate population as reported by the Census Bureau. Populations of states not operating a particular program are excluded. The 1964 rates are for June, based on July 1 population estimates.

f Average payments are expressed per family in ADC, per case in general assistance, and per recipient in all other programs. For 1940, 1950, and 1960, average payments are the average monthly amount of payments (gross of any recoveries) during the year divided by the average monthly number of recipients (or families or cases). The 1964 figures are for June. Except for general assistance, average payment figures include payments in behalf of recipients for medical care, drugs, and so forth.

for general assistance, per capita state-local expenditure, the recipient rate, and the average payment.

The determinant variables include: income level; urbanization; unemployment rate; racial composition; age composition; variables relating to social insurance coverage; and rate of population growth.

*The States' Discretion in Matters of Policy*

Each state has a great deal of control over the number of recipients and virtually total control over the size of payments to recipients in its public assistance programs. Federal standards relate largely to procedure, not to the content or adequacy of the programs. Thus, in determining who is needy and how much assistance is to be paid to those so classified, the states do not operate their public assistance programs under national standards. The Social Security Act also allows the states considerable latitude in setting and interpreting the definitions of "dependent child," "blindness," and "permanent and total disability."[3]

Given this decentralized structure, the possibility exists that a substantial part of the interstate variation in public assistance expenditures results from nonsystematic (and certainly nonquantifiable) factors, particularly the attitudes and policies of states. The more important such influences, the less successful will be any attempt to quantify the determinants of assistance expenditures. Such influences apparently do have important effects on the assistance programs, but significant quantitative relationships are nevertheless to be found.

An attempt was made to identify certain states as having "exceptional" attitudes, either liberal or restrictive, toward the several public assistance programs, and to use dummy variables to separate those states from the others. Results using the dummy variables are not shown, but they are occasionally mentioned in cases where separation of the presumably "extreme" states improved the quality of the empirical results.

The states' important role in making assistance policy justifies

[3] The federal criteria affecting the definition of "dependent child" and "permanent and total disability" are noted below in the discussions of ADC and APTD; there is no federal definition of "blindness." For federal limits on the age, residence, and citizenship requirements that states may set, see note 5.

using states as units of observation. If the programs were operated everywhere under the same rules and standards, it could be argued that states are too large and too arbitrary to permit their use as units of observation. But with a decentralized assistance structure, states are highly significant entities and quite appropriate units.

Table 2 summarizes the extent of interstate variation of public assistance expenditures, recipient rates, and average payments in 1960. For each program, the table shows the highest and lowest state values for these variables and the average values for the nation as a whole.

## The "Quality" of the Empirical Results

The most important feature of the empirical results is perhaps the "qualitative" finding that, despite the states' substantial control over important policy matters, significant relationships in fact exist between the dependent and determinant variables tested.

Measured by the proportion of interstate variation accounted for by the determinants, the results for the recipient rates and the average payments are much more significant than those for per capita expenditures. The reason for this is simple and fundamental: Income level is an important determinant of the assistance program variables, but, as an index of need, income is correlated negatively with the recipient rates, while as an index of ability to spend and of general living standards, it is correlated positively with the average payments per recipient. As a result of these offsetting relationships, income has little statistical significance as an expenditure determinant.

The results are better for OAA than for the other programs. The potential OAA recipient group is clearly defined—those aged sixty-five and over—and there is a good measure available of the relative financial security of the persons in that group—the proportion who receive social insurance benefits. Thus, while rules (for example, limits on property) which govern OAA eligibility and standards for determining need certainly vary among the states, the OAA variables are nevertheless largely determined by clearly defined and easily measured factors: income, age composition, and social insurance coverage.

The general assistance program variables—particularly the recipient rate—are least amenable to explanation by the hypothesized

# TABLE 2. National Averages and Range of Interstate Variations in Assistance Program Variables in 1960[a]

| Program | Per Capita Expenditure (In Dollars) | | | Recipient Rate (Varies; see note) | | | Average Payment (In Dollars) | | |
|---|---|---|---|---|---|---|---|---|---|
| | Low State | U.S. Average | High State | Low State | U.S. Average | High State | Low State | U.S. Average | High State |
| Old Age Assistance | 1.74 (Del.) | 10.69 | 37.08 (Okla.) | 34 (N.J.) | 140 | 518 (La.) | 32.20 (Miss.) | 69.31 | 110.26 (Conn.) |
| Aid to Dependent Children | 1.80 (Tex.) | 5.83 | 12.33 (W.Va.) | 14.3 (N.H.) | 36.2 | 88.2 (W.Va.) | 38.07 (Ala.) | 110.84 | 170.84 (N.Y.) |
| Aid to the Blind | 0.11 (Haw., Md.) | 0.52 | 1.39 (Pa.) | .118 (Conn.) | .602 | 2.912 (Miss.) | 38.55 (Miss.) | 72.57 | 118.32 (Mass.) |
| Aid to the Permanently and Totally Disabled | 0.43 (Tex.) | 1.64 | 4.39 (Okla.) | 1.05 (Cal.) | 3.82 | 10.75 (Miss.) | 32.54 (Miss.) | 65.57 | 128.19 (Conn.) |
| Combined Public Assistance Programs | 5.71 (Va.) | 18.63 | 52.80 (Okla.) | 12.8 (N.J.) | 32.4 | 80.3 (Miss.) | — | — | — |
| General Assistance Programs | 0.01 (Ala.) | 2.39 | 6.56 (Ill.) | 0.04 (Ala.) | 3.96 | 7.92 (Ill.) | 12.99 (Ala.) | 68.75 | 96.66 (Mich.) |

Source: U. S. Bureau of the Census and U. S. Social Security Administration.
[a] All notes in Table 1 apply to this table as well.

determinants. Every state—and in many states, every locality—defines the purpose, coverage, and content of its general assistance program. These characteristics of the general assistance programs vary so widely among the states that it would be remarkable if the standard variables accounted for very much of the interstate variation in the general assistance program variables.

Federal grants to the states for each public assistance program are based on the average monthly assistance payment per recipient. Under the present formula (as of January 1965) for OAA, AB, and APTD, the federal government pays 29/35 of the first $35 of the average payment, plus 50 to 65 percent of the next $35, depending on a state's per capita income. Under the ADC formula, the federal government pays 14/17 of the first $17, plus 50 to 65 percent of the next $13.[4]

To receive federal grants, a state assistance program must have certain characteristics, as follows: (1) The program must be operated throughout the state, by or under the supervision of a state agency, and the state must pay at least some share of the costs. A state agency must set standards for medical institutions if the program provides payments for recipients in such institutions. The

[4] Average payments include medical payments (called vendor payments) on behalf of recipients in states which make such payments. The 1962 public assistance amendments permitted states to combine the OAA, AB, and APTD programs for the calculation of federal grants. Another amendment raised the federal sharing maximum for OAA (or for OAA-AB-APTD, when combined) if the excess of the average payment over the established maximum is comprised of medical vendor payments.

In most ADC families, at least one adult is counted as a recipient in addition to the children.

The grant formula for ADC in 1960 was identical with that now in effect; the 1960 formulae for the adult programs were essentially the same, providing federal payment of 80 percent of the first $30 of the average payment plus 50 to 65 percent of the next $35.

Summary descriptions of public assistance and of the provisions of states' programs are in: U.S. Department of Health, Education, and Welfare, *Serving People in Need: Public Assistance Under the Social Security Act,* Public Assistance Report No. 47 (1964); *Characteristics of State Public Assistance Plans Under the Social Security Act,* Public Assistance Report No. 40 (1960); for provisions that came into effect after 1960, see Public Assistance Report No. 50 (with the same title); *Characteristics of State Public Assistance Plans Under the Social Security Act: Provisions for Medical and Remedial Care,* Public Assistance Report No. 49 (1962).

For general assistance, see: *Characteristics of General Assistance in the United States,* Public Assistance Report No. 39 (1959).

state must also establish a personnel merit system for the staff of its assistance agency. (2) Anyone who wishes to do so must have the opportunity to apply for assistance; assistance must be furnished reasonably promptly to those found eligible; and fair hearings must be provided for applicants or recipients dissatisfied with an assistance agency's decisions. (3) In determining eligibility for assistance and the size of payments, agencies must consider the incomes and resources of applicants, and of recipients (on a continuing basis). That is, the public assistance programs must be based on need, with each recipient's need determined individually. Insofar as possible, there should be intrastate and intraprogram equity in determining eligibility and the amount of assistance payments. (4) Eligibility rules concerning age, residence, and citizenship must not exceed certain limits.[5]

Each state establishes its own assistance standards, which are yardsticks for determining whether a person is needy and the dollar amount of his need. A standard is usually a list of requirements that the state recognizes, such as food, shelter, and clothing, and of dollar allowances for those requirements. The assistance payment is based on the difference between a recipient's requirements, as evaluated by the standard, and any income he may have. The payment sometimes does not cover the entire need as thus evaluated, since states may put restrictions on payments.[6]

States control a number of other aspects of eligibility policy,

[5] Age: Federal grants are not made in aid of OAA payments to persons under age sixty-five nor for OAA programs with minimum age requirements of more than age sixty-five; grants are not made for ADC payments to children over age seventeen nor for APTD payments to persons under age eighteen; there are no federal age rules for AB.

Residence: States' requirements may not exceed five of the last nine years, including continuous residence in the last year, for the three adult programs; the requirement for ADC may not exceed one year.

Citizenship: States may require citizenship, but may not require a certain number of years of citizenship.

[6] Some states put limits on amounts that may be budgeted for certain requirements (for example, shelter), on the total payment to a recipient, and/or on the percentage of evaluated need that may be met by the assistance payment. Also, of course, a recipient may have needs that are not recognized by his state's assistance standard. See: U.S. Department of Health, Education, and Welfare, *Yardstick for Need* (1963); and "State Maximums and Other Methods of Limiting Money Payments to Recipients Under the Special Types of Public Assistance" (September 1964; annual release).

such as rules concerning real and personal property holdings and the financial responsibility of relatives. Recipients also may be required to give a lien or assignment which enables the state to make future recovery, if possible, of some of the cost of providing assistance.

Thus, important characteristics of the public assistance programs for which federal grants are made are largely beyond the control of the federal government. The grants are for support of programs whose general adequacy is determined by the standards of the recipient states.

## Summary of the Empirical Results

Recipient rates vary inversely with income level in all of the public assistance programs. There is a strong statistical relationship; interstate variation in income level can account for over 50 percent of the interstate variation in the proportion of the total population that receives some type of public assistance.

The extent of social insurance coverage can be an important determinant of assistance outlays. The results clearly show that the larger the number of aged persons receiving OASI, the smaller is the need for OAA. Social insurance coverage may also have an influence on AB (since blindness is especially common among the aged) but this does not show clearly in the results. There is a mild indication of negative correlation between the APTD recipient rate and the Disability Insurance beneficiary rate. No direct evidence is found of a relationship between social insurance and ADC.

The unemployment rate appears to be a significant determinant of the OAA and ADC recipient rates, but not of those for AB and APTD. This seems reasonable, for recipients in the latter two groups are presumably much more definitely out of the labor market.

The greater the urbanization of the population, the more likely it would seem that care of the needy will be a social rather than a family function, and urbanization is, in fact, generally associated with higher recipient rates. This is true even when income, which is highly correlated with urbanization, is held constant. However, as might well be expected, urbanization is really significant only with respect to the ADC recipient rate.

Racial composition also has a bearing on public assistance recipient rates; the recipient rates in the programs are positively associated with the nonwhite proportion of the population. However, this relationship is not as strong as one might expect and, somewhat surprisingly, it does not hold at all for ADC.

Recipient rates also tend to be higher in the states that have had the relatively slowest rates of population growth; this relationship is strongest for OAA and APTD.

In contrast to the public assistance programs, the general assistance recipient rate apparently varies less with need than with the ability of state-local governments to support general assistance programs, since the recipient rate is positively correlated with income level.

The poorer states are doubly burdened in the matter of relief, for it appears that blindness, serious disability, and childhood dependency are more prevalent at lower income levels. Relatively larger proportions of the populations of poorer states are potentially eligible for public assistance—by virtue of being blind, disabled, and so forth—and, because of generally lower incomes, relatively larger proportions of these potential recipients in poorer states actually receive public assistance.

AVERAGE PAYMENTS PER RECIPIENT. There are high positive correlations between income level and average monthly payments to assistance recipients. This presumably means that higher-income states have higher assistance standards in terms of items considered in evaluating needs and the dollar values established for them; in addition, recipients in higher-income states may face higher prices.

With the state income level given, there is some tendency for average payments to vary positively with the degree of urbanization of the recipients of assistance. There is also a tendency for the average payment to be smaller the greater the proportion of nonwhite recipients, which may reflect some element of discrimination. Also, nonwhite recipients apparently have lower living standards and therefore smaller evaluated dollar "needs" to be met by assistance payments. In general, state assistance standards do not operate to bring all recipients up to some defined standard of living, but only provide guidelines for putting dollar values on food, shelter, and other requirements. Evaluation of "need" is conducted on an individual basis for each recipient and takes into account his own particular circumstances.[7]

[7] The percentage of the recipients in a public assistance program who are

FEDERAL GRANTS AND PER CAPITA EXPENDITURES. The results for state-local expenditures are almost all weaker than those for federal expenditures. This difference can be attributed to the effects of the federal grant formulae. The grants are based on the average payment per recipient and, in general, the higher that payment the smaller the federal share in it; the federal liability per recipient is absolutely limited by the sharing maxima in the grant formulae. In the case of federal expenditures, therefore, the grant formulae tend to dampen the influence of the higher-income states' relatively high average payments, thus weakening the degree to which the positive correlation of average payment with income offsets the negative correlation of recipient rate with income. Consequently, income has a bit more influence on federal than on state-local expenditures.

It should be noted that the grants have only a limited "equalizing" effect. The negative simple correlation between income and per capita federal expenditures is largely attributable to the higher recipient rates in poorer states; when the recipient rate is held constant, per capita federal expenditure on a public assistance program tends to be invariant with income level. Wealthier states tend to spend more per recipient but poorer states tend to have more recipients per capita. With the recipient rate held constant, the poorer the state, the smaller the per capita expenditure, but the larger the ratio of federal to state-local dollars.[8] The poorer states' "advantage" is that the federal *share* of their public assistance costs is larger; the variability of the share results primarily from the low level

---

also beneficiaries of OASDI was also tested as a determinant of the level of the average payment, on the hypothesis that, with income level held constant, the larger the proportion of recipients with nonassistance income, the lower would be the average assistance payment. However, the coefficients of this variable turned out to be positive, probably because of multicollinearity, and the results are not shown.

[8] The point is illustrated in the correlation of per capita expenditures on the four public assistance programs combined and—as the recipient rate—the ratio of the total number of recipients in the four programs to the total population.

If $X_1$ = total expenditure per capita; $X_2$ = federal expenditure per capita; $X_3$ = state-local expenditure per capita; $X_4$ = personal income per capita; and $X_5$ = recipient rate; then:

$r_{14} = -.203$ $\qquad\qquad\qquad r_{14.5} = .424**$

$r_{24} = -.477**$ $\qquad\qquad\quad\ r_{24.5} = .156$

$r_{34} = .194$ $\qquad\qquad\qquad\ \ r_{34.5} = .524**$

** Significant at the 1 percent level.

The principle holds with respect to each program individually.

of payments to recipients in poorer states rather than from the fact that those states' overall income levels are low.

## Competition Among Programs

There may well be competition among assistance programs—specifically, competition for a limited total amount of state-local funds available for "relief" in each state, and for the goodwill of legislators—but the empirical evidence of the present study is not suited to identifying it.

Interprogram competition might result in a more restrictive assistance standard of need in one program than in others, thus making the average payment or the recipient rate in that program "unexpectedly" low relative to the other programs. However, at any point in time, if a state has a large number of recipients in one program by comparison with numbers of recipients in other states, it tends to have a relatively large number in other programs as well; thus, in a cross section of states, any effects of possible intrastate discrimination among programs are obscured. Similarly, if a state's average payment in one program is relatively low by comparison with other states' payments, its average payments in other programs also tend to be relatively low. Thus, the question of interprogram competition cannot be answered by looking, for example, at the correlation between per capita expenditure for one program and that for another (or all others), because these correlations are all positive and quite high. The question of competition is much better suited to institutional rather than statistical treatment—that is, to an investigation into the manner in which states do, in fact, treat the several programs relative to one another. On that basis, it has generally been observed that ADC is unpopular and operates at a disadvantage in relation to the others.[9]

## The Data

The empirical results are shown in tables which give partial correlation coefficients for the independent variables; those that are statistically significant are clearly marked throughout. (Table A-1

[9] See, for instance: U.S. Advisory Council on Public Assistance, *Report*, Senate Doc. No. 93, 86 Cong. 2 Sess. (1960), especially pp. 18-19; Elizabeth Wickenden and Winifred Bell, *Public Welfare: Time for a Change* (1961), especially Chap. 2.

shows significance levels for the relevant degrees of freedom. The District of Columbia is omitted throughout on the ground that its characteristics are too unlike those of a state and that it does not have a true state's control over its affairs.) The dependent variables and the independent variables common to most programs are summarized in the following paragraphs. Other independent variables are described when introduced.

Per capita expenditures are calculated from Social Security Administration data for calendar year 1960, which show the division of expenditure in each state among the federal, state, and local levels of government. These expenditures are net of any recoveries (for example, from recipients' estates) made during the year. Population data are taken from the 1960 census.

Recipient rates are calculated on the basis of census data as the ratio of the average number of recipients per month during the year to the appropriate population group in the state. The average number of recipients is based on monthly data published by the Social Security Administration.

Average monthly assistance payments are calculated by dividing the average monthly amount of payments (gross of any recoveries) by the average monthly number of recipients. Average payment figures include "vendor payments" in behalf of recipients for medical care. (Total amounts paid to recipients each month are published by the Social Security Administration.)

Per capita income (used as a determinant of expenditures and average payments) is defined as the state's average per capita income for the three years, 1958 to 1960.

"Low income percentage" (used in the analysis of recipient rates) is the percentage of families and unrelated individuals with incomes under $2,000 in 1959, as reported in the 1960 census.

"Nonwhite" population percentage is the percentage of the state's population that is Indian or Negro. This does not include all nonwhites but it was assumed that the assistance programs are affected by racial composition only with respect to these two groups.[10]

---

[10] Although the results might not have been much different had the nonwhite population been defined to include Puerto Ricans and Mexican-Americans as well, such a definition would probably have been more logical.

# TABLE 3. Multiple Regression Analysis of Per Capita OAA Expenditure, 1960

| Dependent Variable: Per Capita OAA Expenditure by Level of Government, 1960[a] | Partial Coefficients of Correlation with the Following Independent Variables: | | | | | | R | $R^2$ | $\bar{R}^2$[d] |
|---|---|---|---|---|---|---|---|---|---|
| | Average Income Per Capita, 1958-60[b] | Percent of Population over Age Sixty-four, 1960 | OASI Beneficiary Rate, 1960[c] | Percent of Population Living in Urban Places, 1960[b] | Unemployment Rate, Spring, 1960[b] | Nonwhite Percent of Population, 1960[b] | | | |
| **Federal and State-Local Combined** | | | | | | | | | |
| (1) | −.2632 | .2435 | | | | | .3331[f] | .1110 | .0731 |
| (2) | −.2607 | .6285[e] | −.7215[e] | | | | .7535[e] | .5737 | .5459 |
| (3) | .0341 | .6452[e] | −.7244[e] | .2320 | .2508 | | .7800[e] | .6084 | .5639 |
| (4) | −.0508 | .6299[e] | −.7503[e] | .2648 | .2554 | −.3017[f] | .8025[e] | .6441 | .5945 |
| **Federal** | | | | | | | | | |
| (5) | .0010 | .6694[e] | −.7844[e] | | | | .8401[e] | .7057 | .6865 |
| (6) | −.1761 | .7095[e] | −.7985[e] | .2461 | .3484[f] | | .8628[e] | .7444 | .7154 |
| (7) | −.2264 | .6967[e] | −.7975[e] | .2654 | .3509[f] | −.2046 | .8690[e] | .7551 | .7209 |
| **State-Local** | | | | | | | | | |
| (8) | .4174[e] | .5255[e] | −.5791[e] | | | | .6172[e] | .3809 | .3405 |
| (9) | .1963 | .5151[e] | −.5669[e] | .1905 | .1328 | | .6368[e] | .4055 | .3380 |
| (10) | .1071 | .4887[e] | −.6317[e] | .2282 | .1326 | −.3389[f] | .6883[e] | .4738 | .4004 |

Source: U. S. Bureau of the Census and U. S. Social Security Administration.

[a] See Table 2 for dollar amounts of per capita OAA expenditures, and Table 1, note d, for an explanation of how per capita expenditures were calculated. Numbers in parentheses identify the results of separate regression tests. For example, lines (1) through (4) show the relationship between a single dependent variable—combined federal and state-local expenditure per capita—and four different combinations of independent variables.

[b] See text, pp. 111 and 113, for definitions of these variables.

[c] Calculated by dividing the number of persons over age sixty-four who were receiving social insurance benefits in December 1960 by the total number of persons over that age as reported by the 1960 Census.

Urbanization is the percentage of the state's population living in urban places as reported in the 1960 Census.[11]

Unemployment is the percentage of the labor force unemployed at the time of the 1960 Census. This figure is used because the regular monthly estimates of total unemployment are not made by state; only insured unemployment is available by state. It was assumed that the assistance programs are more likely to be affected by total unemployment than by insured unemployment.

Percentage change in the population is the percentage change from the estimated figure for July 1, 1955 to the census figure for 1960.

## Old Age Assistance

The partial correlation coefficients in Table 3 show that social insurance is the most important influence on the OAA program; the greater the insurance coverage of the aged population, the smaller the need for and cost of OAA. Income level is a significant determinant of both the recipient rate and the average payment, but these relationships have opposite signs and thus income has little significance in the expenditure results. There is some evidence that the need for and cost of OAA are positively associated with both urbanization and unemployment. Rather surprisingly, the nonwhite percentage of the population is not found to be significant in determining the recipient rate; this may reflect a tendency for nonwhites to support, without public aid, a larger proportion of their dependent persons than do whites. On the other hand, the average OAA payment becomes significantly smaller as the proportion of nonwhites among OAA recipients grows larger; this may be due in part to some form of discrimination.

### Expenditures

In addition to income level, the percentage of the population over age sixty-four is used in Table 3 as a determinant of per capita OAA expenditures. The Social Security Act specifies that states may not establish the minimum age for OAA eligibility at more

[11] The Census defines as urban places with populations of 2,500 or more. A number of the regression models were tested by using instead the percentage living in places of 50,000 or more; the results were very little different.

than sixty-five years, and that no federal grant may be made to assist OAA payments to persons under age sixty-five. A measure of that age group's financial security is provided by the Old-Age and Survivors Insurance beneficiary rate: the proportion of those over age sixty-four receiving social insurance benefits.[12] Presumably, the higher the OASI rate the less extensive will be the need for OAA, particularly if income level is held constant.

As shown in Table 3, line 1, income and the percentage of the population over age sixty-four account for very little of the interstate variation in per capita OAA expenditure, where the dependent variable is the combined expenditure from state-local and federal funds. The important determinant here is the OASI beneficiary rate, which has highly significant negative coefficients. Thus, the larger the proportion of the aged population benefitting from social insurance, the smaller is the per capita OAA expenditure. Additionally, inclusion of the OASI rate makes the percentage of the population over age sixty-four highly significant statistically.

Holding constant the percentage over age sixty-four and the OASI beneficiary rate, per capita OAA expenditure from state-local funds varies positively with income level. This presumably occurs because wealthier states can afford both more liberal OAA eligibility requirements and larger payments per recipient. However, while per capita state-local expenditure varies positively with income, the ratio of federal to state-local dollars varies negatively with income and therefore income is insignificant in the federal expenditure model, as Table 3, line 5, shows.

Social insurance beneficiaries are not necessarily ineligible for OAA; in 1960, some 28.5 percent of the OAA recipients were concurrently benefitting from OASI. The proportion of a state's OAA recipients who also receive OASI benefits varies positively with income, presumably because wealthier states have assistance standards under which OASI beneficiaries are more likely to be ad-

[12] The "OASI beneficiary rate" is the number of persons over age sixty-four receiving social insurance benefits (in December) divided by the total number over age sixty-four. Beneficiaries of social insurance may also receive OAA if, even with their insurance benefit, they are still needy according to their state's assistance standard. OASI beneficiaries greatly outnumber OAA recipients. In 1960, the national OAA recipient rate was 140 per thousand persons over age sixty-four while the OASI beneficiary rate was 638.

judged in need of OAA payments to supplement their insurance benefits.[13] Therefore, the influence of the OASI beneficiary rate is not the same in all states. Although the hypothesis is that the higher the OASI rate the lower the OAA recipient rate, this relationship is in fact relatively less strong in wealthier states. If OAA and OASI were mutually exclusive, the positive correlation between income and state-local expenditure shown in Table 3, line 8, would be wholly attributable to the fact that monthly OAA payments are larger in wealthier states. But since the coverages do overlap, the positive income-expenditure correlation can in some part be attributed to that overlap.

Table 3, line 8, indicates that state-local OAA expenditure is least amenable to "explanation," with only 34.1 percent of its inter-state variation accounted for. In general, all state-local expenditure results are poorer than those for federal or total expenditures. This disparity may be attributed to the states' freedom to make policy decisions (concerning eligibility rules, assistance standards, and so forth) that directly affect their assistance expenditures. Although state-local expenditure is the basis for federal expenditure, the latter is more amenable to "explanation" because the variable-federal-share feature of the grant formula, and the setting of a maximum average payment in which the federal government will share, tend to dampen the influence on federal expenditure of some states' "extreme" attitudes, especially those on the "liberal" side.[14]

Expenditures for OAA may be influenced by additional factors, such as urbanization, unemployment, and racial composition. The results of adding these variables are also shown in Table 3.

Urbanization is hypothesized as positively associated with OAA expenditures because it is presumably associated with weaker family ties and greater "socialization" of the care of the aged, and also

[13] The correlation coefficient between per capita income and the percentage of OAA recipients receiving OASI was .668 in 1960. The number of concurrent recipients is reported periodically in the *Social Security Bulletin;* for 1960 data, see Robert H. Mugge, "Concurrent Receipt of Public Assistance and Old Age, Survivors, and Disability Insurance," *Social Security Bulletin* (December 1960), p. 18.

[14] The use of dummy variables to separate a few presumably "extreme" states from the rest resulted in much larger values of $\bar{R}^2$ for state-local OAA expenditure, and also increased te negative coefficients of income in the models of federal OAA expenditure.

with a smaller probability that aged persons have the independence of home ownership.

Only very high or very low unemployment rates could be expected to have much effect on OAA since most of the elderly are not in the labor force. Very full employment could reduce OAA costs by opening up job opportunities for aged persons who are marginally in the labor force and by improving their relatives' financial circumstances; this apparently did happen during World War II. Very high unemployment rates could, on opposite reasoning, increase dependency on public support.

Racial composition might be expected to influence OAA expenditure through its influence on the recipient rate. Since nonwhites are generally poorer than whites, the larger the nonwhite percentage of the population the greater, presumably, will be the need for assistance. On this reasoning, the percentage of nonwhites in the population should be positively associated with per capita OAA expenditure.

Urbanization, unemployment, and the percentage of nonwhites in the population add little to the explanation of OAA expenditures. Urbanization and unemployment have the expected positive coefficients but, except for unemployment in lines 6 and 7 of Table 3, neither is statistically significant. The insignificance of urbanization is in part attributable to its high correlation with income.

Contrary to expectation, the percentage of nonwhites in the population has coefficients that are negative as well as statistically significant. Similar results for racial composition are found for expenditures on the other assistance programs. The negative signs apparently result from the fact that most states' payments to nonwhite OAA recipients are smaller than their payments to white recipients. Thus, other things being equal, the larger the nonwhite percentage the smaller is the average OAA payment per recipient. Therefore, with the other hypothesized determinants held constant, the larger the nonwhite percentage, the smaller the per capita OAA expenditure (since the nonwhite percentages of the population and of the OAA recipients are highly correlated).

*Recipient Rate*

As shown in Table 4, line 1, almost 43 percent of the interstate variation in the OAA recipient rate can be accounted for by interstate differences in the percentage of the population having "low income." (The income variable is the percentage of families and unrelated individuals with income under $2,000 in 1959.)[15] Thus, it seems clear that regardless of interstate variation in eligibility policies, the OAA program is based on need. While wealthier states may be able and inclined to operate relatively more generous OAA programs, the poorer states nevertheless support larger proportions of their aged on OAA.

The negative correlation between income level and the OAA recipient rate does not result simply from the greater social insurance coverage of the aged in higher-income states. When the OASI beneficiary rate is held constant, there is still a significant negative correlation between income level and the OAA recipient rate.[16] These two variables can account for 72.8 percent of the interstate variation in the OAA recipient rate, and both are statistically significant despite their fairly high intercorrelation.

Unemployment is not quite significant when added to the model, but it does have the expected positive sign and the inclusion of urbanization raises the coefficient of unemployment to a significant level. Thus, there is some indication that even among the aged, higher unemployment leads to higher assistance caseloads. Although neither urbanization nor racial composition is statistically significant, the coefficients of urbanization are at least not negligible and they have the expected positive sign.

Finally, the percentage change in population from 1955 to 1960 is hypothesized as a determinant on the theory that the slower the rate of population growth the more "stagnant" is the state and, therefore, the greater the incidence of need. While the coefficient of the variable is not significant, it does have the expected negative sign. (Racial composition is omitted from line 6 in Table 4, since it is wholly insignificant when added; for the same reason, the population change variable was omitted from Table 3.)

---

[15] Results for the OAA recipient rate are essentially the same, but with slightly smaller multiple correlation coefficients, when per capita income is used instead of the "low-income" variable. This is true, generally, of the recipient rate models for all the assistance programs.

[16] The OASI beneficiary rate varies positively with income level because in higher-income states the labor force is more heavily concentrated in occupations covered by social insurance. However, as OASI coverage has increased and broadened over time, this correlation has weakened.

## TABLE 4. Multiple Regression Analysis of the OAA Recipient Rate, 1960[a]

| Dependent Variable: OAA Recipient Rate, 1960[b] | Partial Coefficients of Correlation with the Following Independent Variables: | | | | | | R | $R^2$ | $\bar{R}^{2c}$ |
|---|---|---|---|---|---|---|---|---|---|
| | Percent of Population with Incomes Below $2,000, 1960 | OASI Beneficiary Rate, 1959 | Unemployment Rate, Spring, 1960 | Percent of Population Living in Urban Places, 1960 | Nonwhite Percent of Population, 1960 | Percent Increase in Population, 1955–60 | | | |
| (1) | .6638[d] | | | | | | .6638[d] | .4407 | .4291 |
| (2) | .3231[e] | −.7306[d] | | | | | .8598[d] | .7392 | .7281 |
| (3) | .3216[e] | −.7413[d] | .2516 | | | | .8693[d] | .7557 | .7398 |
| (4) | .4083[d] | −.6952[d] | .3221[e] | .2718 | | | .8796[d] | .7738 | .7537 |
| (5) | .3928[d] | −.6907[d] | .3268[e] | .2829 | −.0825 | | .8805[d] | .7753 | .7447 |
| (6) | .3855[d] | −.7176[d] | .3334[e] | .3347[e] | | −.2481 | .8875[d] | .7877 | .7636 |

Source: U. S. Bureau of the Census and U. S. Social Security Administration.

[a] See text, pp. 111, 113, and 114, for definitions of independent variables.

[b] See Table 2 for the level of the OAA recipient rate, and Table 1, note e, for the method of calculating this rate.

[c] $\bar{R}^2$ refers to coefficients corrected for degrees of freedom.

[d] Significant at the 1 percent level.

[e] Significant at the 5 percent level.

Why is racial composition statistically insignificant? It is possible, of course, that it has no real bearing on the need for OAA, but this seems unlikely. However, any effects of race may in fact be obscured by intercorrelation among income, the OASI rate, and racial composition. This interpretation seems a bit more likely. It may also be that the recipient rate among nonwhites is held down by a "knowledge factor," for it is quite possible that nonwhites, on balance, are less aware than whites of the availability of public assistance. Finally, there is the possibility that elements of discrimination have an effect on OAA and the other assistance programs, especially ADC; it will be seen in the following section that the percentage of nonwhites in the population has negative coefficients in the ADC recipient rate models. Discrimination would most likely operate through the degree of enforcement of rules regarding property holdings, relatives' responsibility, and so forth (including "suitable home" provisions in ADC). The effect of discrimination would be to keep recipient rates among nonwhites lower than they would "otherwise" be, thus offsetting the influence that was hypothesized for racial composition. An alternative interpretation is that what appears to be the result of discrimination is in fact the result of a greater tendency for nonwhites than for whites voluntarily to "take care of their own." Such a tendency would work to offset the effects of the nonwhites' relatively poorer financial status and could be responsible for the insignificance of the race variable in Table 4 and for its negative correlation with the ADC recipient rate in Table 7. There is evidence suggestive of such a tendency with regard to the support of dependent children, as is indicated in the discussion of ADC. However, it is entirely possible that this apparent alternative to the interpretation which rests on discrimination is in fact itself a result of discrimination. If discrimination tends to keep nonwhites off the public assistance rolls, they have little choice but to "take care of their own" to a greater extent than do whites. In that case, of course, they are not doing so voluntarily.

*Average Monthly Payment*

The size of monthly assistance payments is determined by state-local assistance agencies. States are not obliged to meet 100 percent of need even as evaluated by their own standards, and they may establish maxima for the monthly payments. Each state also decides

# TABLE 5. Multiple Regression Analysis of the Average Monthly OAA Payment, 1960[a]

| Dependent Variable: Average Monthly OAA Payment, 1960[b] | Partial Coefficients of Correlation with the Following Independent Variables: | | | | $R$ | $R^2$ | $\bar{R}^{2}$[c] |
|---|---|---|---|---|---|---|---|
| | Average Income Per Capita, 1958–60 | OAA Recipient Rate, 1960 | Percent of OAA Recipients Living in Urban Places, 1960 | Nonwhite Percent of OAA Recipients, 1960 | | | |
| (1) | .6331[d] | | | | .6331[d] | .4008 | .3883 |
| (2) | .5978[d] | .0815 | | | .6362[d] | .4048 | .3794 |
| (3) | .3793[d] | | .3638[e] | −.4670[d] | .8068[d] | .6510 | .6282 |
| (4) | .5203[d] | .4320[d] | .3799[d] | −.5875[d] | .8462[d] | .7161 | .6909 |

Source: U. S. Bureau of the Census and U. S. Social Security Administration.

[a] See text, pp. 111, 113, and 122, for definitions of independent variables.

[b] See Table 2 for the dollar amount of the average monthly OAA payment, and Table 1, note f , for the method of calculating this payment

[c] $\bar{R}^2$ refers to coefficients corrected for degrees of freedom.

[d] Significant at the 1 percent level.

[e] Significant at the 5 percent level.

whether any of its assistance programs will include medical "vendor payments" in behalf of recipients and, if so, for what medical goods and services.

Table 5 shows the correlation results for the average monthly OAA payment. The hypothesized determinants are per capita income, the OAA recipient rate, the percentage of recipients classified as urban and the percentage of recipients who are nonwhite.

The most obvious hypothesis concerning the average payment is that it varies with the income of the general population. This assumes that assistance standards will (to some extent) vary with general living standards, and also that wealthier states can afford larger assistance payments. As line 1 in Table 5 shows, per capita income differences alone can in fact account for 38.8 percent of the interstate variation in the average OAA payment.

One reason why higher-income states make larger average payments might be simply that they have relatively fewer recipients. However, when the OAA recipient rate is included, income remains highly significant, although correlation between income and the recipient rate reduces the coefficient of income.

It would not be surprising if the recipient rate had a negative coefficient in Table 5, line 2. That would suggest that, whatever the income level, state-local funds are not unlimited and the average payment is affected by a "sharing out" among the recipients of a fixed sum.[17]

Urbanization of the recipients might be positively associated with the average payment because urban recipients probably have less income in kind (for example, implicit rent and home-grown food), have costlier needs (for example, for heating fuel), and may have to pay higher prices for food and shelter. As to the recipients' racial composition, there is no reason to expect that variable to have any systematic influence on the average payment, but it was tested because the nonwhite population percentage has significant

[17] In lines 2 and 4 in Table 5, separation of a few "extreme" states by means of dummy variables not only increases $\overline{R}^2$ but, more importantly, results in more reasonable coefficients for the recipient rate; the coefficient of the rate in line 2 becomes significantly negative while in line 4 it becomes insignificant. In general, for all public assistance programs, the "extreme" state dummies have a larger impact on the average payment results than on those for expenditures or the recipient rate. This is reasonable, since states' control over assistance policy is exercised most directly with respect to payments to recipients.

*negative* coefficients in expenditure models, not only for OAA but for other assistance programs as well.[18]

When the two characteristics of the recipients are added to income, all three variables are significant. Rather unexpectedly, racial composition does indeed have a negative coefficient. One possible explanation of this might be consistent discrimination in the calculation of assistance payments, but it is rather difficult to imagine such a pattern prevailing throughout the country. However, a more subtle form of discrimination could be at work. The generosity of states' assistance standards—applied to all applicants—may be relatively less (given income, certainly an important determinant of assistance standards) the greater the proportion of nonwhites among assistance recipients. The relative prominence of nonwhites on the caserolls could affect the attitudes of state-local policymakers, thus making racial composition something of a proxy for "attitude."

More directly, however, in all but six states the evaluated dollar requirements of the average nonwhite OAA recipient are smaller than those of the average white recipient. Requirements are total monthly dollar needs evaluated under the state's assistance standard, including need that will be met by income from nonassistance sources as well as from the OAA payment. With smaller requirements, it follows that OAA payments to nonwhites will be smaller, and in most states they are. (The race differential is smaller for average payments than for requirements, however, because nonwhites tend to have less nonassistance income.)[19]

The foregoing must have a good deal to do with the negative sign for racial composition in the OAA payment results. But the

---

[18] Recipients' characteristics are from a 1960 survey. For findings, see: U.S. Department of Health, Education, and Welfare, *Characteristics and Financial Circumstances of Recipients of Old Age Assistance, 1960, Part I—National Data and Part II—State Data*, Public Assistance Report No. 48 (1961 and 1962, respectively).

Percentage nonwhite includes all nonwhites except in Hawaii, whose figure is adjusted to include only Indians and Negroes; the figure for Vermont is estimated. The urbanization and racial composition of the recipients are highly correlated with the same characteristics of the population at large ($r = .87$ and .86, respectively). Thus, very similar results are obtained using the population percentages. This is noted because state data on recipients' characteristics were available only for OAA (for 1960) and ADC (for 1958), and in other average payment models the general population percentages had to be used.

[19] *Ibid., Part II*, Tables 44-45.

question remains: Why, in almost all states, are nonwhites' requirements smaller than those of whites? Two reasons for this can be suggested.

First, nonwhite recipients apparently have lower living standards than do whites. Within any state, the average nonwhite recipient is more likely to cook and heat with wood, and less likely to have central heating, refrigeration, or running water. Therefore, the nonwhites' requirements for housing, fuel, and the like probably tend to be less costly.

Second, a considerably smaller proportion of nonwhite than of white recipients lives in institutions, such as nursing homes and nonpublic homes for the aged, and the dollar requirements of institutionalized recipients are a good deal higher than are those of other recipients. (In 1960 the proportions institutionalized, nationally, were 2.4 percent of the nonwhites and 10.7 percent of the whites; among the states reporting this proportion by race, all showed a higher proportion of institutionalized recipients among whites.)[20]

It is likely that both these factors contribute to the white-nonwhite differential in average requirements of (and thus in average payments to) OAA recipients. Nevertheless, the possibility of discrimination cannot be ruled out; for one thing, it may well have some bearing on the large race differential in the proportion of recipients in institutions. Furthermore, significant negative coefficients are found for the nonwhite percentage in the average payment models for the other assistance programs—including ADC, in which institutionalization is rare.[21]

## Aid to Dependent Children

The ADC program is more strongly affected by the "nonsystematic" factor of state attitudes than OAA, and thus statistical results for the program are weaker. Urbanization and unemployment appear to be significant determinants of the cost of ADC. A variable measuring the prevalence of childhood dependency has significant

[20] *Ibid.,* Tables 19, 20, 23-33, 46, 48.
[21] Available data on the characteristics of ADC families are not broken down by race; no state data on AB or APTD recipients' characteristics were available when this study was conducted.

positive association with expenditures and with the recipient rate, but only when the nonwhite population percentage is held constant. The latter variable is, unexpectedly, negatively correlated with both expenditures and the recipient rate. The significant *negative* coefficient of the race variable as a recipient rate determinant is the most interesting of the ADC results.

In part, this may well reflect some degree of discrimination. Although there is evidence suggesting a tendency for the nonwhite community to support without public funds a larger proportion of its dependent children than does the white community, there is no proof that the tendency is voluntary. Rather, as was suggested in the discussion of OAA, it could result from discrimination in ADC.

Social insurance has little measurable effect on ADC. To be sure, OASDI is largely replacing ADC in supporting those children with whom the original assistance legislation was primarily concerned—those whose fathers are dead. But there are so many other causes of childhood dependency that expanding social insurance coverage has not led to a decline in the need for ADC nor even to an increase in the proportion of ADC recipients also benefitting from social insurance. ADC and OASDI interact at only a few points, where death and, more recently, disability, are involved; OASDI is quite unrelated to the broken families and social dislocation that underlie most ADC families' need for assistance.[22]

## Dependency

For ADC eligibility, a child must not only be needy but also "dependent," which the Social Security Act defines as deprived of support by reason of a parent's death, prolonged absence, or physical or mental incapacity. Thus, the ADC caseload and cost must be in part determined by the prevalence of such "dependency," which presumably varies among the states. An attempt was made to determine whether this interstate variation can be measured and used as

[22] In late 1958, 221,000 (10.3 percent) of the children receiving ADC were classed as being needy because of the father's death; at that time, 1,378,000 children under eighteen received social insurance benefits as survivors of deceased workers. Only 27,000 of the children were concurrently receiving both ADC and Survivors Insurance. For a summary of data from a survey of ADC families in 1958, see Robert H. Mugge, *Characteristics and Financial Circumstances of Families Receiving Aid to Dependent Children, Late 1958,* U.S. Department of Health, Education, and Welfare, Public Assistance Report No. 42 (1960). See also Mugge, in *Social Security Bulletin.*

a determinant of the ADC program variables. Several variables that might serve this purpose were investigated; the one chosen for use was the proportion of children living with their mother only, among all children under age eighteen living with one or both parents. As measured by this variable, childhood dependency is more prevalent the lower a state's income level, the larger its nonwhite population percentage, and the more urbanized its population.[23]

There are two points to note concerning the relationship between race and dependency. First, among persons aged thirty to forty-five—a group which must include most of the parents of young children—the nonwhite death rate is well over twice that of whites.[24] Second, the nonwhite percentage may be a fairly good proxy for the incidence of illegitimacy. No illegitimacy variable is included in the ADC models because data on illegitimate births are available from only thirty-four states. In those states, however, the ratio of illegitimate births to all births is about ten times as large among nonwhites as among whites; and the ratio of total illegitimate births to total births is highly correlated with the nonwhite population percentage.[25]

## Expenditures

Results for ADC expenditures are shown in Table 6. Four of the six determinants—income, urbanization, unemployment, and racial composition—were also used for OAA expenditures. The other two are the percentage of the population in the age group eligible for ADC, and the "dependency" variable described above.[26]

[23] The "low-income" percentage, urbanization, and the nonwhite percentage can account for 78.2 percent of the interstate variation in the dependency variable, with all three independent variables significant at the 1 percent level. The other possible "dependency" variables that were investigated are similarly related to income, urbanization, and race. These others included: the percentage of children under age eighteen not living with both parents; the percentage of women over fourteen and ever married, who are separated, widowed, or divorced; the percentage of women over fourteen, ever married but not widowed, who are separated or divorced; the percentage of children under age eighteen who receive any type of OASDI benefit.

[24] U.S. Public Health Service, *Vital Statistics of the United States, 1960,* Vol. II, Sec. 1 (1961), Tables 1-D, 1-T.

[25] Using 1957 illegitimacy ratios from the thirty-four reporting states, Spearman's rank correlation coefficient is .919. For illegitimacy data see: U.S. Department of Health, Education, and Welfare, *Illegitimacy and Its Impact on the Aid to Dependent Children Program* (1960), Table 4.

[26] In most states the age variable is the percentage of persons under age

# TABLE 6. Multiple Regression Analysis of Per Capita ADC Expenditure, 1960[a]

| Dependent Variable: Per Capita ADC Expenditure by level of Government, 1960[b] | Partial Coefficients of Correlation with the Following Independent Variables: | | | | | | | | | |
|---|---|---|---|---|---|---|---|---|---|---|
| | Average Income Per Capita, 1958–60 | Percent of Population Under Age Eighteen, 1960 | Unemployment Rate, Spring, 1960 | Percent of Population Living in Urban Places, 1960 | Nonwhite Percent of Population, 1960 | Percent of Children Living with Mother Only, 1960[c] | Percent Increase in Population, 1955–60 | R | $R^2$ | $\bar{R}^2$[d] |
| **Federal and State-Local Combined** | | | | | | | | | | |
| (1) | −.1187 | .1684 | .4175[f] | .3448[e] | | | | .4923[f] | .2424 | .1750 |
| (2) | −.2695 | .1836 | .4734[f] | .4115[f] | −.3541[e] | | | .5808[f] | .3373 | .2620 |
| (3) | .0381 | .3560[e] | .3305[e] | .1474 | −.5376[f] | .4377[f] | | .6814[f] | .4643 | .3896 |
| (4) | −.1378 | .1495 | .4170[f] | .3400[e] | | −.0737 | | .4965[f] | .2465 | .1609 |
| (5) | .1051 | .4246[f] | .3043[e] | .2137 | −.5709[f] | .4884[f] | −.2564 | .7067[f] | .4995 | .4161 |
| **Federal** | | | | | | | | | | |
| (6) | −.2835 | .1340 | .4142[f] | .2742 | | | | .4882[f] | .2384 | .1707 |
| (7) | −.3425[e] | .1392 | .4396[f] | .3077[e] | −.2078 | | | .5208[f] | .2713 | .1885 |
| (8) | −.0001 | .3477[e] | .2743 | −.0050 | −.5212[f] | .4848[f] | | .6706[f] | .4497 | .3729 |
| (9) | −.1654 | .1503 | .3716[e] | .2090 | | .0897 | | .4945[f] | .2445 | .1587 |
| (10) | .0302 | .3625[e] | .2577 | .0265 | −.5308[f] | .5036[f] | −.1180 | .6763[f] | .4574 | .3670 |
| **State-Local** | | | | | | | | | | |
| (11) | .2078 | .1634 | .2840 | .3432[e] | | | | .6017[f] | .3620 | .3052 |
| (12) | −.0109 | .1889 | .3717[e] | .4433[f] | −.4617[f] | | | .7057[f] | .4980 | .4410 |
| (13) | .0825 | .2329 | .2946[e] | .3146[e] | −.3846[f] | .1537 | | .7139[f] | .5097 | .4413 |
| (14) | −.0434 | .0985 | .3749[e] | .4420[f] | | −.3132[e] | | .6516[f] | .4246 | .3592 |
| (15) | .1843 | .3718[e] | .2606 | .4096[f] | −.4544[f] | .2670 | −.3695[e] | .7594[f] | .5767 | .5062 |

Source: U. S. Bureau of the Census and U. S. Social Security Administration.
[a] See text, pp. 111, 113, and 125, for definitions of independent variables.
[b] See Table 2 for the dollar amount of the per capita ADC expenditure, and Table 1, note d, for the method of calculating this figure.
[c] This is the number of children under eighteen years old living with their mother only, expressed as a percentage of all children under eighteen living with one or both parents.
[d] $\bar{R}^2$ refers to coefficients corrected for degrees of freedom.     [e] Significant at the 5 percent level.     [f] Significant at the 1 percent level.

Per capita income has statistically insignificant coefficients except in line 7 (for federal expenditure), probably because of both multicollinearity and the offsetting influences that income has on expenditures. The "equalizing" effects of the federal grants appear to be mild, since, with other variables held constant, the coefficients of income in the federal expenditure models are negative but generally not significant.

Urbanization and unemployment are generally significant, and, with one exception, have positive signs. These variables should be important as ADC expenditure determinants. The unemployment rate can be expected to be more significant for ADC than for the other public assistance programs because the ability of mothers of dependent children to support them is probably quite sensitive to general employment conditions; it is also likely that desertions of fathers are more common, and support from absent fathers less adequate, when the unemployment rate is high. One can expect ADC to be especially sensitive to urbanization because of its association with family disintegration.

The nonwhite percentage of the population has significant negative coefficients, rather than the positive coefficients that would seem more probable in view of the sizable positive correlation between that percentage and childhood dependency. As an indication of the forces producing this result, results omitting the nonwhite percentage are also shown. The only determinant significantly affected by that omission is the "dependency" variable; the important interrelationship, among the determinants, is that between race and dependency. Given the presumed extent to which a state's children are potential ADC recipients (that is, the prevalence of "childhood dependency"), ADC expenditure is *smaller* the larger the nonwhite population percentage. Because dependency and race are highly correlated, the former is not a significant determinant of ADC expenditures unless the latter is held constant.

The negative coefficients of the nonwhite percentage are not

---

eighteen, but in two states the eligibility limit is age sixteen, and in one state it is age fourteen. In some twenty of the states with limits of age eighteen, children aged sixteen and seventeen are eligible only if attending school but this condition has been ignored in calculating the percentage of the population eligible for ADC (and in calculating the ADC recipient rate). This procedure perhaps unwisely ignores the probability that a large proportion of the sixteen- and seventeen-year-olds in poor families drop out of school.

due simply to a tendency for monthly ADC payments to be smaller
the larger the nonwhite percentage (both of population and of recipient families), though such a relationship does exist (as shown in
Table 8). The negative coefficients of the race variable are also attributable to a much more surprising relationship: Holding constant
the "prevalence of dependency," there is significant *negative* correlation between the nonwhite population percentage and the ADC
recipient rate itself (as shown in Table 7). The meaning of that relationship is considered below.

The ADC expenditure results are much weaker than those for
OAA. Although there is no single highly important factor which
influences ADC, such as social insurance coverage in the case of
OAA, somewhat better results were expected. Their weakness suggests the possibility that the states' control over eligibility and standards, coupled with their diverse social structures and attitudes, result in ADC expenditures being determined in large degree by nonquantifiable factors. The ADC program differs markedly from
OAA in that the recipients' characteristics and the causes of need
are much less homogeneous in ADC. Need for ADC often arises
from socially condemned behavior, and ADC apparently enjoys
less public sympathy than other public assistance programs. ADC is
probably much more affected than is OAA by rules governing eligibility and payments. These vary widely among states because they
are fashioned by each jurisdiction in light of its own social conditions and attitudes. The variety of such rules, combined with the
variety of causes of need for ADC, could well mean that nonquantifiable influences on expenditures are much more important for
ADC than for OAA.[27]

*Recipient Rate*

Although the ADC recipient rate models fit the data fairly well,
the results are weaker than are those for the OAA recipient rate. It
is not unreasonable to attribute a good deal of the unexplained

[27] However, separation of a few presumably "restrictive" states by means of a
dummy variable added virtually nothing to the explanatory power of the ADC
expenditure models. It might have been worthwhile to have tested the state (or
local) percentage of combined state-local expenditure in the public assistance expenditure models, on the thesis that the smaller the state share, the greater the
local control and the more "restrictive" the program.

variance in the ADC rate to the effects of the states' varying attitudes and different ADC rules.

A review of the states' ADC eligibility rules supports such an attribution. The program was established to meet need that was expected to be of long duration, and Congress had in mind cases where the father had died. Death is perhaps the only really indisputable cause of lasting need; it is not susceptible to qualifications and definitions, as are "incapacity" and "prolonged absence." The proportion of ADC cases in which need is caused by factors other than death, with eligibility determined under varying state rules, has grown steadily. The states' control over eligibility rules and their application means that they can, in administering ADC, express attitudes toward illegitimacy, underemployment, illiteracy, and the like. State policies vary in regard to, among other things: school attendance, work requirements for both children and adults in the ADC family, relatives with whom and circumstances in which ADC children may live, responsibility of and support from absent fathers and other relatives, "suitable home" requirements, eligibility of unborn children, and so on.[28]

The ADC recipient rate is the number of child recipients per thousand persons in the eligible age group. While this rate ranged (in 1960) from 88.2 in West Virginia to 14.3 in New Hampshire (with a nationwide rate of 36.2), there was little interstate variation in the average number of children per ADC family. Among 87.3 percent of all ADC families in 1960, need was great enough for the adult caretaker to be considered an ADC recipient.[29] The interstate variation in this percentage was not wide nor did it appear to follow any discernible pattern.

Table 7 summarizes the results for the ADC recipient rate. Income is an important explanatory variable, except when the depen-

---

[28] For a discussion of the influence of state policy on ADC recipient rates at an earlier date, see Elizabeth Alling and Agnes Leisy, *Aid to Dependent Children in a Postwar Year: Characteristics of Families Receiving ADC, June 1948*, Federal Security Agency, Public Assistance Report No. 17 (1950), pp. 20-26.

[29] This means that the adult's needs are included in calculating the amount of assistance to be paid and that the adult is counted as a recipient in calculating the federal grant. However, many states with maximum payment provisions make no allowance in their maxima for adult recipients; the maxima are stated in dollars per child, regardless of whether an adult's needs are included in the family's need.

# TABLE 7. Multiple Regression Analysis of the ADC Recipient Rate, 1960[a]

| Dependent Variable: ADC Recipient Rate, 1960[b] | Partial Coefficients of Correlation with the Following Independent Variables: | | | | | R | $R^2$ | $\bar{R}^2$[d] |
|---|---|---|---|---|---|---|---|---|
| | Percent of Population with Incomes Below $2,000, 1959 | Unemployment Rate, Spring, 1960 | Percent of Population Living in Urban Places, 1960 | Non-white Percent of Population, 1960 | Percent of Children Under Eighteen Living with Mother Only, 1960[c] | | | |
| (1) | .5166[e] | | | | | .5166[e] | .2669 | .2517 |
| (2) | .6258[e] | .4454[e] | | | | .6789[e] | .4609 | .4258 |
| (3) | .2113 | .3978[e] | .1184 | | .3426[f] | .7240[e] | .5242 | .4819 |
| (4) | .5402[e] | .4528[e] | .4200[e] | −.1069 | | .6835[e] | .4671 | .4197 |
| (5) | .2843 | .4070[e] | .0552 | −.4848[e] | .5631[e] | .7975[e] | .6361 | .5948 |

Source: U. S. Bureau of the Census and U. S. Social Security Administration.
[a] See text, pp. 111 and 113, for definitions of independent variables.
[b] See Table 2 for the level of the ADC recipient rate, and Table 1, note e, for the method of calculating this rate.
[c] See Table 6, note c.
[d] $\bar{R}^2$ refers to coefficients corrected for degrees of freedom.
[e] Significant at the 1 percent level.
[f] Significant at the 5 percent level.

dency proxy is included in the equation; because of collinearity, the role of income is then reduced. By itself, income variation can account for about 25 percent of the interstate variation in the ADC recipient rate.

Unemployment is clearly a significant factor in determining the recipient rate. It is particularly reasonable that unemployment should be significant with regard to ADC, since many ADC families include persons who are at least potential members of the labor force.

Urbanization plays a significant role so long as the dependency proxy is not included. Presumably, the frequency of broken families and of illegitimacy, and the need of dependent children for public financial aid, vary positively with urbanization.

Interpretation of the role of the nonwhite percentage is complicated by collinearity among it, urbanization, income, and dependency. There is more dependency among nonwhite than among white children; in late 1958, though fewer than 10 percent of all families were nonwhite, more than 40 percent of the ADC families were nonwhite.[30]

Therefore, the ADC recipient rate could well be expected to vary positively with the nonwhite percentage. The insignificance of that percentage in line 4, Table 7, is at least partly attributable to multicollinearity.[31] However, a more interesting explanation of its insignificance can be derived from the unexpected result in line 5: With the prevalence of childhood dependency held constant, the ADC recipient rate has a significant *inverse* relationship with the nonwhite percentage. These results may be interpreted as follows: The larger the proportion of the population that is nonwhite, the greater is the incidence of childhood dependency. However, given the prevalence of such dependency, the larger the nonwhite proportion of the population, the smaller is the proportion of children who

[30] Mugge, *Characteristics . . . of Families Receiving ADC,* p. 14. As was pointed out in footnote 23, the "dependency" variable has significant positive correlation with the nonwhite percentage, even when income is held constant.

[31] However, the observation for West Virginia has a substantial effect on the results; if that observation is excluded, the nonwhite percentage has a significant positive coefficient in line 4, and in line 5 its coefficient, though still negative, is not significant. West Virginia has an exceptionally high recipient rate and a small nonwhite percentage.

Use of the dummy variable to separate the states presumed to be "exceptionally restrictive" had little effect on the results in Table 7.

receive public financial aid. This can be taken to reflect: (1) elements of discrimination in the administration of ADC and/or (2) a white-nonwhite differential in the extent to which dependent children are supported without public aid. There is evidence suggesting that such a difference exists but, as was noted in the foregoing discussion of OAA, the difference may itself result from discrimination.

One possible form of "discrimination" was mentioned in connection with the OAA recipient rate results: the possibility that state-local government attitudes toward an assistance program are affected by the racial composition of the recipients. It is also possible that state ADC eligibility rules tend to discriminate between whites and nonwhites. Rules concerning "suitable homes," school attendance, prosecution of fathers who have deserted, or identification of unmarried fathers, may disqualify more nonwhite than white children who are otherwise eligible. Then, with income and dependency held constant, the proportion of children receiving ADC might well vary inversely with the nonwhite percentage. If such rules are applied with equal force to whites and nonwhites, this hypothesis implies that there are substantial white-nonwhite differences in the social environmental circumstances of needy children. However, the enforcement of such rules could itself be used as a means of discriminating against nonwhites.

On the other hand, it is possible that, while dependency is more prevalent among nonwhites, they voluntarily support without public aid a larger proportion of their dependent persons than do whites. There is at least one piece of empirical evidence tending to support this hypothesis: An estimated 9.2 percent of the surviving white children under age eighteen who were born out of wedlock were receiving ADC in late 1958; the comparable figure for nonwhite children was 15.6 percent. Yet nonwhite adoptions are much less common than white adoptions; an estimated 70 percent of white illegitimate children, but only some 3 to 5 percent of such nonwhite children, are given for adoption.[32] Thus the race differential in the proportion of illegitimate children receiving ADC is surprisingly small.

[32] U.S. Department of Health, Education, and Welfare, *Illegitimacy and Its Impact*, p. 8. In late 1958, 10.9 percent of white ADC families and 33.5 percent of nonwhite ADC families were classed as being in need because the parents were not married. See Mugge, *Characteristics . . . of Families Receiving ADC,* Tables 5-7.

The figures can be interpreted as roughly indicating that some 80 percent of nonwhite illegitimate children neither receive ADC nor have been adopted, while the comparable figure for whites is around 20 percent. This certainly suggests that nonwhite dependent children (and similarly, perhaps, aged persons) may be *relatively* less dependent on public support than are whites. The unresolved question is whether this is a voluntary tendency or the result of discrimination in the public assistance programs.

## Average Payment

The average ADC payment is calculated in this study as the average per family rather than per recipient. However, since these two payment figures are very highly correlated ($r = .98$), it makes little difference which is chosen. Correlation results appear in Table 8.

Interstate differences in income alone can account for 35.2 percent of the interstate variation in the average ADC payment.[33] Income remains highly significant when the recipient rate is added, but the significant negative coefficient of the rate suggests that there is some element of sharing out of a fixed amount of state-local funds among ADC families.

The urbanization of the recipient families is not statistically significant, probably because of collinearity with income; its coefficients do, however, have the expected positive signs.[34] The nonwhite percentage of the families has significant negative coefficients. That percentage is not simply acting as a proxy for the ADC recipient rate; with the rate included, there is no marked change in the coefficients of the other hypothesized determinants.

The results in Table 8 suggest essentially the same conclusions as were suggested by the OAA payment results: Income level is a

---

[33] The average number of children per family was found to be highly insignificant. In ADC, as in the other programs, separation of a few "extreme" states had a larger impact on the average payment results than on those for expenditures or the recipient rate. In Table 8, such separation resulted in higher values for $\overline{R}^2$, for the coefficient of income, and for the negative coefficient of the recipient rate.

[34] Data from Mugge, *Characteristics . . . of Families Receiving ADC,* Tables 1-4. Nonwhite percentage is estimated for Vermont and adjusted for Hawaii; see note 18. Largely similar results are obtained if the characteristics of the population rather than of the ADC families are used.

# TABLE 8. Multiple Regression Analysis of the Average Monthly ADC Payment, 1960[a]

| Dependent Variable: Average Monthly ADC Payment, 1960[b] | Partial Coefficients of Correlation with the Following Independent Variables: | | | | $R$ | $R^2$ | $\bar{R}^{2c}$ |
| --- | --- | --- | --- | --- | --- | --- | --- |
| | Average Income Per Capita, 1958–60 | ADC Recipient Rate, 1960 | Percent of ADC Families Living in Urban Places, Late 1958 | Nonwhite Percent of ADC Families, Late 1958 | | | |
| (1) | .6044[d] | | | | .6044[d] | .3653 | .3521 |
| (2) | .5266[d] | −.3162[e] | | | .6548[d] | .4288 | .4045 |
| (3) | .4877[d] | | .2210 | −.5545[d] | .7944[d] | .6310 | .6069 |
| (4) | .4777[d] | −.1810 | .1760 | −.5438[d] | .8020[d] | .6431 | .6114 |

Source: U. S. Bureau of the Census and U. S. Social Security Administration.

[a] See text, pp. 111, 113, and 133, for definitions of independent variables.
[b] See Table 1 for the dollar amount of the average monthly ADC payment, and Table 1, note f, for the method of calculating this payment.
[c] $\bar{R}^2$ refers to coefficients corrected for degrees of freedom.
[d] Significant at the 1 percent level.
[e] Significant at the 5 percent level.

highly significant determinant of the average payment. Given income, the urbanization and racial composition of the recipient families both have a bearing on the ADC payment, but the latter characteristic is the important one and its influence is negative.

The negative coefficients of the nonwhite percentage may be due to a race differential *within* states in the calculated requirements of ADC recipients, such as appears to be the case in the OAA program. Data on ADC families available when this study was made excluded a breakdown of family requirements by race, but there would seem to be less ground for such a differential in ADC than in OAA, since ADC payments are rarely made for persons in institutions. To account objectively for a differential in requirements, there remains only the possibility of a race differential in recipients' living standards; but such a differential seems less probable among a state's neediest families with children than among its neediest elderly persons. Also, ADC assistance standards are generally so low that it is hard to imagine the evaluated requirements of nonwhite families being consistently lower than those of whites. However, some "discrimination" may exist, possibly in the form of a reflection of the recipients' overall racial composition in the attitudes of state-local policymakers.

## Aid to the Blind

The capacity of statistical methods to account for the size and cost of AB is limited by our ignorance of the size of the blind population and our consequent inability to make proper allowance for interstate variation in the prevalence of blindness. The prevalence of blindness very probably varies inversely with income level and directly with the proportion of nonwhites and aged persons in a state's population. The age and race variables do have significant positive coefficients in the expenditure and recipient rate models, but there is no way of knowing how well the interstate variation in these variables measures the interstate variation in the prevalence of blindness. The weakness of the AB results may also be attributable in some part to randomness in the interstate variation in the true prevalence of blindness since, lacking an actual census of blindness, attempts to estimate its prevalence must proceed on the assumption that its variation is basically attributable to variation in measurable factors—such as age and race.

*Estimating the Prevalence of Blindness*

There has never been a national census of the blind. However, estimates have been made for 1940, 1952, and 1960 of the prevalence of blindness by states. The estimates were intended to measure prevalence according to the definition of blindness most commonly accepted in this country, and they were based on two assumptions: (1) that the prevalence of blindness varies among the states, and (2) that the three most important factors which account for interstate variation are differences in the proportion of the population which is nonwhite, in the proportion of the population which is elderly, and in public health standards. The prevalence thus estimated for each state in 1960 was tested as a determinant variable in the AB expenditure and recipient rate models, but statistically more significant results were achieved simply by using age and racial composition as proxies for the prevalence of blindness, and only the latter results are shown.[35]

The infectious diseases which can cause blindness are more likely to affect persons who have, or live in areas that have, a relatively low standard of living (especially with regard to public health and medical facilities). Moreover, causes (such as diabetes and glaucoma) that may be random in their incidence probably cause actual blindness more frequently in persons whose socioeconomic status is

---

[35] The Census Bureau once made decennial enumerations of the blind but stopped after the 1930 census because the count appeared to be very unreliable.

The estimates of the prevalence of blindness for the three years were made by Ralph Hurlin, for many years a consultant to the Social Security Administration. Hurlin estimated the relative prevalence of blindness in each state, using an index constructed by weighting the state-to-national-average ratios for the percentage over age sixty-four, the percentage nonwhite, and the infant death rate (representing public health standards); he then derived the actual prevalence by tying each state's index to the reported prevalence in North Carolina, which has a fairly dependable census of its blind population. For Hurlin's work, see: "Estimates of Blindness in the United States," *Social Security Bulletin* (March 1945); "Estimated Prevalence of Blindness in the United States, July 1952," *Social Security Bulletin* (July 1953); "Estimated Prevalence of Blindness in the United States and in Individual States, 1960," *Sight Saving Review* (Spring 1962).

According to the definition most common in this country, a person is blind if his better eye, with correcting lens, can recognize objects only within one-tenth or less the distance at which the normal eye can recognize them. Most states' AB programs use this definition and also provide that a certain limitation of the breadth of the visual field is considered equally disabling. See Gabriel Farrell, *The Story of Blindness* (1956), pp. 202-05.

low than in those whose status is higher. Therefore, it can be expected that both income level and racial composition are related to the prevalence of blindness. In addition, age composition will have a bearing on the overall prevalence because blindness is much more common among the aged than among the population at large. Cataracts and atrophy of the optic nerve or the retina are the major age-connected causes, and much of the blindness afflicting the aged is unavoidable and incurable.[36]

There is no definition of blindness in the Social Security Act. Thus the possibility exists that considerable interstate variation in expenditure and recipient rates results from differing state policies and attitudes that find expression in decisions on whether applicants are blind within the states' definitions.[37]

## Expenditures

Income level and two hypothesized proxies for the prevalence of blindness—the percentage of the population which is nonwhite and the percentage over age sixty-four—were tested as expenditure determinants. No allowance is made for the states' different age limits for AB eligibility, because that factor is assumed to have no significant effect on interstate expenditure variation.[38] Results are

[36] For a discussion of the causes of blindness, see *ibid.*, Chaps. 17 and 18.

[37] Although a fairly commonly accepted definition of blindness exists, it is not known how flexibly the states actually apply their definitions to applicants for AB. A number of states include in their AB definitions statements such as "vision so defective as to prevent performance of ordinary activities for which eyesight is essential." There is at least the possibility that significant interstate differences in the AB caseload result from different definitions of blindness, or different degrees of flexibility in applying them.

The interstate variation in the AB recipient rate and in state-local expenditure is influenced by the fact that some states include in their AB programs "blind pensioners" who receive financial aid from state-local funds but are not counted as AB recipients by the federal government. Such states were classed as "exceptionally liberal" in constructing dummies for "extreme" states for AB. Use of the dummies showed that expenditure in a few "liberal" states contributes a great deal to the variance of state-local, and thus of total, AB expenditure.

[38] Inclusion of the percentage of the population in the age group eligible for AB makes no difference in the expenditure results. Although twenty-two states had age limits for eligibility in 1960, all but one of those states had a lower limit only. If many had upper limits (say age sixty-five) then interstate age and eligibility differences might well lead to significant differences in caseloads and expenditures. Among children, however, blindness is rare and blindness accompanied by serious need very rare; therefore, it is unlikely that much of the interstate variation in the AB program variables arises from the states' different age limits for eligibility.

# TABLE 9. Multiple Regression Analysis of Per Capita AB Expenditure, 1960[a]

| Dependent Variable: Per Capita AB Expenditure by Level of Government, 1960[b] | Partial Coefficients of Correlation with the Following Independent Variables: | | | | | | R | $R^2$ | $\bar{R}^2$[c] |
|---|---|---|---|---|---|---|---|---|---|
| | Average Income Per Capita, 1958–60 | Nonwhite Percent of Population, 1960 | Percent of Population Over Age Sixty-Four, 1960 | OASI Beneficiary Rate, 1960 | Unemployment Rate, Spring, 1960 | Percent of Population Living in Urban Places, 1960 | | | |
| Federal and State-Local Combined | | | | | | | | | |
| (1) | .1085 | .4327[d] | .2808 | | | | .4629[d] | .2143 | .1631 |
| (2) | .2247 | .2930[e] | .3822[d] | −.3372[e] | | | .5510[d] | .3036 | .2417 |
| (3) | .1677 | .3118[e] | .4393[d] | −.3594[e] | .2189 | .0037 | .5852[d] | .3425 | .2508 |
| Federal | | | | | | | | | |
| (4) | −.1752 | .5627[d] | .2475 | | | | .6789[d] | .4610 | .4259 |
| (5) | −.0611 | .4493[d] | .3462[e] | −.3225[e] | | | .7190[d] | .5170 | .4741 |
| (6) | .0504 | .4776[d] | .4056[d] | −.3585[e] | .1570 | −.1367 | .7417[d] | .5502 | .4875 |
| State-Local | | | | | | | | | |
| (7) | .2836 | .2352 | .2544 | | | | .3397[e] | .1154 | .0577 |
| (8) | .3635[e] | .1007 | .3369[e] | −.2829 | | | .4315[d] | .1862 | .1139 |
| (9) | .2138 | .1064 | .3857[d] | −.2916 | .2180 | .1025 | .4743[d] | .2250 | .1169 |

Source: U. S. Bureau of the Census and U. S. Social Security Administration.
a See text, pp. 111, 113, and 114, for definitions of independent variables.
b See Table 2 for dollar amounts of per capita AB expenditures, and Table 1, note d, for the method of calculating these expenditures.
c $R^2$ refers to coefficients corrected for degrees of freedom.   d Significant at the 1 percent level.   e Significant at the 5 percent level.

shown in Table 9. While the proportion of interstate variation in expenditure accounted for by the three variables in small, age and racial composition do make rather sizable contributions. As is the case with the public assistance programs generally, the state-local expenditure results are decidedly poorer than are those for federal expenditures.[39]

Three additional variables hypothesized as having a bearing on the extent to which blind persons require AB were the OASI beneficiary rate (among persons over age sixty-four), unemployment, and urbanization. Only the OASI rate, which has the expected negative coefficients, makes a significant explanatory contribution. Since blindness is especially prevalent among the aged, it is reasonable to expect that their financial security will have a bearing on the need of the blind for AB. It was assumed that the overall OASI rate is a reasonably good proxy for the OASI rate among blind persons over age sixty-four.

Unemployment and urbanization should have less effect on AB than on OAA or ADC. There is no reason to think that either variable has any systematic bearing on the prevalence of blindness and it is unlikely that either has a very strong influence on the extent of need for AB among the blind. However, some of the factors generally hypothesized as tending to associate urbanization with greater need for assistance—weaker family ties, larger cash requirements, and so forth—presumably play a role in AB. On the other hand, blind persons' opportunities for training and employment probably increase with urbanization, thus tending to reduce their need for AB. Thus it is not surprising that unemployment and urbanization are statistically insignificant in Table 9.[40]

The interstate variation in AB expenditures remains largely unexplained, and it cannot be determined to what degree the weak results are attributable to the unknown interstate variation in the true prevalence of blindness. The AB results contrast sharply with those for OAA, in the case of which the size and financial circumstances of the potential recipient group were easily measured. The problem

[39] In AB programs, there is an additional difference between state-local and federal expenditure which results from inclusion of "blind pensioners" in the reported number of AB recipients in some states; see note 37.

[40] Neither the beneficiary rate for Social Security disability insurance, nor the percentage change in population from 1955 to 1960, makes any improvement in the results when added as expenditure determinants.

in identifying determinants of the AB program variables differs from
that mentioned in connection with the ADC expenditure results—
that ADC may well be "nonsystematically" influenced by wide interstate variation in social structures and conditions, and in attitudes.
In contrast to ADC recipients, AB recipients are by definition a
homogeneous group with respect to the basic cause of their need;
and their need is not bound up with social problems nor are its causes
generally open to doubt or challenge. On the contrary, the blind
probably enjoy greater public goodwill than does any other handicapped or disadvantaged group.

The comparative rareness of blindness may be in part responsible for the generally weak AB expenditure and recipient rate results. It has been estimated that only some 0.2 percent of the population are blind.[41] If the blind are such a small group, then determinant variables that treat each state as a unit could well be much less
successful in measuring interstate variation in conditions (of unemployment, for example) which influence the need for and expenditure on AB than they are in measuring variation in conditions
which influence OAA and ADC, for which the "potentially eligible" groups are much larger.

### Recipient Rate

Each state's recipient rate is based on the total population, rather than on the subgroup that is within the age limits for AB
eligibility.[42]

The "true" AB recipient rate—among the blind—presumably
depends on the extent to which the blind are needy enough to qualify for AB, and thus on their ability to support themselves through
employment, or on the adequacy of their support from other
sources (property, relatives, social insurance, and so forth). However, even if the "true" recipient rate were known, investigation of
its determinants would be complicated by the mandatory exemption
of some earned income from the calculations that determine AB
eligibility and assistance payments. This exemption, intended to encourage self-help, could blur the effects of interstate differences in
blind persons' opportunities for employment and in their earnings.
In states where employment opportunities for the blind are relative-

[41] This was Hurlin's estimate for 1960.
[42] Results using the recipient rate based on the population in the eligible age
group were similar but weaker; see note 38.

ly good, the earnings exemption might contribute to making AB recipient rates higher than they would otherwise be.[43]

Table 10 shows results of testing hypothesized determinants of the AB recipient rate, with the age and race variables assumed to be proxies for the prevalence of blindness.[44] It is clear that the lower the state's income level the larger is the proportion of the population which receives AB; income variation alone accounts for 39.5 percent of the interstate variation in the recipient rate. That result is undoubtedly due in part to a greater prevalence of blindness in lower-income states, but it is impossible to separate the influence of income level *per se* from its relationship to the prevalence of blindness.

Use of the two hypothesized proxies for the prevalence of blindness leads, as would be expected, to problems of multicollinearity. Nevertheless, it is probably safe to conclude that lower-income states have higher AB recipient rates even after allowance is made for the greater prevalence of blindness in those states; that is, their blind people are in greater need of AB because their potential for self-support is smaller and because they are less likely to have adequate support from other sources.

The OASI beneficiary rate is included in Table 10, line 4, along with unemployment and urbanization, and it is highly insignificant. Indeed, no matter what other hypothesized determinants were included, the OASI rate made only the most marginal difference in the fit of the AB recipient rate models; it was not significant and its inclusion had little effect on the coefficients of the other variables, although it did have negative coefficients. These results surely do not prove that the AB recipient rate is significantly affected by the OASI coverage of the aged, but in view of the imperfections of the recipient rate variable, they cannot be taken as disproving that hypothesis.

[43] From 1950 to mid-1962, the first $50 per month was exempted; in 1962 the exemption was raised to $85 plus 50 percent of earnings over $85. A permissible earnings exemption for OAA—later to become mandatory—and a limited permissible exemption for ADC, were introduced in the 1962 amendments to the Social Security Act.

[44] Separation of a few "extreme" states by dummies improved the results but not by a great deal. If the "true" AB recipient rate among the blind were available, the dummy for "liberal" states should certainly make a difference, since some of those states have integrated their own "blind pension" plans into AB and the pensions are based on less stringent needs tests than is AB.

# TABLE 10. Multiple Regression Analysis of the AB Recipient Rate, 1960[a]

| Dependent Variable: AB Recipient Rate, 1960[b] | Partial Coefficients of Correlation with the Following Independent Variables: | | | | | | R | $R^2$ | $\bar{R}^{2}$[c] |
|---|---|---|---|---|---|---|---|---|---|
| | Percent of Population with Incomes Below $2,000, 1959 | Nonwhite Percent of Population, 1960 | Percent of Population Over Age Sixty-Four, 1960 | Unemployment Rate, Spring, 1960 | Percent of Population Living in Urban Places, 1960 | OASI Beneficiary Rate, 1960 | | | |
| (1) | .6380[d] | | .1935 | | | | .6380[d] | .4071 | .3948 |
| (2) | .3320[e] | .3815[d] | .2310 | .1885 | | | .7026[d] | .4926 | .4606 |
| (3) | .2872 | .3332[e] | .2048 | .1885 | .1236 | | .7180[d] | .5155 | .4605 |
| (4) | .2345 | .3333[e] | | .1875 | .1122 | −.0101 | .7180[d] | .5156 | .4480 |

Source: U. S. Bureau of the Census and U. S. Social Security Administration.
[a] See text, pp. 111, 113, and 114, for definitions of independent variables.
[b] See Table 2 for the level of the AB recipient rate and Table 1, note e, for the method of calculating this rate.
[c] $\bar{R}^2$ refers to coefficients corrected for degrees of freedom.
[d] Significant at the 1 percent level.
[e] Significant at the 5 percent level.

In 1960, the Disability Insurance (DI) part of OASDI had not been effective long enough to have had a perceptible impact on AB, and inclusion of the DI beneficiary rate made no improvement in the AB results. DI benefits, calculated as though the worker were retiring at age sixty-five, are payable to insured workers under sixty-five who are so disabled as to be "unable to engage in any substantial gainful activity." Benefits were first paid in July 1957, but until November 1960 disabled workers under age fifty were not eligible. DI benefits can be expected to reduce the need for AB among persons who become blind during their working lives; in 1960, there probably were some persons who would have been AB recipients had DI not existed. Anyone whose blindness and inability to support himself qualify him for AB, and who has been working in covered employment, would very likely be entitled to DI benefits.[45]

Urbanization and unemployment add little to the explanation of the recipient rate. It was noted above that there is less reason to expect these variables to be significant in the case of the AB than in the case of OAA or ADC, and they might very well be of negligible importance even if the "true" AB recipient rate among the blind were known.

## Average Payment

The results for the average monthly AB payment, shown in Table 11, are quite similar to those for the average OAA payment. In addition to income and the recipient rate, the determinants are the racial composition and urbanization of the population, which are presumed to be proxies for the respective percentages of the AB recipients.[46]

Per capita income differences alone can account for 48.1 percent of the interstate variation in the average AB payment. The

[45] For DI eligibility, the disability must be expected to last indefinitely and must be such that the applicant is unable to do any substantial gainful work. Thus, a person with a visual handicap as great or even greater than the usual AB blindness criterion is not necessarily eligible for DI; but neither is a person with a less severe visual handicap necessarily ineligible. See U.S. Department of Health, Education, and Welfare, *If You Become Disabled,* Social Security Administration Pub. No. OASI-29 (January 1962).

[46] State data on the characteristics of AB recipients were not available, necessitating the use of the population characteristics. See notes 18 and 34.

# TABLE 11. Multiple Regression Analysis of the Average Monthly AB Payment, 1960[a]

| Dependent Variable: | Partial Coefficients of Correlation with the Following Independent Variables: | | | | | | |
|---|---|---|---|---|---|---|---|
| Average Monthly AB Payment, 1960[b] | Average Income Per Capita, 1958–60 | AB Recipient Rate, 1960 | Percent of Population Living in Urban Places, 1960 | Nonwhite Percent of Population, 1960 | $R$ | $R^2$ | $\bar{R}^{2^0}$ |
| (1) | .7013[d] | | | | .7013[d] | .4918 | .4812 |
| (2) | .6446[d] | −.1218 | | | .7066[d] | .4993 | .4780 |
| (3) | .3613[e] | | .2860[e] | −.3882[d] | .7680[d] | .5898 | .5631 |
| (4) | .3688[e] | .1086 | .2963[e] | −.3855[d] | .7711[d] | .5946 | .5586 |

Source: U. S. Bureau of the Census and U. S. Social Security Administration.
[a] See text, pp. 111 and 113, for definitions of independent variables.
[b] See Table 2 for the dollar amount of the average monthly AB payment, and Table 1, note f, for the method of calculating this payment.
[o] $R^2$ refers to coefficients corrected for degrees of freedom.
[d] Significant at the 1 percent level.
[e] Significant at the 5 percent level.

144

higher-income states' larger average payments are not attributable simply to their lower recipient rates; with the addition of the rate, shown in Table 11, line 2, the coefficient of income, though lower, remains significant.[47]

The nonwhite percentage is tested simply to ascertain whether, in AB as in other programs, it will have the unexpected significant negative coefficients. The two population characteristics and income are all significant in line 3, and the nonwhite percentage does indeed have a negative coefficient. That percentage is not acting simply as a proxy for the AB recipient rate, for its negative coefficient remains significant when the recipient rate is included.

The results in Table 11 lead to conclusions and questions similar to those suggested by the OAA payment results. Income level is a very important determinant of the average payment. Despite correlations (positive and negative, respectively) with income, the urbanization and the nonwhite percentage of the population both influence the level of the payment, with racial composition the more significant of the two. It is possible that nonwhite AB recipients' requirements are lower than those of white recipients, as in OAA, which would suggest that the nonwhites have lower living standards. A race differential in requirements may also arise from a differential in the proportion of recipients in institutions, although a smaller proportion of AB than of OAA recipients is in institutions.[48] The question raised previously remains—whether some form of "discrimination" plays a role in determining assistance payments.

## Aid to the Permanently and Totally Disabled

The APTD expenditure results indicate that the tested relationships are quite weak. This may be due in part to the fact that the

[47] As with the analogous model of the average OAA payment, addition of the dummies for "extreme" states to line 2 in Table 11 makes the coefficient of the recipient rate significantly negative, thus suggesting some "competition" among the recipients of AB.

[48] When the present study was being conducted, only summary national data concerning the characteristics of AB recipients were available. These data, from a 1962 survey, include no information about recipients' requirements by race or by living arrangement. At the time of the survey, 7.5 percent of the AB recipients were in nursing homes and other institutions, including nonpublic homes for the aged. See U.S. Department of Health, Education, and Welfare, *Characteristics of*

program is newer than the others and in 1960 was apparently still in the phase of initial expansion. Interstate expenditure variation may therefore be less amenable to explanation by quantitative determinants than it would be if the program had reached a "settled" maturity. However, there is another important reason for the weak results. The cost of the program depends basically on the number of persons who are "permanently and totally disabled," and that number simply is not known. Since states are permitted a good deal of latitude in defining disability for APTD eligibility, interstate variation in the number of eligible persons is very probably affected by differing definitions, as well as by real variation in the number who would be counted under a uniform definition. In view of this, it is surprising that reasonably good results are found for the APTD recipient rate.

As in the other programs, lower-income states provide APTD for larger proportions of their populations of eligible age. This probably results in part from a greater prevalence of disability in those states, although there is no clear-cut evidence to support that point. The possibility is suggested, however, by the fact that income level is negatively correlated with the proportion of the population receiving vocational rehabilitation services and with the proportion receiving Disability Insurance benefits.

The recipient rate and the cost of APTD have been growing at a substantial pace ever since the program started. Part of this growth can reasonably be attributed to the worsening of employment prospects for the least skilled, least educated, least productive people, and to overall economic decline in some regions. APTD in some states has been taking in persons whose mental or physical disability would not, under better economic circumstances, be a "permanent and total" barrier to self support. Thus, for efficient utilization of the nation's human resources, it is important that rehabilitative and remedial treatment actually be provided to all recipients who can profit thereby; otherwise, APTD could become a growing human scrap heap.

The outlook for the APTD recipient rate and expenditure level depends heavily on prevention—through education and training, retraining of those displaced by economic change, and better medical care for the poorest groups. The average APTD recipient has

---

*Recipients of Aid to the Blind—Findings of the 1962 Survey: National Totals* (March 1964).

very little education and skill. The need for APTD will exist whenever such a person, whose self-support potential is precarious at best, suffers any physical or mental disability in addition to his other handicaps.

### Defining "Permanent and Total Disability"

The interstate variation of the APTD program variables is subject to two influences that cannot be quantified: (1) the variety of state definitions of permanent and total disability and their interpretation at the case level; and (2) the number of people who are "permanently and totally disabled," even by any single definition.

According to the Social Security Administration, "permanent and total disability" generally means a permanent physical or mental impairment which substantially prevents an individual from engaging in a useful occupation within his competence. A statement of this sort is to be found in many states' APTD eligibility definitions, but the definitions vary a good deal since the concepts involved are anything but precise.[49] Sizable interstate variation in APTD caseloads probably results from interstate differences in such factors as: (1) the criteria used to judge totality and permanence; (2) the weight given, in evaluating disability, to age, training, and similar factors bearing on a person's competence for a useful occupation; and (3) the consideration given to whether employment in a useful occupation, for which the disabled person is competent, is actually available in his community.

In the empirical investigation of the APTD program variables, a variable based on vocational rehabilitation data is postulated as a rough proxy for the prevalence of disability. This measure, which is far from satisfactory but apparently the best available, is the proportion of the population aged eighteen to sixty-four which was undergoing vocational rehabilitation in June 1960; the measure is called the "V.R. case rate." The assumption that this ratio is a proxy for the overall prevalence of disability is very tenuous, but since vocational rehabilitation and APTD deal with two fairly dis-

---

[49] For summaries of states' definitions as of 1959, see U.S. Department of Health, Education, and Welfare, *Characteristics of State Public Assistance Plans Under the Social Security Act*, Public Assistance Report No. 40 (1959). The only specific requirement for eligibility is that recipients must be at least eighteen years old. Federal law does not even require a medical examination of applicants, though federal administrative rulings do call for a review (at some level) of case data concerning the disability factor, before assistance is given.

## TABLE 12. Multiple Regression Analysis of Per Capita APTD Expenditure, 1960[a]

| Dependent Variable: Per Capita APTD Expenditures, by Level of Government, 1960[b] | Partial Coefficients of Correlation with the Following Independent Variables: | | | | | | | R | $R^2$ | $\bar{R}^{2}$[e] |
|---|---|---|---|---|---|---|---|---|---|---|
| | Average Income Per Capita, 1958–60 | Percent of Population Living in Urban Places, 1960 | Unemployment Rate, Spring, 1960 | Nonwhite Percent of Population, 1960 | Percent Increase in Population, 1955–60 | DI Beneficiary Rate,[c] 1960 | VR Case Rate,[d] 1960 | | | |
| **Federal and State-Local Combined** | | | | | | | | | | |
| (1) | −.2828 | .2593 | .0089 | −.0110 | −.3143[f] | | | .3165[f] | .1002 | .0102 |
| (2) | −.2888 | .3545[f] | −.0055 | .0446 | −.3083 | .0625 | | .4348[g] | .1891 | .0851 |
| (3) | −.2872 | .3548[f] | −.0284 | .0090 | −.2822 | | | .4385[g] | .1922 | .0646 |
| (4) | −.2844 | .4127[g] | −.0572 | .0389 | | −.0863 | .3245[f] | .5266[g] | .2773 | .1406 |
| **Federal** | | | | | | | | | | |
| (5) | −.3837[f] | .1885 | .0301 | .1673 | −.2248 | | | .5627[g] | .3166 | .2483 |
| (6) | −.3873[f] | .2554 | .0205 | .2062 | −.2154 | .1074 | | .5926[g] | .3511 | .2679 |
| (7) | −.3860[f] | .2561 | −.0210 | .1326 | −.1810 | | | .5989[g] | .3586 | .2573 |
| (8) | −.3905[f] | .3226[f] | −.0519 | .1713 | | −.0540 | .3475[f] | .6604[g] | .4361 | .3294 |
| **State-Local** | | | | | | | | | | |
| (9) | −.1282 | .2978 | −.0144 | −.1940 | −.3651[f] | | | .4018[g] | .1615 | .0776 |
| (10) | −.1274 | .4098[g] | −.0330 | −.1416 | −.3633[f] | .0044 | | .5227[g] | .2733 | .1801 |
| (11) | −.1271 | .4098[g] | −.0323 | −.1265 | −.3428[f] | | | .5227[g] | .2733 | .1586 |
| (12) | −.1164 | .4484[g] | −.0540 | −.1082 | | −.1069 | .2531 | .5655[g] | .3198 | .1911 |

Source: U. S. Bureau of the Census and U. S. Social Security Administration.

a See text, pp. 111 and 113, for definitions of independent variables.
b See Table 1 for the dollar amounts of per capita APTD expenditures, and Table 1, note f, for the method of calculating these expenditures.
c The number of Disability Insurance beneficiaries in December, 1960, divided by the number of persons aged fifty to sixty-four in the population according to the 1960 Census.
d The proportion of the population aged eighteen through sixty-four which was undergoing vocational rehabilitation in June, 1960.
e $\bar{R}^2$ refers to coefficients corrected for degrees of freedom.
f Significant at the 5 percent level.
g Significant at the 1 percent level.

tinct groups of the disabled, it can at least be assumed that the "V.R. case rate" is not simply a proxy for the APTD recipient rate itself. During the 1950's, only about 12 percent of those accepted for vocational rehabilitation were chiefly dependent on public relief when accepted. As noted previously, the "V.R. case rate" varies inversely with income level.[50]

## Expenditures

The Social Security Act sets age eighteen as the minimum age for APTD eligibility, and it permits states to set a maximum age. Nevertheless, the "percent of population eligible" was highly insignificant in the APTD expenditure models, and results which include it are not shown. The insignificance of that variable is rather surprising, since the group excluded from APTD eligibility in some states and included in others is those aged sixty-five and over. *A priori,* one would expect a higher incidence of serious disability (plus need) in that group than among those aged eighteen to sixty-four, and the eligibility of older persons should have a bearing on per capita expenditure. (In 1960, twenty-eight of the forty-five states with APTD limited it to persons under age sixty-five.) However, the statistical insignificance of the "percent of population eligible" does not necessarily disprove that hypothesis, for interstate differences in the definition of disability may be large enough to obscure the effects of varying age limits.

The first variables hypothesized as APTD expenditure determinants are income, urbanization, unemployment, and racial composition. (See Table 12.) Although it is no less likely that urbanization has a bearing on APTD than on other public assistance programs, there is little reason to expect that unemployment has a significant effect. Physical or mental disability (combined with handicaps of age, education, location, and so forth) is presumably the major barrier to the employment of actual and potential APTD recipients; labor market conditions are probably of very secondary importance. Nevertheless, in regions of serious and chronic labor

[50] All states operate vocational rehabilitation programs with federal grant assistance; these programs provide diagnosis, training, placement, sheltered employment, and other services. During fiscal 1960, nearly 300,000 persons were on the vocational rehabilitation rolls for some period of time, as compared with an average of about 360,000 APTD recipients during calendar 1960.

surplus, the APTD caseloads may be rather higher than they would be if unemployment were less severe.[51] The nonwhite population percentage may be directly related to the prevalence of "permanent and total disability," insofar as assistance agencies consider education and skills when evaluating the seriousness of a given impairment. The self-support potential of a person with a given handicap is probably smaller, on the average, if he is nonwhite than if he is white.

The expenditure results, based on the four variables, are very poor. They suggest that urbanization, in addition to income, has some noticeable effect on APTD spending and that unemployment does not. The negligible coefficients of the nonwhite percentage reflect its positive correlation with the recipient rate and its negative correlation with the average APTD payment.[52] Addition of the population growth variable improves the results. Its negative coefficients indicate that the states experiencing slower rates of population growth (from 1955 to 1960) spend more on APTD. This implies that the need for APTD is relatively greatest in states whose population growth and economy are relatively stagnant, and that the program probably has a tendency to assist persons who are "left behind" in the general expansion of the economy.

The Disability Insurance part of contributory social insurance might be expected to have an influence on APTD. Insured workers who are so disabled as to be "unable to engage in any substantial gainful activity" are eligible for DI benefits equivalent to the Old Age benefits they would receive at retirement age.[53] One might expect that, *ceteris paribus,* the larger the number of DI beneficiaries the smaller the APTD caseload and the cost of APTD, but only insignificant positive coefficients are found for the DI

[51] This can be inferred from the description of conditions in one depressed mining region, in Harry M. Caudill, *Night Comes to the Cumberlands* (1963), Chap. 18.

[52] At the state-local level, elimination of a few presumably "extreme" states results in a very large improvement in the fit of the expenditure models. For example, in the case of line 9 in Table 12, corrected $\overline{R}^2$ rises from .078 to .481. Thus, much of the interstate variation in APTD spending can be attributed to the "exceptional" behavior of a few states.

[53] Until November 1960, eligibility was limited to disabled workers aged fifty to sixty-four; the lower age limit was then eliminated. In December 1960, there were about 430,000 disabled-worker DI beneficiaries in the forty-five states that had APTD programs, compared with an average of about 360,000 APTD recipients during 1960.

beneficiary rate (the number of DI beneficiaries in December 1960 divided by the population aged fifty to sixty-four). However, the DI rate itself is undoubtedly correlated positively with the prevalence of disability and this would tend to give it positive rather than negative coefficients. Therefore, the hypothesized proxy for that prevalence, the Vocational Rehabilitation case rate, is added to the expenditure model. Its inclusion improves the fit of the models but has little effect on the coefficients of the other variables. However, the DI beneficiary rate, though still statistically insignificant, does acquire the negative sign that would be expected if the prevalence of disability were truly accounted for. Nevertheless, very little of the interstate variation in APTD expenditures has been explained. Indeed, in view of our ignorance of the true prevalence of serious disability, it is impossible to attach much significance to any of the expenditure results.

*The Recipient Rate*

In view of the lack of data on the prevalence of disability and the variety of possible definitions, the results for the APTD recipient rate are fairly satisfactory. For this investigation, the rate for each state is based on the population within the state's age limits for eligibility.

The recipients of APTD are those persons among the disabled population who have the least training and education. A 1962 survey found that only 22 percent had completed more than eight years of school, while 18 percent had not completed even one year; the median number of years completed was five. Furthermore, one-fifth had never been employed nor occupied in homemaking, nearly 12 percent had previously been occupied only in homemaking, and another 39 percent had last been employed as unskilled workers or farm laborers, or as domestic servants.[54]

Variations in income level alone can account for 47 percent of the interstate variation in the APTD recipient rate. (See Table 13.) A person with a given disability is more likely to need APTD in a lower-income state because his private resources (property, family support) are smaller, or because he has less education and skill, or,

[54] See U.S. Department of Health, Education, and Welfare, *Characteristics of Recipients of Aid to the Permanently and Totally Disabled, Findings of the 1962 Survey: State Tables* (June 1964), Tables 8, 9, 15, 19, 20.

TABLE 13. **Multiple Regression Analysis of the APTD Recipient Rate, 1960[a]**

| Dependent Variable: APTD Recipient Rate, 1960[b] | Partial Coefficients of Correlation with the Following Independent Variables: | | | | | | | | | |
|---|---|---|---|---|---|---|---|---|---|---|
| | Percent of Population with Incomes Below $2,000, 1959 | Nonwhite Percent of Population, 1960 | Percent of Population Living in Urban Places, 1960 | Unemployment Rate, Spring, 1960 | Percent Increase in Population, 1955–60 | DI Beneficiary Rate[c] | VR Case Rate[d] | $R$ | $R^2$ | $\bar{R}^2{}_e$ |
| (1) | .6994[f] | | | | | | | .6994[f] | .4822 | .4701 |
| (2) | .4572[f] | .3353[g] | | | | | | .7351[f] | .5404 | .5185 |
| (3) | .3809[g] | .2859 | .1043 | .1715 | | | | .7463[f] | .5570 | .5127 |
| (4) | .3544[g] | .3409[g] | .1731 | .1647 | −.2562 | | | .7656[f] | .5861 | .5330 |
| (5) | .3515[g] | .2759 | .1728 | .1053 | −.2466 | .1337 | | .7704[f] | .5935 | .5293 |
| (6) | .3430[g] | .3396[g] | .2482 | .0781 | −.2188 | −.0520 | .3989[g] | .8113[f] | .6582 | .5935 |

Source: U. S. Bureau of the Census and U. S. Social Security Administration.
[a] See text, pp. 111 and 113, for definitions of independent variables.
[b] See Table 2 for the level of the APTD recipient rate, and Table 1, note e, for the method of calculating this rate.
[c] See Table 12, note c.
[d] See Table 12, note d.
[e] $R^2$ refers to coefficients corrected for degrees of freedom.
[f] Significant at the 1 percent level.
[g] Significant at the 5 percent level.

152

possibly, because jobs that he might be able to perform are less available. While there seems little reason to expect a relationship between income and the prevalence of many types of disability (for example, disability due to heart disease, epilepsy, orthopedic impairment), it is probable that lower-income areas have a greater prevalence of disability resulting from inadequate medical care, poor nutrition, low public health standards, and so forth.

The nonwhite population percentage is also significant and bears a positive sign, as shown in line 2, Table 13. Since the education and skill levels of nonwhites are generally lower, a given disability can be expected to pose a more serious economic hardship for a nonwhite. Also, it is conceivable that extensive Negro migration has increased the need for APTD among disabled Negroes, since the movement into urban, industrial labor markets perhaps reduces the availability of family support and family employment for marginally productive persons.

As to unemployment, if a state reserves APTD only for the completely incapacitated, then general employment conditions will affect the recipient rate only by affecting relatives who might support the disabled. In other states, however, some persons may receive APTD at least partly because they are unemployed. In regions with declining industries or an increasing rate of displacement of unskilled labor, some disabled persons who formerly managed to support themselves, at least at a minimal level, may no longer be able to get by on their own. Similarly, urbanization is associated with greater dependence on full-time paid employment in impersonal labor markets, and thus may reduce a disabled person's opportunities for earning some income.

Both unemployment and urbanization have positive coefficients, as hypothesized, but neither is statistically significant. In fact, their combined contribution, shown in line 3, Table 13, is so small that corrected $\bar{R}^2$ is reduced. However, the population change variable improves the explanatory power of the model and it has a negative sign, thus suggesting the possible implications mentioned in the discussion of expenditures results.

As in the results for APTD expenditures, the DI beneficiary rate is statistically insignificant, and its coefficient has a negative sign only when the proxy for the prevalence of disability is included. While the use of that proxy improves the explanatory power

TABLE 14. Multiple Regression Analysis of the Average Monthly APTD Payment, 1960[a]

| Dependent Variable: | Partial Coefficients of Correlation with the Following Independent Variables: | | | | $R$ | $R^2$ | $\bar{R}^2$[c] |
|---|---|---|---|---|---|---|---|
| | Average Income Per Capita, 1958–60 | APTD Recipient Rate, 1960 | Percent of Population Living in Urban Places, 1960 | Nonwhite Percent of Population, 1960 | | | |
| Average Monthly APTD Payment, 1960[b] | | | | | | | |
| (1) | .7083[d] | | | | .7083[d] | .5018 | .4902 |
| (2) | .5613[d] | −.1417 | | | .7154[d] | .5118 | .4886 |
| (3) | .3079[e] | | .1901 | −.4483[d] | .7772[d] | .6041 | .5750 |
| (4) | .3008 | .0523 | .1816 | −.4258[d] | .7779[d] | .6052 | .5656 |

Source: U. S. Bureau of the Census and U. S. Social Security Administration.
[a] See text, pp. 111 and 113, for definitions of independent variables.
[b] See Table 2 for the dollar amount of the average monthly APTD payment, and Table 1, note f, for the method of calculating this payment.
[c] $\bar{R}^2$ refers to coefficients corrected for degrees of freedom.
[d] Significant at the 1 percent level.
[e] Significant at the 5 percent level.

of the model, it results in little improvement in the significance of the other hypothesized determinants.

Other forms of the recipient rate model, omitting some variables, give results (not shown) which suggest that urbanization is somewhat more significant than unemployment. In particular, it appears that inclusion of the proxy variable for the prevalence of disability generally increases the significance of urbanization and decreases that of unemployment. Thus, given income and the prevalence of disability, the APTD recipient rate rises with urbanization but is unaffected by unemployment. This seems reasonable.

## Average Payment

As in the other programs, income level is a highly significant determinant of the average APTD payment, as Table 14 shows. Differences in per capita income alone can account for nearly half the interstate payment variation. Given income, the recipient rate is negatively but not significantly correlated with the average payment, which may point to a certain degree of "competition" among recipients for available funds.[55] The other results in Table 14 are also similar to those for the average payment in the other programs, and they point to similar conclusions. Given income, the average payment is significantly smaller the larger the nonwhite population percentage (presumably a proxy for the nonwhite percentage of the recipients). Urbanization may have some effect but its substantial correlation with income leaves this uncertain.

In the discussion of results for the average OAA payment, it was suggested that a white-nonwhite differential in the proportion of recipients in institutions may contribute to a race differential in their requirements and thus in their assistance payments. Not surprisingly, the proportion of recipients in institutions is larger in APTD than in any other public assistance program. This increases the possibility that a race differential in that proportion (if there is one) will lead to a differential in the average payment large enough to be observed.[56]

[55] When the presumably "extreme" states were separated by the use of dummy variables, the negative coefficient of the recipient rate became significant.

[56] As is true of all programs except OAA, published data on APTD recipients' living arrangements and financial circumstances are not broken down by race.

**TABLE 15. Multiple Regression Analysis of Per Capita Expenditure on Four Public Assistance Programs Combined, 1960[a]**

| Dependent Variable: Per Capita Expenditure on Four Public Assistance Programs Combined, by Level of Government, 1960[b] | Partial Coefficients of Correlation with the Following Independent Variables: | | | | | | | | | | |
|---|---|---|---|---|---|---|---|---|---|---|---|
| | Average Income Per Capita, 1958–60 | Percent of Population Under Age Eighteen, 1960 | Percent of Population Over Age Sixty-Four, 1960 | Unemployment Rate, Spring, 1960 | Percent of Population Living in Urban Places, 1960 | Nonwhite Percent of Population, 1960 | OASI Beneficiary Rate, 1960 | Percent Increase in Population, 1955–60 | R | R² | $\bar{R}^2$[c] |
| **Federal and State-Local Combined** | | | | | | | | | | | |
| (1) | −.3294d | .1169 | .2941d | .2637 | .3574d | | | | .4573e | .2091 | .1193 |
| (2) | .0157 | .3283d | .6326e | .4275e | .4366e | −.2968 | −.7475e | | .8080e | .6529 | .5951 |
| (3) | .0320 | .3757d | .6277e | .4230e | .5004e | −.3014 | −.7656e | −.2742 | .8240e | .6790 | .6164 |
| **Federal** | | | | | | | | | | | |
| (4) | −.5043e | .0397 | .2036 | .2852 | .3095d | | | | .5758e | .3316 | .2557 |
| (5) | −.1973 | .2947 | .6437e | .4959e | .3909e | −.2186 | −.7902e | | .8692e | .7556 | .7149 |
| (6) | −.1903 | .3259d | .6366e | .4913e | .4310e | −.2182 | −.7987e | −.1972 | .8747e | .7651 | .7193 |
| **State-Local** | | | | | | | | | | | |
| (7) | −.0233 | .1902 | .3578d | .2030 | .3698d | | | | .4864e | .2366 | .1499 |
| (8) | .2028 | .2998d | .5356e | .2801 | .4059e | −.3111d | −.6034e | | .7179e | .5154 | .4347 |
| (9) | .2268 | .3518d | .5263e | .2688 | .4809e | −.3172d | −.6309e | −.2894 | .7456e | .5560 | .4694 |

Source: U. S. Bureau of the Census and U. S. Social Security Administration.
[a] See text, pp. 111, 113, 114, and 125, for definitions of independent variables.
[b] See Table 2 for the dollar amount of per capita expenditure for the combined public assistance programs, and Table 1, note d, for the method of calculating this expenditure.
[c] $\bar{R}^2$ refers to coefficients corrected for degrees of freedom.   [d] Significant at the 5 percent level.   [e] Significant at the 1 percent level.

156

# Four Public Assistance Programs Combined

Each public assistance program was investigated separately because each deals with a distinct group of the needy and because a different set of uncertainties and unknowns is relevant to each. However, it is appropriate to give some attention to the expenditures and recipient rate for the four public assistance programs combined. Results for the combined programs are reported in Tables 15 and 16. Expenditure per public assistance recipient—the "average public assistance payment"—was not calculated because its interstate variation would be affected by the varying distributions of states' public assistance recipients among the several programs; more specifically, the larger the proportion of ADC recipients, the smaller will be the "average public assistance payment" per recipient. The models of the combined public assistance variables are fitted to data from all states.[57]

The only determinant used here that has not been used previously is the variable which measures the composition of the labor force. It is significant in the recipient rate results but not in the expenditure results, for which it is not shown. For the same reason, the rate of population growth is shown only in the expenditure results, since it was highly insignificant in the recipient rate models.

Since OAA was the largest program in dollar terms in 1960, the level of OAA expenditure significantly influences the level of total public assistance expenditures. Therefore, it is not surprising that the two variables specifically related to OAA—the percentage of the population over age sixty-four and the OASI beneficiary rate —are highly significant determinants of combined public assistance expenditures. The coefficients of the other variables turned out as one would expect on the basis of the expenditure results for the individual programs. Unemployment and urbanization are significant with positive signs; the percentage of the population under age

[57] Since some states did not have APTD programs in 1960, it might seem that higher and more "meaningful" coefficients would result from fitting the combined-program models only to the states operating all four programs. However, the results were nearly identical whether the models were fitted to all states or only to the states operating all programs. This was true not only for 1960 but also for 1950 and 1940, despite the fact that in 1940 eleven states did not operate one or more of the programs.

## TABLE 16. Multiple Regression Analysis of the Recipient Rate in Four Public Assistance Programs Combined, 1960[a]

| Dependent Variable: Recipient Rate in Four Public Assistance Programs Combined, 1960[b] | Partial Coefficients of Correlation with the Following Independent Variables: | | | | | | | R | $R^2$ | $\bar{R}^2$[d] |
|---|---|---|---|---|---|---|---|---|---|---|
| | Percent of Population with Incomes Below $2,000, 1960 | Unemployment Rate, Spring, 1960 | Percent of Population Living in Urban Places, 1960 | Percent of Population Under Age Eighteen, 1960 | Percent of Population Over Age Sixty-Four, 1960 | OASI Beneficiary Rate, 1960 | Employment Composition, 1960[c] | | | |
| (1) | .7381[e] | | | | | | | .7381[e] | .5449 | .5354 |
| (2) | .7972[e] | .2924[f] | .5108[e] | | | | | .8181[e] | .6692 | .6476 |
| (3) | .8127[e] | .3898[e] | .5842[e] | .3103[f] | .3019[f] | | | .8410[e] | .7073 | .6740 |
| (4) | .5613[e] | .5249[e] | .5122[e] | .3888[e] | .5501[e] | | | .8922[e] | .7959 | .7674 |
| (5) | .8196[e] | .3054[f] | .4610[e] | .3531[f] | .3445[f] | −.5503[e] | .2020 | .8481[e] | .7192 | .6800 |
| (6) | .5593[e] | .4304[e] | .2912 | .4908[e] | .6332[e] | −.6205[e] | .3924[e] | .9096[e] | .8274 | .7986 |

Source: U. S. Bureau of the Census and U. S. Social Security Administration.
[a] See text, pp. 111, 113, 114, and 125, for definitions of variables not noted here.
[b] See Table 2 for the level of the recipient rate in the combined programs, and Table 1, note e, for the method of calculating this rate.
[c] The percentage of employed persons engaged in industries other than agriculture, forestry, and fishing.
[d] $\bar{R}^2$ refers to coefficients corrected for degrees of freedom.
[e] Significant at the 1 percent level.
[f] Significant at the 5 percent level.

158

eighteen is significant, or nearly so, and it also bears a positive sign. As was the case in the expenditure results for all programs except AB, the coefficients of the nonwhite percentage are negative—presumably because that percentage is negatively correlated with the average assistance payments. As was generally true for expenditures on the individual programs, income is not significant.

The social insurance status of a state's aged population may perhaps be called a "key element" which determines the level of public assistance expenditures in the state. Omission of the OASI beneficiary rate from Table 15 not only lowers the multiple correlation coefficients significantly, but also decreases the coefficients of other hypothesized determinants.

The models in Table 16 test determinants of the proportion of a state's population which receives support from one of the four programs; the combined public assistance recipient rate is the total number of recipients in the four programs divided by total population. (The Social Security Act provides that no individual may receive assistance through more than one public assistance program at any one time.)

As was true in the case of each public assistance program separately, the hypothesized determinants can account for a much larger proportion of the interstate variation in the combined public assistance recipient rate than in combined public assistance expenditures. The lower a state's income level, the larger is the proportion of the population which receives some type of public assistance; income level alone can account for over half of the interstate variation in the public assistance recipient rate. Unemployment and urbanization, hypothesized as factors that should generally tend to increase recipient rates, both have significant positive coefficients when added to income. The highly significant coefficients of urbanization shown in Table 16 support the hypothesis that, at any general income level, greater urbanization results in weaker family ties and larger cash needs and thus in greater need for assistance.

Inclusion of age variables allows for interstate variation in the proportions of the population in the age groups relevant to the two largest programs—OAA and ADC. With the percentages of the population under age eighteen and over age sixty-four held constant, both unemployment and urbanization have even larger coefficients. The two age variables are significant, as would be expected.

More than two-thirds of the interstate variation in the proportion of the population which receives public assistance is accounted for without inclusion of the OASI beneficiary rate, but that rate is nevertheless highly significant when it is included. This reflects the importance of the OASI rate as a determinant of the OAA recipient rate, its probable bearing on the AB rate, and the possibility that it reflects to some degree the extent to which fatherless children and disabled workers are covered by social insurance.

The combined public assistance recipient rate is apparently the only variable, among those this study investigates, which is affected by labor force composition. The results imply that the smaller the proportion of the labor force employed in agriculture, forestry, and fisheries, the larger the overall public assistance recipient rate.

The nonwhite population percentage was highly insignificant in all the versions of the public assistance recipient rate model. Its inclusion generally served only to reduce somewhat the coefficient of income. These results, which are not shown, reflect the generally small coefficients of the racial composition variable in the recipient rate models for the individual public assistance programs.

## Public Assistance Administrative Expenditures

Expenditures for administering public assistance are of interest because they basically reflect the average amount of social-work effort expended per recipient of public assistance. The larger that average, the greater is the amount of staff effort presumably being devoted to the guidance and counselling of recipients, over and above the fundamental staff responsibilities of investigation and periodic rechecking.

The results in Table 17 show that, in each public assistance program, average administrative expenditure per case per month has a substantial positive correlation with income, whether or not the recipient rate is held constant; and, given income, administrative expenditure per casemonth is smaller the higher the recipient rate. These results indicate that the ratio of professional staff to assistance recipients varies positively with income level, which can be

**TABLE 17.** Multiple Regression Analysis of Administrative Expenditure Per Casemonth in Four Public Assistance Programs, 1960

| Independent Variable: Administrative Expenditure Per Casemonth, Four Public Assistance Programs, 1960 | Partial Coefficients of Correlation with the Following Independent Variables: | | R | R² | R̄²[a] |
|---|---|---|---|---|---|
| | Average Income Per Capita, 1958–60 | Recipient Rate in the Program, 1960 | | | |
| OAA | .7247ᶜ | | .7247ᶜ | .5252 | .5153 |
| ADCᵇ | .6598ᶜ | | .6598ᶜ | .4354 | .4237 |
| AB | .6692ᶜ | | .6692ᶜ | .4478 | .4363 |
| APTD | .7372ᶜ | | .7372ᶜ | .5435 | .5329 |
| OAA | .6149ᶜ | −.3145ᵈ | .7564ᶜ | .5722 | .5540 |
| ADCᵇ | .5948ᶜ | −.2923ᵈ | .6955ᶜ | .4837 | .4617 |
| AB | .6116ᶜ | −.1055 | .6738ᶜ | .4540 | .4307 |
| APTD | .6000ᶜ | −.0336 | .7427ᶜ | .5516 | .5303 |

Source: U. S. Bureau of the Census and U. S. Social Security Administration.
ᵃ R̄² refers to coefficients corrected for degrees of freedom.
ᵇ Administrative expenditures for ADC are expressed in terms of per family per month; for all other programs, they are expressed per recipient per month.
ᶜ Significant at the 1 percent level.
ᵈ Significant at the 5 percent level.

taken to represent a state's "ability" to spend on assistance. This is what would be expected in view of the fact that, in 1960, federal grants for administrative expenditures were a flat 50 percent of outlays.[58]

The goal of public assistance, as stated in the Social Security Act, is not only to furnish financial aid but also to provide social

[58] Expenditures for administering the four public assistance programs in 1960 were $275 million, an amount equal to 8.2 percent of total assistance payments in the four programs. The federal share was 49.7 percent, slightly less than the possible 50 percent because small amounts of expenditure in a few states were ineligible for federal sharing. The monthly administrative expenditure per recipient (per family in ADC) is shown below, with the ratio of administrative expenditures to assistance payments (expressed as a percentage) for each program in 1960.

| | *OAA* | *ADC* | *AB* | *APTD* |
|---|---|---|---|---|
| Administrative expenditure per casemonth (in dollars): | 4.30 | 11.98 | 6.18 | 7.48 |
| Administrative expenditure as a percent of total assistance payments: | *6.3* | *10.8* | *8.5* | *11.4* |

worker services to help the needy achieve the greatest possible economic and personal independence. The costs of such services are considered administrative expenditures "necessary to proper and efficient program operation" and thus they are eligible for federal administrative expenditure grants. However, in contrast to the grants for assistance payments, the administrative expenditure grants are made on a flat percentage basis, with no federal maxima and no provision for "equalization"; also, each state determines what, if any, services will be provided by its welfare agencies.[59]

Although the level of staff salaries naturally has some bearing on the level of administrative costs, administrative expenditure per casemonth in each public assistance program can be considered a proxy for the ratio of professional staff to assistance recipients. The ratio cannot be calculated for the individual programs because most agency staff members work on more than one public assistance program (and many work on general assistance or child welfare programs as well).[60]

The results shown in Table 17 indicate that poorer states cannot afford staff/recipient ratios as large as those of wealthier states because they are doubly burdened: they have more recipients relative to population and smaller resources (per capita and, even more so, per recipient). The amount of social casework per recipient is

[59] In 1960, administrative expenditure grants were a flat 50 percent of total expenses. The first move toward federal standards for agency services was made in the 1962 public assistance amendments, which gave federal authorities the power to specify certain minimal requirements for the service features in the states' programs. In states meeting the requirements, the federal share of the costs of rendering "service" was to expand to 75 percent.

[60] Although it is not possible to classify professional staff members by assistance program, an overall ratio of professional staff to recipients can be calculated for the states in 1960 by using data on staff working primarily on assistance rather than child welfare programs. This ratio is highly correlated with the "average" administrative expenditure per public assistance case, which is calculated as total administrative expenditures in the public assistance programs divided by total recipients (counting families, not persons, in ADC); Spearman's rank correlation coefficient is .87. In thirty-four states, the reported number of professional staff working primarily on assistance programs included those working on general assistance as well as public assistance, and in those states, the denominator of the staff/recipient ratio includes the number of general assistance cases. See U.S. Department of Health, Education, and Welfare, *Public Social Welfare Personnel, 1960* (1962). Services for public assistance recipients are discussed in Helen B. Foster, *Services in Public Assistance: The Role of the Caseworker*, Public Assistance Report No. 30 (1957).

smallest in states having the largest proportions of dependent persons in their populations (that is, in states with the largest recipient rates).[61]

If there is a "national interest" in securing some national minimum standard of professional social work per assistance recipient, it would be logical to institute a policy under which the federal share of administrative costs varies inversely with income. However, a variable grant formula would not guarantee the desired result unless the grant were conditioned upon the maintenance of such a standard; otherwise, poorer states might simply reduce their own outlays for administration, thus leaving the total unchanged.

It can be expected that administrative expenditures per public assistance case will increase as more emphasis is put on social casework. The point pressed by federal authorities, and attested by the cases reported in the social work journals, is that increases in such expenditures pay large returns in the form of future decreases in public assistance expenditures. As would be expected, the largest returns are apparently found in the ADC program.[62]

## General Assistance

The available general assistance data are seriously inadequate for use in investigating determinants of the general assistance program variables, and no attempt was made to investigate general assistance in any detail. Tables 18, 19, and 20 simply show the results

[61] Except at very small scales of operation—far smaller than those actually prevailing—it would not be reasonable to expect that there are any "economies of scale" in the staff/recipient ratio, such that the "desirable" or efficient ratio falls as the absolute size of the operation increases. It could be argued that one reason why administrative costs per casemonth are higher in higher-income states is that those states pay higher salaries. However, there does not appear to be an especially large correlation between salary level and income per capita. The median salary of caseworkers appears on inspection to be strongly influenced by regional patterns, which is not surprising. Some data on salaries and characteristics of welfare personnel are contained in U.S. Department of Health, Education, and Welfare, *Public Social Welfare Personnel, 1960.*

[62] Paradoxically, there is only a limited, optional provision for an exemption of earnings from calculations of need and of assistance payments in ADC. A mandatory exemption was enacted for AB in 1950 and a permissive one, later to become mandatory, for OAA in 1962—both with the stated intent of fostering self-reliance and self-support. This paradox is probably a reflection of congressional distrust of ADC recipients relative to those in the other public assistance programs.

TABLE 18. Multiple Regression Analysis of Per Capita General Assistance Expenditure, 1960[a]

| Dependent Variable: Per Capita General Assistance Expenditure, 1960[b] | Partial Coefficients of Correlation with the Following Independent Variables: | | | | | | | |
|---|---|---|---|---|---|---|---|---|
| | Average Income Per Capita, 1958–60 | Unemployment Rate, Spring, 1960 | Percent of Population Living in Urban Places, 1960 | Nonwhite Percent of Population, 1960 | State Share of Cost, 1960 | $R$ | $R^2$ | $\bar{R}^{2}$[c] |
| (1) | .6071[d] | | | | | .6071[d] | .3686 | .3552 |
| (2) | .6035[d] | .2111 | | | | .6298[d] | .3967 | .3705 |
| (3) | .3556[e] | .2249 | .0440 | −.1780 | | .6450[d] | .4160 | .3629 |
| (4) | .3629[e] | .1756 | .0110 | −.1864 | .0797 | .6479[d] | .4197 | .3523 |

Source: U. S. Bureau of the Census and U. S. Social Security Administration.
[a] See text, pp. 111, 113, and 167, for definitions of independent variables.
[b] See Table 2 for the dollar amount of per capita expenditure for general assistance programs, and Table 1, note d, for the method of calculating this expenditure.
[c] $\bar{R}^2$ refers to coefficients corrected for degrees of freedom.
[d] Significant at the 1 percent level.
[e] Significant at the 5 percent level.

of fitting to the available data some of the determinants used for the public assistance programs. The results indicate that general assistance programs are most extensive in states with high income; not only the average payment but also the recipient rate is positively correlated with income level. It appears that the scope of noncategorical relief financed wholly from state-local funds depends heavily on the financial resources of state-local governments. However, as compared with the public assistance programs, the states' general assistance programs are so varied in nature that little of the interstate variation in the general assistance program variables can be attributed to systematic response to variation in quantifiable determinants other than income. The general assistance caseload, and thus expenditure, in a number of states is probably responsive to employment conditions, but even the unemployment rate is insignificant in the general assistance models.

The general assistance programs vary immensely with regard to purpose, standards, eligibility rules, and all other characteristics.[63] The programs are generally characterized by stringency of one or more types: very limited assistance standards; low maximum payments; low percentages of evaluated need met; and limited periods for which assistance may be received. In most states, responsibility and control are shared between state and local governments, but in about one-third of the states, general assistance is administered and financed entirely by local governments.

A serious deficiency of the general assistance data is that the monthly figures (used to calculate recipient rates and average payments) exclude noncash payments and cases receiving only such payments, although noncash payments are a large part of the general assistance total in many states, covering food and shelter as well as medical care. The annual data used to calculate expenditure per

[63] In 25 percent of the states, general assistance is available only for short-term or emergency needs and another 25 percent provide general assistance on a continuing basis only in a few specified circumstances (usually for chronically ill persons not eligible for public assistance); these are the two most common uses of general assistance in many other states. Ineligibility of "employable" persons and of families with "employable" members is not uncommon. For transients and persons who are not legal residents, most states provide only emergency medical care, if that. A summary of states' general assistance provisions as of 1959 is contained in U.S. Department of Health, Education, and Welfare, *Characteristics of General Assistance in the United States,* Public Assistance Report No. 39 (1959).

**TABLE 19. Multiple Regression Analysis of General Assistance Recipient Rate, 1960[a]**

| Dependent Variable: General Assistance Recipient Rate, 1960[b] | Partial Coefficients of Correlation with the Following Independent Variables: | | | | | $R$ | $R^2$ | $\bar{R}^{2c}$ |
| --- | --- | --- | --- | --- | --- | --- | --- | --- |
| | Percent of Population with Incomes Below $2,000, 1959 | Unemployment Rate, Spring, 1960 | Percent of Population Living in Urban Places, 1960 | Nonwhite Percent of Population, 1960 | State Share of Cost, 1960 | | | |
| (1) | −.5017[d] | | | | | .5017[d] | .2517 | .2358 |
| (2) | −.5050[d] | .0725 | | | | .5057[d] | .2557 | .2233 |
| (3) | −.1470 | .1139 | .1599 | −.1075 | | .5255[d] | .2762 | .2104 |
| (4) | −.1536 | .0332 | .1059 | −.1352 | .1925 | .5505[d] | .3030 | .2219 |
| (5) | −.4939[d] | | | | .2180 | .5360[d] | .2872 | .2562 |

Source: U. S. Bureau of the Census and U. S. Social Security Administration.
[a] See text, pp. 111, 113, and 167, for definitions of independent variables.
[b] See Table 2 for the level of the general assistance recipient rate, and Table 1, note e, for the method of calculating this rate.
[c] $\bar{R}^2$ refers to coefficients corrected for degrees of freedom.
[d] Significant at the 1 percent level.

capita do include noncash payments for medical items, but the extent of coverage of other noncash payments is not clear.[64]

There is a distinct seasonal pattern in the monthly level of general assistance cases. They increase during the winter to a peak in March, then decline steadily to a low in September. This presumably reflects the fact that the purpose of most general assistance programs is to provide bare subsistence in cases of great hardship, which would be more frequent during the winter. By contrast, there is no apparent seasonal variation in the number of recipients in the public assistance programs, which generally meet continuing need on a long-term basis.

The share of general assistance costs borne by state governments is hypothesized as a determinant on the theory that the content and coverage of a state's program may be more liberal the larger the share of the cost borne by the state rather than the localities. The results for expenditures do not support this hypothesis, although the average payment and recipient rate results do give it some support.

The most important feature of the recipient rate results is that the rate is positively correlated with income level. This can be taken to mean that the higher the state's income level, the more comprehensive and generous is its general assistance program, in terms of the assistance standard and the eligibility rules governing the types of needy persons that may receive general assistance.[65]

As expected, the average payment per general assistance case has a high positive correlation with income level. In fact, the share of interstate variation accounted for by income (52.3 percent) is larger than that accounted for by income in any of the four public assistance programs. The state share of the cost is also significant, suggesting that the greater the state financial role in general assistance, the more liberal is the assistance standard and/or the larger is the percentage of evaluated need met by the general assistance

[64] Some general assistance payments in some states are made to public assistance recipients, generally for medical needs or for transportation to receive medical care. The number of such supplementation cases is small, and in all but a few states these payments are a very small share of total general assistance expenditures.

[65] Neither inclusion of the labor force composition nor of the percentage change in population, 1955-60, made any improvement in the general assistance results.

TABLE 20. Multiple Regression Analysis of Average Monthly General Assistance Payment Per Case, 1960[a]

| Dependent Variable: Average Monthly General Assistance Payment Per Case, 1960[b] | Partial Coefficients of Correlation with the Following Independent Variables: | | | | | | | |
|---|---|---|---|---|---|---|---|---|
| | Average Income Per Capita, 1958–60 | General Assistance Recipient Rate, 1960 | Percent of Population Living in Urban Places, 1960 | Nonwhite Percent of Population, 1960 | State Share of Cost, 1960 | R | R² | R̄²[c] |
| (1) | .7303[d] | | | | | .7303[d] | .5333 | .5234 |
| (2) | .7394[d] | | | | .3540[e] | .7693[d] | .5918 | .5740 |
| (3) | .6775[d] | .2253 | | | .3125[e] | .7827[d] | .6125 | .5868 |
| (4) | .4580[d] | | .2374 | −.2809 | .3602[e] | .8004[d] | .6408 | .6080 |
| (5) | .4473[d] | .1396 | .2135 | −.2434 | .3288 | .8048[d] | .6478 | .6068 |

Source: U. S. Bureau of the Census and U. S. Social Security Administration.

[a] See text, pp. 111, 113, and 167, for definitions of independent variables.

[b] See Table 2 for the level of the average monthly general assistance payment, and Table 1, note f, for the method of calculating this payment.

[c] R̄² refers to coefficients corrected for degrees of freedom.

[d] Significant at the 1 percent level.

[e] Significant at the 5 percent level.

payment. Thus, the wealthier the state, the more liberal is its general assistance program with respect both to the types of need covered and to the content of the assistance standard. Therefore, it is not surprising that the recipient rate has a positive (though not significant) coefficient when used as a determinant of the average payment, as shown in line 3, Table 20. With income held constant, the higher the recipient rate the more comprehensive or liberal is the program and therefore the larger is the average payment.

## Prospects for the Public Assistance Programs

Although "need" for public assistance at any point in time varies inversely with income, a rising income level over time will not necessarily decrease the need for or expenditures on public assistance. There are always needy persons who are very much at a disadvantage relative to the general population. The very existence of public assistance programs facilitates the identification and alleviation of need that would otherwise be ignored or dealt with by piecemeal public or voluntary measures. Because the public assistance programs are available they are used.

### Income Levels

A rising income level means generally rising living standards and concomitant changes in the criteria of need. Higher incomes lead to higher standards against which "need" is measured. Monthly assistance payments can be expected to rise with rising income levels and expenditures may therefore continue to grow even in programs with falling caseloads.[66]

Rising income levels will probably be accompanied by increasing social disorganization and economic maladjustment. More specifically, rising labor productivity worsens the position of the unskilled, the poorly educated, aging workers in declining industries, and others unequipped for full participation in the modern labor force. Rising income levels are likely to be accompanied by rising (or at least stable) recipient rates in ADC and APTD, though probably not in OAA or AB. The ADC and APTD programs deal with need among groups—members of broken families and the disabled

[66] Over time, the ratios of the national average assistance payment in each public assistance program to national per capita income have been quite stable.

—in which the incidence of non-self-supporting status may well remain constant, or even increase, despite overall growth in income levels and productivity.

## Urbanization

Urbanization will presumably continue to exert upward pressure on assistance caseloads and expenditures. In each public assistance program, greater urbanization is associated with higher recipient rates and larger payments to recipients. Urbanization is associated with social disorganization, in the form of broken families and generally weaker family ties. Also, urbanization may well mean fewer opportunities for marginally productive persons—those handicapped by age, disability, education, and so forth—to earn at least a minimum living, because urban labor markets are oriented toward full-time employment and impersonal competition among job seekers. Furthermore, it is likely that the real content of a minimum living standard, the cost of that standard, and the proportion of the cost that must be met by assistance payments, are all higher in urban than in rural areas.[67]

## Unemployment

Unemployment is generally not a highly important determinant of the public assistance program variables, except in ADC, but it is not insignificant. This is reasonable, for all programs but ADC deal largely with persons whose age or handicaps make then "unemployable" in the traditional sense. The ADC program, however, deals with families in which there is usually an "employable" person (in the sense of being able-bodied), and the proportion of potentially eligible families actually requiring ADC will depend in part on general employment conditions.

Since 1961, states have been permitted to extend ADC coverage to families in which both parents may be present and which are in need specifically because of unemployment. This development, which naturally increases the sensitivity of ADC to employment conditions, marked the first overt move toward using public assistance for relief of persons clearly in the labor force.

[67] However, some groups of potential public assistance recipients may be better off if they live in urban areas. In particular, greater urbanization may mean that the blind and disabled have greater opportunities for sheltered employment or for training and rehabilitation.

Since all public assistance programs except ADC deal with persons who are generally outside the labor force and only a few of whom would benefit from full employment, the achievement and maintenance of full employment would by no means end the need for public assistance, as the experience of World War II showed. On the other hand, a higher unemployment rate could be expected to exert some additional upward pressure on public assistance recipient rates and expenditures.

That there is some impact of unemployment on general assistance can be seen from time series data for the postwar period. In years of rapid expansion, general assistance cases fell by an average of 63,000. They fell by an average of 5,000 in years of slow growth, and rose by 71,000 in recession years.

## Dependency, Blindness, Disability

Childhood dependency is apparently becoming more prevalent —despite the decreasing frequency of deaths of fathers of young children—because divorce, separation, and illegitimacy are becoming more frequent. It is very likely that the ADC recipient rate will continue to rise.

Improved public health standards and wider access to medical care, which have accompanied rising income levels, are probably helping to reduce the prevalence of blindness except, perhaps, among the aged; much age-connected blindness is unavoidable. Thus, there is reason to think that the AB recipient rate will continue to fall unless the growth of the aged population is so great that it offsets the effects of the declining overall prevalence of blindness. Even that might not impede the decline in the AB rate, because of the steadily increasing probability that a person reaching age sixty-five enjoys social insurance coverage. Thus, more of those who become blind because of age will have income from an OASDI benefit.

The future trend of the prevalence of serious disability is unclear, because the term "permanent and total disability" is imprecise. There continues to be a stratum of "marginal" people—poorly educated, without skill, with little or no mobility or adaptability— whose relative disadvantage grows as the value to the economy of unskilled labor diminishes. Such marginal workers find it difficult indeed to support themselves if they are also handicapped by physical or mental disabilities, and they are likely to end up on the APTD rolls. The extent to which APTD takes on the burden of supporting persons who have some disability, and who lack the training to support themselves in a high-skill economy, will depend on how states define "permanent and total disability," and on the weight they give to education, training, and the existence of employment opportunities.

If APTD increasingly supports persons whose dependency results as much from inability to adjust to economic change, or from levels of productivity too low for their employment, as it does from actual disability, then policymakers should intensify and enlarge programs for rehabilitation and vocational training in APTD.

*Social Insurance*

Old-Age and Survivors Insurance has provided much of the support of the aged and OASI can be expected to continue to supplant OAA, leaving to the latter only the needy among the small proportion of the future aged population that will not have social insurance coverage. Of course, some OASI beneficiaries require OAA to supplement their social insurance benefits and this will continue to be true. Nevertheless, OASI will continue to supplant OAA so long as the purchasing power of OASI benefits does not deteriorate seriously.

Survivors Insurance has come to meet a large part of the need that the framers of ADC had in mind—need due to a father's death —and Disability Insurance should protect some additional families from the need for ADC. But social insurance provides no help for the major causes of childhood dependency—those related to family disorganization—nor does it constitute a safeguard for children in families that have never acquired insured status.

Both DI and OASI should tend increasingly to reduce the need for AB, while DI should tend to reduce somewhat the need for APTD. However, there will always be blind and disabled persons who have been handicapped from an early age and who have never acquired OASDI coverage, and who therefore will potentially remain dependent on public assistance.

*Changes in the Coverage of Public Assistance*

It has been proposed in recent years that public assistance should discard the categorical structure of rules under which it has operated since 1935, and provide general, noncategorical income security. Such proposals usually reflect a desire to assist all the needy without regard to age or cause of need, though there are other reasons.[68]

The extent to which this happens will in the long run be determined by fundamental attitudes of the population and the policies of government. The rapidly rising costs of ADC may ultimately be limited by changes in private and public attitudes toward birth control. As the anti-poverty program begins to break the cycle of poverty through its efforts to promote higher levels of educational attainment and work skills, lower recipient rates should result for several categories of assistance, including ADC, APTD, and general assistance.

Last, as this study has shown, expenditures are influenced not just by objective economic variables, but by the subjective attitudes of the electorate, of state and local governments, and of the federal government. It remains to be seen how these attitudes will be affected in coming years by the reapportionment of state legislatures, by a greater emphasis on training and rehabilitation as opposed to pure income maintenance, by increases in the number of mothers who hold jobs, and by the civil rights revolution.

[68] For example: greater freedom for states to shape their assistance programs as they see fit; greater simplicity and less red tape in operation; and greater potential for public assistance to play a contracyclical role by paying benefits to the unemployed.

# APPENDIX

# Tables Showing Levels of Significance and Number of Observations Used in the Regression Analyses

**TABLE A-1. Absolute Values Above Which Partial and Multiple Correlation Coefficients Are Significant, at 5 Percent and 1 Percent Levels**

| | | Number of Observations | | Absolute Values Above Which Coefficients Are Significant, at the: | | df |
|---|---|---|---|---|---|---|
| | 50 | 49 | 45 | 5 Percent Level[a] | 1 Percent Level[a] | |
| | 1 | | | .2787 | .3605 | 48 |
| | 2 | 1 | | .2816 | .3646 | 47 |
| | 3 | 2 | | .2845 | .3683 | 46 |
| | 4 | 3 | | .2875 | .3721 | 45 |
| | 5 | 4 | | .2906 | .3760 | 44 |
| Number of | 6 | 5 | 1 | .2940 | .3801 | 43 |
| Independent | 7 | 6 | 2 | .2973 | .3843 | 42 |
| Variables | 8 | 7 | 3 | .3007 | .3886 | 41 |
| | | 8 | 4 | .3044 | .3931 | 40 |
| | | | 5 | .3082 | .3978 | 39 |
| | | | 6 | .3120 | .4026 | 38 |
| | | | 7 | .3160 | .4076 | 37 |
| | | | 8 | .3202 | .4128 | 36 |

[a] A partial or multiple correlation coefficient can be accepted as significantly different from zero, with 5 percent and 1 percent probabilities of error, if its absolute (unsigned) value exceeds the values shown, for various degrees of freedom.

**TABLE A-2. Number of Observations Used in Regression Analyses**

| OAA | ADC | AB | APTD | All Public Assistance Programs Combined | General Assistance Programs |
|---|---|---|---|---|---|
| 50 | 50 | 50 | 45 | 50 | 49 |

174

JOHN W. DORSEY

# The Mack Case:
# A Study in Unemployment

ON OCTOBER 31, 1961, the Mack Truck Company shut down its engine and transmission manufacturing plant at Plainfield, New Jersey, and moved its operations to Hagerstown, Maryland. This is a study of the workers affected by the Mack relocation.

The first part of the study traces the events leading up to the plant relocation and then, on the basis of personal interview records, compares the sociological and economic characteristics of the workers who followed the company to Maryland with the characteristics of those who did not. Workers' stated reasons for transferring or not transferring are also discussed.

The second part of the study deals with the re-employment problems of those workers who did not transfer with the company. Again using the personal interview method, the characteristics of the workers and their employment experience in the nine months following the shutdown are analyzed. Where possible, data collected by the state Employment Service are also presented.

The third part of the study is an examination of household budgets of those workers who remained unemployed for more than six months. It deals with the adjustments in family expenditures and the loss in family income which resulted from the shutdown.

* University of Maryland.

The Mack plant shutdown offered an opportunity to examine intensively the mobility and re-employment problems of one group of industrial workers. It was a vivid example of many of the problems created during the process of industrial relocation and it raised issues that are relevant for large sectors of our industrial community today. More specifically, the Mack case was selected for study for the following reasons: (1) It offered an opportunity to combine an analysis of inter-plant labor mobility with an analysis of unemployment. Since the two problems are closely related, I considered it important to study them together. (2) The Mack Company offered unusually large severance payments to workers who were left behind when the plant relocated. This situation made it possible to examine in detail the effects of payments on the mobility and re-employment of the workers. (3) The New Jersey State Employment Service had set up a special program to put workers affected by the shutdown back to work as soon as possible. The existence of the special project meant that much information and research assistance was available through the state of New Jersey which might not otherwise have been available. Moreover, the Commissioner of Labor and Industry in New Jersey expressed a strong interest in the research proposal and put the facilities of his office at my disposal.

## Relocation of the Mack Plant

The two most important reasons for the plant shutdown were the outdated character of physical plant and outmoded wage practices.

### Background

The Plainfield plant was built in 1910 and was not at all suited to those modern production methods which were necessary to maintain the Mack Company's competitive position in the industry. The plant was actually a series of separate buildings connected by passageways. Some buildings were two or three stories high and included floors which sometimes were not on the same level as floors in adjacent, connected buildings. There were only a limited number of truck bays, no extensive parking areas for trucks waiting to load and unload, and only minimal freight elevator facilities convenient to the different sections of the plant complex.

The wage structure in the plant consisted of a base rate which workers received for producing a daily quota, plus an incentive wage for everything over this norm. The quotas had not been revised sufficiently over the years to allow for increasing mechanization. As a result it was relatively easy for workers to produce 200 to 300 percent of their quota in less than eight hours of work and thus receive very high weekly wages.

In 1954 the company came to the union for relief from the wage practices. The company argued that it was unable to compete because a profit squeeze had set in. In view of this the union accepted a cut in pay averaging over 20 cents an hour on the base rate. In 1955, after the new contract had been signed, the company started working the men overtime because there was a flood of unfilled orders, and the union felt that it had been deceived.

In 1958, during the contract negotiations of that year, company complaints began again. In a letter to the employees on October 10, 1958, the company indicated its dissatisfaction with the incentive wage situation, which at that time provided an average incentive rate for Mack workers of over $3.50 an hour, as compared with the average rate elsewhere in the automotive-truck manufacturing industry of $2.51 an hour.[1] In addition, the letter complained about the profit squeeze, falling sales, and the difficult competitive position of the company's products. The Master Shop Agreement which was signed in late 1958 did not meet the company's specifications, and the decision to relocate at a new plant was announced in the fall of 1959. By this time Mack workers were averaging about $144 in gross pay each week.

Instead of conducting a vigorous campaign to keep wages in line with those in other comparable firms in New Jersey, Mack had taken the path of least resistance and yielded to the union wage demands.

## The Decision to Relocate

Due to poor plant facilities and high wages, the company's profit position and place in the industry had been slipping in the 1950's. Mack decided to rebuild its operations around a new, highly automated plant where levels of production could be raised and

---

[1] Copies of all letters discussed in this paper will be found in my unpublished doctoral dissertation, "The Mack Case: A Study in Unemployment" (Harvard University, 1963).

unit wage costs held down—preferably in an area far enough away from Plainfield to escape the influence of Local 343 of the United Automobile Workers. The company planned to go after competitive government contracts and also to build up its business in the Common Market countries. The Fantus Company, a consultant on plant location, was hired to recommend a suitable new site. Fantus recommended Hagerstown, Maryland.

Hagerstown is a city of about 50,000 and the county seat of Washington County, Maryland. It had been a depressed area for several years due to the decline of the Fairchild Aircraft Company, Hagerstown's major employer since World War II, when the "Flying Boxcar" was in its prime. With the advent of jet aircraft and missiles, Fairchild's position in the industry had begun to fall and, in the years following the Korean War, the company laid off about 7,000 workers.

### The Transfer of Workers

In June 1960, the Mack Truck Company announced in a letter to its employees that construction would begin immediately on a new plant in Hagerstown, but that the Plainfield plant would not be closed before October 20, 1961. Enclosed in the letter was a detailed description of the "extremely favorable" separation and retirement benefits which the company had proposed to the union for those workers who stayed in New Jersey. These benefits were approximately double the benefits required by the existing contract. Although this letter stressed the benefits which workers who stayed behind would receive, it said little about the conditions which would prevail at the new plant. It pointed out only that Hagerstown was an area of "severe and continuing unemployment," that there would be no incentive pay system in Hagerstown for at least two years, if at all, and that the average rate at Hagerstown's largest manufacturing plant (Fairchild Aircraft) was $2.53 an hour. In addition, the letter indicated that transferred employees would receive full supplementary unemployment benefits, pension and vacation credits, and a $200 relocation allowance, but that seniority for purposes of layoff, recall, and promotion would be determined at the new plant.

The company made two additional points in its letter. First, since the severance and retirement benefits which the company proposed to pay were in excess of their contract obligations, it stipulated that any worker who participated in a strike or slowdown of production would be denied that portion of the payment which was in excess of contract requirements. More important, perhaps, a questionnaire was to be sent out very soon asking each worker whether or not he would accept transfer. As the letter put it, "Any employee who answers the questionnaire by stating that he is available for transfer but later refuses an offer to transfer, will be limited to the benefits prescribed by the contract and will not be entitled to receive any of the additional rights or benefits proposed by the company." The letter did not explicitly say that those workers who answered "no" would not be given a chance to change their minds. It only hinted at this point by stating that "The Company must also be able to rely on the answers given." The conditions outlined in this letter were company proposals which had not yet been negotiated with the union, but since they were in excess of contract obligations, the company anticipated their acceptance.[2] Nowhere in the letter was there any mention of seniority or age requirements for transferring with the company. The letter did not suggest that everyone who requested transfer would be accepted; it simply left this question unstated.

At this point the workers faced a major dilemma. If they answered "no" to the survey and accepted the company's offer of increased benefits, they had to remain with the company until the plant shutdown and then face the prospect of unemployment at a time when many of their fellow workers were also in the job market. On the other hand, if they answered "yes" to the survey, they had to be prepared to relocate at the company's discretion or lose their right to receive the additional benefits. Of the 2,700 employees who participated in the survey, about 1,200 indicated their willingness to accept an offer of transfer. Supervisory and administrative employees were accorded separate treatment by the company and were invited to transfer according to the job requirements of the new plant.

Apparently dissatisfied with the results of the first survey, the company announced in another letter of February 3 that a "second and final" survey would be conducted among those employees who

---

[2] Under the existing contract the company's only obligation was to discuss with the union the subject of worker transfers.

answered "yes" on the first survey in order to give them "an opportunity to change their answer" and thus to share in the company's
"double benefit" program. Some new information was presented in
this letter. The company revealed that production standards at the
new plant would "be established by the company at a work pace
considerably higher than that now prevailing in Plainfield," that
many of the transferred workers would have to accept new job classifications, and that for purposes of layoff, recall, and promotion,
Plainfield employees would maintain their seniority in relationship
to each other, but that the relationship of Plainfield employees to
new employees at Hagerstown would have to be negotiated later.
The letter concluded by reminding the employees that "this is your
last and only chance to change your answer if you wish to be eligible for the double benefits."

About the time that the second questionnaire went out to the
workers, the international union sent a letter to its members outlin-
ing the union's efforts and policies. The letter described the existing
situation as follows:

Company officials have expressed a willingness to work out an early
retirement and severance program for employees who do not move to
Hagerstown; however, we have not been able to reach an agreement which
would give an opportunity for everyone to go to Hagerstown who wants to
go. The company has agreed to recognize the UAW at the Hagerstown
location and to negotiate a contract covering wages and working conditions after a number of people have been employed at the Hagerstown
plant.

The letter further urged all members to wait until after the union
meeting scheduled for February 12 before returning their questionnaire since representatives of the international would attend the
meeting to discuss the problems involved. Also at this time, one of
the local television stations showed a documentary film about Hagerstown, Maryland, which presented the city as one of the nation's
leading depressed areas. When tabulated, the second survey showed
about 650 employees still anxious to transfer to the new plant.

By mid-April the company and the union had finally agreed on
the terms of a separation and transfer agreement. The agreement
contained for the most part the company's proposals previously discussed; however, there were some modifications. All employees

who answered "yes" on the second survey would be offered employment in Hagerstown, provided: (1) that the employee had the ability to perform the work to which he would be assigned; (2) that the employee should not have attained his 58th birthday before October 20, 1961; and (3) that he should have attained a minimum of three years of seniority as of October 20, 1961. Although items (2) and (3) were clear, item (1) created much confusion among the workers since the new plant would require many different skills, and many workers were not completely certain that they would be able to perform the new jobs. Also under the agreement, the company received full rights to establish rate structures, classifications, production standards, and all other conditions of employment in the initial operation of the Hagerstown plant, but no details were offered concerning these. Finally, the seniority of Plainfield employees regarding layoff and recall was preserved with some minor exceptions. A copy of this final relocation program was mailed to the employees on April 25.

On September 29, in a letter to the employees, the company announced its decision to close the Plainfield plant effective November 1. The company also announced then a third survey for the purpose of giving eligible employees who had previously indicated they wanted to transfer an opportunity to change their minds without forfeiting their rights in the double-benefit program. At the same time the company announced another increase in pension benefits, supplementary unemployment benefits, and separation payments. On this third survey only 250 employees indicated that they desired to transfer.

Finally, on October 31, in a special referendum, the membership of Local 343 ratified the separation and transfer agreement. Thus, after more than one year of negotiation and persuasion, conducted in an atmosphere of confusion, the company was committed to take less than one-tenth of the Plainfield hourly employees to Hagerstown. On the other hand, the company was committed to the most generous separation and retirement program accorded to similar workers under any UAW contract. In offering these benefits the company was clearly motivated by a desire to discourage as many as possible of the Plainfield employees from transferring in order to prevent a labor situation like the one in Plainfield from developing at the new plant. One company official, K. E. Warrick,

Director of Industrial Relations, put it mildly in a personal interview when he said: "We did not encourage them to transfer." It would appear in retrospect that the company's policy was one of being specific and generous concerning the conditions of separation and retirement while being vague and parsimonious concerning conditions at the new plant. By the third survey the conditions at the new plant concerning seniority had been made clear, but the question of wages was still unsettled. However, many workers, perhaps fearing loss of the double benefits, had already said "no" on one of the two previous surveys and thus had no chance to change their minds. It might be said that the company had successfully persuaded many workers to stay in New Jersey.

*The Survey*

A survey of workers was designed to answer two related questions about transfers between the old and new Mack plants: (1) Why were some workers willing to transfer and others not? (2) What was the influence, if any, of the extraordinary amount of separation pay and unemployment compensation on the workers' decisions?

The analysis in this section is based on the results of two random samples—one taken in New Jersey among workers who had decided not to transfer or who had not yet transferred, and the second in Maryland among workers who had already transferred.[3] Three approaches were used:

(1) A comparison of sociological characteristics of employees transferring and not transferring.

(2) An open-end question which required respondents to list the factors in their decision and to arrange these factors in the order of their importance.

(3) A limited-choice question in which each worker was presented with a definite list of factors and asked to arrange them in the order of their importance in his decision.

The information was gathered in the above order so that the answers to the unlimited-choice question would not be influenced by the suggestions made in the limited-choice question. In the anal-

[3] Details of sampling procedures may be found in Appendix B.

ysis, each variable was considered separately as a factor in the transfer decision and was then viewed in relation to other variables. For each variable considered, tables were prepared which compared workers who transferred with those who did not, and chi-square tests were used to determine whether the observed differences were significant. Production and nonproduction workers were analyzed separately where it was felt that their behavior might be different. Only workers who were eligible to transfer under the transfer agreement were considered. A correlation matrix of all variables was prepared and searched for interrelationships among explanatory variables.[4]

Since this analysis was necessarily tedious, I shall not burden the reader with great detail, but merely summarize the most significant relationships.[5]

## Factors in Workers' Decisions

A worker's willingness to transfer depended upon whether his attachment to his job was greater than his attachment to his area of residence, and on the attractiveness of the terms on which he could transfer as compared with the terms offered him to stay behind.

The most important characteristics which determined the attachment to job and area appeared to be occupation, seniority, and years lived in the area.

Among occupational groups, professional workers (in general, management personnel) showed by far the greatest tendency to transfer. This was to be expected since the terms of transfer were better for professionals than for other groups. They were promised wages at least as high as those they received in Plainfield and payment of all their moving expenses. Clerical and white collar workers showed the least tendency to transfer, perhaps because many of them were females whose husbands were employed by other firms in New Jersey. A fairly high percentage of foremen transferred to Maryland. Among production workers the transfer rate was higher for skilled workers than for semiskilled or unskilled workers.

There are many factors which might contribute to the area at-

---

[4] The multiple regression technique could not be used because of multicollinearity and because no proper dependent variable could be defined.

[5] The interested reader can find the data and a more complete analysis in my dissertation (see note 1).

tachment of a worker—home ownership, family size, years lived in an area, employment status of other family members, and a great many intangibles. Only one of these factors, years lived in the area, appeared to be significant; workers who had lived near Plainfield, New Jersey, for long periods of time showed less tendency to transfer than those who had not.

Seniority, which may be considered a measure of job attachment, was also an important variable. Since many advantages accrued to workers from length of service, the more senior workers might have been expected to have had higher transfer rates. The data supported this hypothesis. None of the other variables tested seemed important.[6]

## Reasons for Workers' Decisions

As part of the survey, each respondent was asked to list the reasons why he was or was not transferring. The interviewer simply recorded whatever reasons the respondent gave, then asked him to arrange his reasons in the order of their importance in his decision.

Among those workers who had transferred or were waiting to transfer, a group of variables reflecting *job attachment* seemed to be most important. Job attachment included job security, seniority, company pensions, the promise of promotion, and whether the worker "liked his job."

Workers interviewed in New Jersey who had not transferred and were not planning to do so similarly were asked the reasons for their decision and were also asked to arrange them in the order of importance. Factors expressing *area attachment* were clearly most important. Home ownership, a preference for the area, and children in school were all frequently mentioned. Among the other factors, the expectation of lower pay at the new plant was named most often.

The expectation of lower pay at the new plant and the expected

---

[6] The original data for each of the variables, adjusted for different sampling proportions, were subjected to a chi-square test for all eligible workers and for production workers alone. The test revealed whether the difference between transferring workers and nontransferring workers was greater for each variable than would have been expected from the total distribution of that variable. It should be stressed that these tests showed the significance of variation in a particular factor without allowing for the effects of other variables. Many of the variables were correlated.

loss of seniority were relatively more important among production workers than among nonproduction workers. For both groups the area attachment factors were most frequently mentioned.

During the course of the interview each respondent who was eligible to transfer but had declined was handed a card on which was printed the following list of six reasons:

(1) I have children in school.
(2) I expected lower wages in Hagerstown.
(3) I have friends here and like the area.
(4) I own my home and do not wish to sell it.
(5) Moving is too expensive.
(6) I felt that my severance pay and unemployment compensation would give me a chance to find a good job.[7]

The most important factor by far was the prospect of lower wages at the new plant. The other factors in the order of their importance were: preference for the area, home ownership, separation pay and unemployment compensation, children in school, and finally, the expense of moving.

## Separation Pay and Unemployment Compensation

The unusual combination of large separation payments, at a median level of about $2,000, and unemployment compensation, which in most cases was $50 a week, distinguishes the Mack case from other similar situations. Whether in fact separation pay and unemployment compensation combined to make New Jersey seem more attractive than Maryland is hard to determine. The reasons for transferring volunteered by the workers themselves, though, would indicate that these factors were not important. In the list of answers to the open-end question, only ten of the 211 respondents mentioned separation pay or unemployment compensation as a factor. Three of them said the two payments were the most important reason for not transferring, three ranked them second, and four said they were third in importance.

[7] There were a series of six cards, each with the order of the items changed. They were used for six consecutive interviews to avoid any bias imposed by the order of the choices. The worker was asked to arrange the items in the order of importance in his decision.

However, when a worker was confronted with the list of six reasons and asked to arrange them in the order of their importance in his decision not to move, the situation changed; this factor gained in importance and for nonproduction workers seemed very important indeed. After these subjective and objective tests each respondent was asked the specific question: "Suppose you had received no severance pay and no unemployment compensation; would you have been more likely to transfer to Hagerstown?" In reply, thirty-four said "yes," 155 said "no," and twenty-two said they were not sure. The thirty-four positive responses represented 18 percent of those who answered either "yes" or "no."

Interviewers recorded comments of workers about severance pay and unemployment compensation. These comments ranged from complete denials of any influence, such as: "Not much at all," and "I was interested only in wages and seniority"; to statements like: "They were quite important," and "They made it worthwhile for me to stay." The comment most frequently recorded was that separation pay and unemployment compensation, while not in themselves crucial factors in the mobility decision, did create an atmosphere in which it was financially possible for some workers who otherwise might have transferred to stay behind and take their chances on finding a new job. Some of the statements recorded were: "I didn't want to jeopardize my sizable severance for a job where the conditions were uncertain"; "It didn't really influence my decision not to transfer, but it enabled me to wait for a while to find a good job"; "I knew that separation pay and unemployment compensation would give me a chance to look for a job"; "They enabled me to set up my own business and stay here"; "I wanted to start raising a family so severance and unemployment compensation gave me a start."

## Summary of Influences on the Relocation Decision

The conclusion is that most workers felt a strong attachment to their New Jersey homes—an attachment conditioned by their years in the area, home ownership, children in school, and family ties. The prospect of leaving their homes to accept lower wages in a strange new area did not appeal to them. The cushion provided by separation pay and unemployment compensation made it possible for them to remain in New Jersey without fear of starvation.

On the other hand, some employees felt a strong attachment to their jobs with Mack. For some, job attachment outweighed area attachment in importance. This was especially true of nonproduction workers who did not face lower wages at the new plant and of older production workers whose age made their chances for re-employment in New Jersey difficult. These were the workers who transferred to the new plant.

In a similar study of the shutdown of an automobile plant in California, Gordon and McCorry felt that age, skill, number of children and years lived in the area were all important variables in the transfer of workers. They concluded that transfer rates were highest among the older, the least skilled, those with the largest families, and those who had lived at their last address for a relatively short period of time. Also, on the open-end question those authors used, job security and "a favorable attitude toward the job" were cited as the most important reasons for transferring, while area attachment appeared to be the most important reason for not transferring. The Gordon-McCorry study differs from this one in many respects, however, and its results cannot be considered entirely comparable with my own.[8]

## Re-employment Experience After the Shutdown

Plainfield, New Jersey, is a small city located about thirty miles southwest of New York City. Although Plainfield itself has a population of only about 50,000, it is part of a larger urban complex of nearly 100,000. The city is not an industrial center, and its economy rests more on its role as a shopping center and well-to-do residential area than on manufacturing.

Of the more than 3,000 Mack employees, only about 600 lived in the city of Plainfield, where the plant was located, and another 600 lived in the urban complex around Plainfield. Nearly 900 lived in the New Brunswick and Highland Park area, and another 300 in Somerville—both ten to twenty miles from Plainfield. The rest were scattered over the state, with small concentrations in Perth Amboy

[8] Margaret S. Gordon and Ann H. McCorry, "Plant Relocation and Job Security," *Industrial and Labor Relations Review*, Vol. 11 (October 1957), pp. 13-36. For an interesting discussion of the willingness of employees of the Armour Company to transfer to plants in other cities, see Richard Wilcock and Walter Frank, *Unwanted Workers* (Free Press, 1963), pp. 100-13.

(fifteen to twenty miles), Elizabeth (fifteen to twenty miles), and Newark (twenty to twenty-five miles). Some commuted from distant areas, such as Paterson (thirty to forty miles), Red Bank (forty-five to fifty miles), and Toms River (forty-five to fifty miles).

At the time of the shutdown, most of the Mack-affected area was experiencing moderate unemployment (from 3.0 to 5.9 percent). The northern areas of the state around Newark and Jersey City and the area to the southeast of Plainfield around Perth Amboy had been classified as areas of substantial unemployment (6.0 to 8.9 percent), but Newark and Perth Amboy were removed from the labor surplus list in 1962; thus both areas experienced rising employment rates during the months following the Mack layoff.

*The New Jersey State Employment Service Project*

The New Jersey State Employment Service (NJSES) set up a special experimental project to deal with the Mack shutdown. This project provided an exceptional source of data on the workers' job-seeking experience. It also provided an opportunity to examine the merits of this kind of approach by a state employment service to a mass layoff.

The project consisted of several phases. First, a pre-layoff registration program was conducted in the Plainfield union hall, where about half of the Mack employees were interviewed and classified, and many were also tested and counseled. This relieved the local Employment Service offices of much work in the early days of the layoff.

Second, a special questionnaire for a job supply survey was sent to 3,600 employers in the area to be affected by the layoff to determine what openings were available. By the time of the shutdown on October 31, 1961, over 800 responses had been received indicating over 500 vacancies, about half of which seemed suitable for Mack workers.

Third, special steps were taken in the local offices. Mack workers were located geographically in areas served by twenty-one NJSES offices. Eighty percent of the workers were concentrated in four offices—Plainfield, Highland Park, Somerville, and Perth Amboy. In each of the twenty-one offices, one or more "Mack specialists" were designated to be responsible for finding jobs for Mack workers. All of the records for former Mack employees were kept separate from the regular files so that accurate reporting would be possible.

A central Mack office was established in Trenton with a coordinator and a labor analyst. The central office had the task of coordinating the activities of the twenty-one local offices and of aggregating their reports. The Trenton office was also asked to inform appropriate authorities in Washington of the progress of the project and of any insights into employment problems. The state Commissioner of Labor and Industry took a personal hand in the project by calling upon employers to hire former Mack employees and by holding meetings of NJSES personnel to make them aware of the importance of the project.

*Workers' Response to the Project*

During the first two months, the twenty-one local offices made a combined total of 2,380 call-ins of former Mack workers for definite referral. Of these, about 70 percent reported to the local office, and 730 were referred to an employer. However, only ninety-one were hired.[9]

In the four local offices most affected by the Mack shutdown, there were 9,036 non-Mack workers seeking work on October 31, 1961, and 2,388 Mack workers. During November and December these four offices made 1,353 placements of non-Mack workers but succeeded in placing only forty-nine Mack workers.

In mid-December, the Employment Service mailed 2,700 questionnaires to former Mack employees. The first 1,000 respondents who indicated that they were still unemployed were selected for home interviews to determine their attitudes toward returning to work. The results of the interviews conducted by the professional Employment Service interviewers are shown in Table 1.

After this evaluation was made, those workers who were considered active in the labor market were singled out for special attention. They were re-interviewed and an effort was made to find

[9] A "call-in" is a request by the Employment Service for a worker to report to his local office to discuss a particular job opening. When the worker reports to the local office, the interviewer evaluates his qualifications for the job, and if the worker is found to be satisfactory, the interviewer "refers" the worker to an employer. The worker may then accept the "referral." If he accepts, he may or may not be hired by the employer. If he rejects the referral without good reason, he may be denied unemployment compensation. "Good reason" may be low pay, as compared with previous wages, or an "unreasonable" commuting distance.

**TABLE 1. Results of New Jersey Employment Service
Survey of Former Mack Workers**

| Type of Response to Unemployment | Number of Workers | Percent |
|---|---|---|
| Very active in labor market; following all leads with no restrictions | 292 | 29.5 |
| Active in labor market; some restrictions as to wages or distance | 158 | 16.0 |
| Not active; definite restrictions | 145 | 14.7 |
| Using age as an excuse for not looking for work | 135 | 13.7 |
| Minimum effort to seek work; "sitting back and waiting" | 96 | 9.7 |
| Not able to locate respondent | 89 | 9.0 |
| Already working | 74 | 7.5 |
| Total | 989 | 100.0 |

Source: NJSES survey of former Mack workers.
Note: Details may not add to totals due to rounding.

jobs for them.

During the first three months of 1962, Employment Service efforts continued and were even intensified. There were many call-ins each month, but many of those called in refused referrals to employers. The major reasons for these refusals were low wages and the relatively long commuting distances to job demand areas.

A Bergen County aircraft manufacturer decided to try positive recruitment in the Mack-affected area by lowering his usual job specifications and expressing a willingness to take trainees. The net result was that 641 Mack workers responded to call-ins in the four major local offices, but 469 of these said the distance was too far (about thirty-five miles from Plainfield). Five days of all-out recruitment resulted in six placements. It seemed apparent that any attempt to channel Mack workers to demand areas was doomed to failure. Therefore, efforts by the Employment Service to make more local placements were increased. The efforts concentrated on achieving realistic occupational classifications, providing testing and counseling, and encouraging workers to enroll in late afternoon or evening vocational school courses.[10] These efforts were in vain.

[10] Workers who enroll in daytime vocational courses may lose their eligibility for unemployment compensation in New Jersey, although there is some disagreement on the interpretation of the law.

## Employers' Response to the Project

In addition to *worker* reluctance to accept jobs in the demand areas and to work for lower rates of pay than Mack had paid, the problem of *employer* hostility was growing in importance. Rumors spread rapidly throughout the state concerning the strong union at Mack and the attitudes of the Mack workers. It became very difficult for the Employment Service to use Mack workers to fill large orders from employers. For example, two weeks after the opening of a branch plant of a large can company in the Mack area, twenty-five former Mack workers were hired and the hiring of up to 250 more was promised. After hearing that these former Mack employees were plotting against the local United Steelworkers Union to replace it with their own, the employer informed the NJSES that he would take no more Mack workers. About the only course open to the local offices was to concentrate on single placements.

Illustrative of the growing employer hostility were some comments made by former Mack workers on questionnaires sent out by the NJSES:

It is a known fact throughout New Brunswick that no one had anything good to say about Mack men.

The personnel manager told me that he was sorry, but he was told not to hire Mack workers.

As soon as they found out I was from Mack Truck the excuses came rolling out . . . I have over 100 applications in and no job, have reasoned with all excuses but to no avail.

All I can say is that Mack Trucks left a poor taste of its employees in the state of New Jersey.

Whenever I was interviewed, and stressed I was in the union at Mack Truck, I would get an answer such as: "We'll call you; there's no union here; I heard about Mack Truck's union." You'd think I belonged to the Communist party. . . . Well, I think I could write here all day, but I guess I have to solve my own problem.

One prospective employer advised me not to write down on my applications that I had worked at Mack.

In fact, one man in a tool company told me outright: "You guys from Mack are no good and we don't want you."

During the months of April through June, Employment Service activity declined for a number of reasons: (1) Local offices in the central Mack area had few suitable jobs to offer. (2) Outside employers, due to past experience and rumor, were not in general interested in recruiting Mack workers. (3) Employment Service interviewers were frustrated by their repeated unsuccessful efforts to place Mack workers.

At the end of June there were seventy-six former Mack workers enrolled in training. The Middlesex County Vocational School in New Brunswick—located in the heart of the Mack-affected area—had sixty-five of these, and the Thomas A. Edison Vocational School in Elizabeth had eleven. All of these workers were training in machine trades to upgrade their skills. Of the sixty-five enrolled at the Middlesex School, only twenty-two completed the course and most of them were able to get jobs right away. The forty-three drop-outs gave the following reasons for their decision:

| Reason for Leaving | Number |
|---|---|
| Got job on own | 10 |
| Physical disability | 2 |
| Too old to learn | 8 |
| Afraid to change skill | 5 |
| Instruction too general | 3 |
| Would not pay $5.00 fee | 4 |
| No explanation | 11 |

Placement activity declined again in July, August, and September. As a result of this, the extra personnel who had been allocated to the local offices in the central Mack area were withdrawn and returned to their regular duties. The Mack files were still kept separate in the local offices and placements, when they were possible at all, were still made from them. From this point on, the Employment Service project consisted for the most part of research to try to find out why the project had not been as successful as anticipated in placing workers in new jobs, and also, to appraise the merits of the project as a method for handling future mass layoffs.

The NJSES had hoped that by concentrating on Mack placements, it would be able to find new jobs for former Mack employees rapidly and thereby minimize the impact of the shutdown. Yet no matter how active Employment Service interviewers were in calling-in former Mack workers, the number of placements remained fairly constant. The three most successful periods for placements were during the first few weeks after the shutdown, in the few weeks after the Christmas holidays, and in the spring as the unemployment compensation claims ran out and spring construction work began. Yet total placements were less than 400. Normally, the NJSES placed in a job one out of every twelve or thirteen applicants who responded to a call-in. If the normal ratio had held, about 900 Mack workers would have been placed in jobs. But of course this is not a fair basis of comparison. Because of the special project, Mack workers were called-in over and over again. One low-paying, distant job may have been offered to and refused by dozens of Mack workers.[11]

It is likely that the expectations of the NJSES were too high, and that in fact the project was relatively successful. Yet there is little doubt that the project could have been more successful than it was. Some of the reasons for its limited success were as follows:

First, the project was inadequately planned. Although the NJSES was aware of the impending Mack shutdown two years before it occurred, it did not develop plans for handling the situation until shortly before the closing. Moreover, much of the initial planning was done by personnel not experienced in local office operations.

The mass registration which took place at the union hall could have been a useful technique. In this particular project its usefulness was impaired by the fact that many inexperienced Employment Service personnel were used. As a result, many former Mack employees were given improper skill classifications, compounding placement difficulties and requiring later reclassification.

Moreover, a permanent Mack coordinator was not selected until weeks after the plant shutdown. Much of his time, and that of his labor analyst, was spent in preparing reports for consumption in Washington and in negotiating with Washington about what should

[11] Studies of other plant shutdowns have revealed that relatively few workers in a similar situation find jobs through the state Employment Service. For example, in the study by Myers and Shultz, only about 3 percent of the employed workers, following a plant shutdown, had found jobs through the state Employment Service. Data in the Mack case indicate that about 8 percent of the employed workers had found jobs through the NJSES. Charles A. Myers and G. P. Shultz, *Dynamics of a Labor Market: a Study of Labor Mobility, Job Satisfaction, and Company and Union Policies* (Prentice-Hall, 1951), pp. 98-99.

be included in these statistical studies. If the coordinator had been able to use more of his time to push the job development and placement activities, perhaps better results would have been achieved. The diversion of his energies was in part due to the fact that the NJSES is a state agency, but is wholly financed by the federal government.

A second reason for the limited success of the project was poor communication between the policy-makers and those charged with carrying out policies. It was apparent to me that there was considerable mistrust between the office of the Commissioner of Labor and Industry (policy-makers) on the one hand and the NJSES and its field staff (policy implementers) on the other. As a result, the Commissioner's office lacked an understanding of local office problems and the NJSES was unable to carry out policies quickly and effectively.

Other reasons for the limited success of the project included the attitude of the Mack workers themselves and employer resistance to hiring them—topics discussed in detail above.

The Employment Service's principal alternative to the special-project approach was to treat the workers laid off by the plant closing just as they did other unemployed persons. The people best qualified to evaluate the special project were the Employment Service personnel who worked on it. Using a special questionnaire, I surveyed the Employment Service personnel. Of the thirty-five people sent questionnaires, twenty-nine responded. When asked whether or not they favored handling future mass layoffs in a similar way, the result was:

| Should the "Special Project" Technique Be Used in the Future? | Number of Employment Service Respondents |
|---|---|
| No | 22 |
| Yes | 3 |
| Partially | 2 |
| Do not know | 1 |
| No answer | 1 |

One reason for this negative reaction was the fact that the special project disrupted the normal duties of the Employment Service. Twenty-six respondents said this was so; only two took the opposite view.

It is clear that the number of Employment Service staff members used on the project and the number of call-ins was disproportionate to the number of placements. Moreover, the maintenance of separate records for Mack workers and the necessity of sending weekly reports to the central Mack coordinator placed an extra administrative burden on the local offices.

From October 1961 to June 1962, the Mack project cost the NJSES more than $75,000. Over $40,000 of this can be attributed directly to special requirements of the project. This large expenditure of time and money resulted in only about 350 hirings of Mack workers. The most pertinent question—how many former Mack workers would have been hired and at what rate if there had been no special project—cannot be answered, nor can the number of losses of hirings of non-Mack workers as a result of the Employment Service's concentration on Mack workers be determined. In spite of its shortcomings, I believe the project to have been a useful experiment. Although it was hampered by inadequate planning and communication and by the specific problems associated with Mack workers, it was a qualified success. The mass registration technique employed at the outset proved to be a useful method of relieving the burden on the local offices. Moreover, the project demonstrated the need for more effective counseling of workers regarding the realities of the job market and for federal retraining programs which were not available at that time.

*Summary of Survey Findings*

The principal findings of the survey of workers who remained in New Jersey when the Mack plant moved are presented below. Following this summary, an econometric model is used to explain the workers' re-employment experience.

A random sample of survey respondents in New Jersey was selected in July and August 1962, and classified into six groups on the basis of employment experience between the shutdown and the day respondents were interviewed. These classes are listed in Table 2.

At the time of the survey, nine to ten months after the shutdown, 64 percent of the respondents were back at work, 23 percent were unemployed but seeking work, and the rest were out of the labor force or waiting to transfer to the new plant.[12]

[12] For tables showing detailed survey results, see Appendix A.

**TABLE 2. Employment Experience of Workers Who Remained in New Jersey Nine to Ten Months After the Shutdown**

| Category | Number | Percent |
|---|---|---|
| 1. Out of work for entire period | 71 | 19 |
| 2. Unemployed at time of survey but held a job for a while | 15 | 4 |
| 3. Employed at time of survey after more than two weeks of unemployment | 185 | 50 |
| 4. Employed within two weeks after the shutdown | 51 | 14 |
| 5. Out of the labor force | 37 | 10 |
| 6. Awaiting transfer to the new plant[a] | 8 | 2 |
| Total | 367 | 100 |

Source: Interviews with random sample of former Mack workers.
[a] Nine other respondents were awaiting transfer, but they had taken temporary jobs and were placed in category 3.

Of the 251 respondents in the survey who were employed or had been employed at some time since the shutdown, sixty-two had held two jobs, twelve had held three jobs, and two had held four jobs. The industrial distribution of these new jobs reveals that although most of them were in manufacturing, only a small number were in the Mack-related field of aircraft and auto manufacturing.

Wages in the new jobs did not compare at all favorably with those at Mack. Only 13 percent of the respondents were receiving $100 or less each week at Mack while 55 percent received $100 or less in their new jobs. Surprisingly enough, even with the lower wages in their new jobs, many former Mack workers were working over forty hours each week.

An analysis of commuting distances showed that for respondents with new jobs, the median round-trip distance from home to work was about five miles less for their new jobs than it had been for their jobs with Mack.

Most of the respondents with new jobs seem to have found them on their own initiative or through the help of a friend. When asked whether they considered their new jobs permanent, a large number indicated that they were looking for something better.

About 10 percent of the workers in the sample had withdrawn from the labor force. Most of them were older people who retired prematurely. Some had searched unsuccessfully for a job. Thirteen were over fifty-eight years old and were collecting a pension but claimed to be still in the labor force. After the shutdown, forty-two housewives went to work because of family financial need and eight others were looking for work at the time of the interview.

## An Econometric Analysis of Re-employment Experience

Why were some workers re-employed more rapidly than others? A multiple regression model is developed below to explain why some were still unemployed nine months after the shutdown and to account for the reasons others found jobs quickly. The variables selected for inclusion in the model were age, education, skill, em-

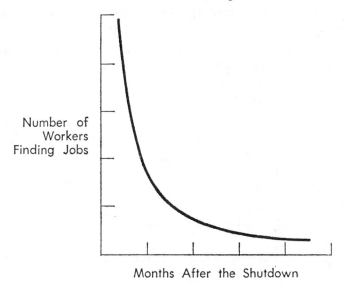

Months After the Shutdown

ployment impact on the area of residence in New Jersey, and sex-family status.

The dependent variable in the model was the number of months after the shutdown before which a worker found his next job. There was a problem in defining the dependent variable for those workers who were still unemployed at the time of the survey. This was resolved by assuming that since the survey was conducted nine to ten months after the shutdown, many of the workers who were unemployed at that time would find jobs in the months following the survey. The total number of months of unemployment experienced can be approximated by extrapolating the curve showing the number of workers returning to work each month. The curve looks much like a rectangular hyperbola, as shown above, and the approximate value for the average number of months of unemployment, found by spreading the experience of the seventy-one unemployed workers along the curve until they are exhausted and averaging the result, was thirteen months. The dependent variable thus took values between one and ten for employed workers and a value of thirteen for unemployed workers.

The age variable was the worker's age on July 1, 1962.

There were several choices available for the education variable. It could have been defined as the number of years of formal schooling, but it was clear from data on incomes by educational level that the important differences in educational experience were not differences in years of formal training but rather differences between some high school training and the holding of a high school diploma, and between some high school training and none at all. On the basis of this knowledge, educational attainment was classified into six categories, as follows:

(1) Under seven years.
(2) Seven to eleven years.
(3) High school diploma.
(4) Some college.
(5) College degree.
(6) More than four years of college.

For sex and family status, dummy variables representing six categories, as follows, were used:

(1) Single female.
(2) Married female whose husband was working.
(3) Married female whose husband was not working.
(4) Single male.
(5) Married male whose wife was working.
(6) Married male whose wife was not working.

Similarly, dummy variables were used for the six occupational-skill categories discussed earlier: professional, clerical and white collar, foremen, skilled, semiskilled, and unskilled.

To test for the effect of Mack's closing on the labor market of the area in which the worker lived, a variable defined as the num-

**TABLE 3. Summary of Final Regression Analysis of the Relation Between Months of Unemployment and Selected Variables**[a]

| Variable | Regression Coefficient | Standard Error |
|---|---|---|
| Age | .1514 | .0235 |
| Area impact | 57.3002 | 21.6100 |
| Education | −1.5809[b] | .6402 |
| Single female | −5.1254 | 1.9553 |
| Married female whose husband was not working | −2.7719 | .9371 |
| Married male whose wife was working | −4.7602 | 1.2669 |
| Single male | −2.7340 | 1.3194 |
| Married male whose wife was not working | −4.9338 | 1.2002 |
| Clerical-white collar worker | −1.2467 | 1.8054[c] |
| Foreman | −1.4032 | 2.3928[c] |
| Skilled | −3.9408 | 1.9133 |
| Semiskilled | −1.8621 | 1.7703[c] |
| Unskilled | −2.3444 | 1.8338 |

Source: Interviews with random sample of former Mack workers.
[a] $R = .5455$; $F = 9.64$; $S_y = 3.6340$; degrees of freedom = 296.
[b] Logarithmic form used.
[c] Not significant.

ber of Mack workers in the area as a percentage of the total nonagricultural employment in that area was introduced. The hypothesis to be tested was that the impact of the layoff was localized by area with workers living in the most affected areas experiencing longer periods of unemployment. The variable ranged from 2.66 percent in Plainfield to almost zero in some of the most distant areas.

The final regression equation is summarized in Table 3. As might be expected, age was the most important independent variable. Its coefficient was highly significant and accounted for about half of the explained variation by showing that the older a worker, the longer he was unemployed.

The area impact variable was positive and significant. A worker living in those labor market areas most affected by the shutdown experienced a longer period of unemployment than a worker living in the least affected areas. For example, a worker living in Plainfield took on the average one and a half months longer to find a job than a worker living in Jersey City.

Education had a negative coefficient which was statistically significant; the greater the educational attainment of the worker, the shorter was the frictional adjustment period.

The dummy variables representing sex and family status all had negative coefficients which were statistically significant. They may be ranked in the order of size of their coefficient—that is, from the shortest frictional period to the longest, as follows:

| Coefficient | Category |
|---|---|
| −5.1254 | Single female |
| −4.9338 | Married male whose wife was not working |
| −4.7602 | Married male whose wife was working |
| −2.7719 | Married female whose husband was not working |
| −2.7340 | Single male |
| In constant (6.8351) | Married female whose husband was working |

Those workers who occupied important positions as breadwinners in their families seemed to go back to work more quickly than others. Married males and single females were more successful in obtaining jobs than were those in other groups. Married females with working husbands were least successful in finding jobs. It may be that some of these women were really out of the labor force or only in the labor force to the extent that they would accept a job which met very rigid specifications. Although the coefficients shown above are statistically significant, the categories "single female" and "married female whose husband was not working" were based on few observations (six and three, respectively). In the case of a "married female whose husband was not working," the husband in fact re-entered the labor market after the shutdown in two of the three cases.

Several of the dummy variables representing six occupation-skill classifications were clearly not significant statistically, but it was not reasonable to omit some and retain others since they were mutually exclusive categories. According to an "F" test on the $R^2$ before and after the addition of these dummies, their total contribution to the explained variation is significant. If coefficients are ranked in the order of the length of the frictional period associated with each, from shortest to longest, the following order results:

| Coefficient | Category |
|---|---|
| −3.9408 | Skilled |
| −2.3444 | Unskilled |
| −1.8621 | Semiskilled |
| −1.4032 | Foremen |
| −1.2467 | Clerical-white collar |
| In constant (6.8351) | Professional |

The first category (skilled) is the only one which is clearly statistically significant. The fourth (foremen) and sixth (professional) categories each were based on only four observations.

Skilled workers had little difficulty in finding jobs. There were none in the sample who were unemployed at the time of the survey. The poor showing of clerical workers can be explained by the relatively large number of women in this group whose husbands were employed. It may be that these women, feeling little financial pressure, were only nominally in the labor force.

The unskilled workers were second to the skilled workers in re-employment success. Almost 80 percent of them were employed at the time of the survey. On the other hand, the semiskilled group, which was larger than any other in the Mack layoff, had the greatest problems of adjustment. Their wage expectations turned out to be unrealistic in light of the fact that their nontransferable skills were no longer of much value. As a result, their period of unemployment was the longest among the three categories of production workers.

The people best qualified to judge the Mack work force from the standpoint of skill were the Mack "specialists" of the New Jersey State Employment Service. These persons evaluated the skill level of the more than 2,800 former Mack employees who came to the service for help.[13] A questionnaire was mailed to the more than thirty "specialists" to determine their views. Many of these people were also interviewed personally, but it was felt that an anonymous questionnaire would give them an opportunity to express their opinions frankly without fear of censure or recrimination.

In the context of Employment Service assistance, a skilled machinist is versatile, can use precision instruments (such as a micrometer), and can read blueprints. A semiskilled worker can operate one machine well but lacks the versatility which the skilled worker possesses. Moreover, his specialized skill is frequently not transferable, since other industries may have no use for his narrow specialty. Thus a semiskilled worker is frequently not useful in small machine shops which require great versatility of a small number of workers who must perform a variety of tasks; such a worker may also be excluded from large industrial enterprises which cannot use his partic-

---

[13] See the above description of the NJSES special project for former Mack workers.

ular talent or which easily maintain a supply of workers with his talent.

According to the NJSES "specialists," the Mack workers were for the most part less skilled than non-Mack workers who held the same nominal job title. Of the twenty-three "specialists" who returned the questionnaire, twenty said that Mack workers were less skilled than non-Mack workers carrying the same job title, and three said they had the same level of skill. One "specialist" who came into contact with about 1,200 Mack people estimated that only three or four were skilled machinists, three or four were skilled tool and diemakers, and three were journeyman electricians, but that most "knew only one machine, couldn't read blueprints, use precision instruments, or make set-ups."

Obviously, a cross-section model of this kind leaves much unexplained variation. Some workers were fortunate and stumbled upon a job quickly; others did not. Some workers were naturally enthusiastic, energetic, and ambitious and through persistence found a job rapidly. Others were lethargic and indifferent. Detailed analysis of individuals of course revealed an enormous number of variables, many of them nonquantifiable. Among the many factors which could not be quantified and specifically included in the model, the most important were perhaps employer resistance to hiring former Mack employees (discussed above) and the attitudes of the workers themselves. The latter problem is discussed below.

It was impossible to evaluate quantitatively the importance of employer resistance to hiring Mack workers as an influence on the length of the frictional adjustment period of the workers. Perhaps it affected all workers equally and hence only the average rather than the relative adjustment period was changed. More likely, however, was the possibility that the workers most affected were those in the Plainfield and Highland Park areas where the impact of the shutdown was greatest. Employers were in many cases willing to hire one or several Mack workers but were often afraid to hire very many of them. This is perhaps one of the reasons for the significance of the area impact variable in the regression model, although certainly it is not a perfect representation of the problem.

## Wages in the New Jobs

The Mack workers who were re-employed after the shutdown in general received a considerably lower wage than they had re-

**TABLE 4. Median Gross Weekly Wages at Mack and in
New Jobs by Months of Unemployment**

| Months After Shutdown | Number Re-employed | Median Wage at Mack | Median Wage on New Job | New Wages as Percent of Mack Wages[a] |
|---|---|---|---|---|
| 1 | 60 | $141 | $94 | 77 |
| 2 | 21 | 122 | 92 | 78 |
| 3 | 27 | 133 | 87 | 73 |
| 4 | 20 | 139 | 101 | 72 |
| 5 | 27 | 134 | 95 | 71 |
| 6 | 25 | 130 | 87 | 63 |
| 7 | 28 | 145 | 90 | 62 |
| 8 | 17 | 131 | 70 | 56 |
| 9–10 | 16 | 134 | 87 | 72 |

Source: Interviews with random sample of former Mack workers.
[a] Median of the ratio computed for each individual.

ceived at Mack. Their median gross weekly wage at Mack had been
$137, but in the new job was only $85—a decrease of $52 per
week. Those who found jobs within six months after the shutdown
received a median wage of $93 per week, while those who took
over six months to find employment received only $80. Table 4
shows the number of months workers required to find new jobs and
the median pay in both former and new employment. Seventy-one
workers not re-employed at the time of the survey are excluded.
Their median wage at Mack was $134.

Relative to their wages at Mack, those who were re-employed
early seemed to fare best. Workers who were employed in the first
and second months after the shutdown received median wages
which were 77 percent and 78 percent, respectively, of their Mack
wages; those re-employed in the eighth month obtained new wages
which were only 56 percent of their Mack wages. After the second
month the median of the new wage as a percentage of the old declined steadily until the ninth month when it rose again sharply. The
mean ratio remained relatively constant for the first four months and
then fell consistently until the ninth month when it rose sharply. This
unexpected increase was related to the fact that the median age
dropped from forty-nine years in the eighth month to forty-three
years in the ninth month, and to the fact that median years of education rose from 8.2 in the eighth month to 11.2 in the ninth month.
As a result, this group received better wages. What remains unexplained is why, with comparative advantages of age and education,

they remained unemployed for such an extended period. Perhaps the group includes persons who waited in the hope of finding a superior job and eventually realized that they would not equal their Mack wage, or possibly this anomaly is a statistical peculiarity which resulted from the small sample of workers falling into this category.

## Worker Attitudes Toward Job-Seeking and Financial Security

In view of the high wages paid at Mack and the large separation payments which many workers received, one might have expected their job demands to be somewhat more selective than those of the average job-seeker in New Jersey. One of the purposes of this study was to examine worker attitudes toward job-seeking and to find out what influence, if any, separation payments and other payments had on the search for a new job.

When asked how the Mack employees compared with non-Mack employees in job demands, the twenty-three Employment Service "specialists" who felt qualified to answer the question found Mack workers on the whole to be more selective. In fact, twenty-two believed the former Mack employees were more selective than other applicants they had interviewed; only one "specialist" felt their selectiveness was the same as that of non-Mack workers, and none asserted that they were less selective.

According to the "specialists," the most important variables in the Mack workers' job demands were distance to work and type of job, in that order. One "specialist" cited as an example a case in which thirty-five former Mack people were called in by the NJSES for consideration as trainees at a large steel company, located about twenty miles away, which offered a starting wage of $2.49 an hour plus bonus. Only seven of the thirty-five accepted a referral by the NJSES to this plant's employment office. Six of the seven passed all tests and were offered jobs. Five refused the job; one accepted but quit after two months.

Here are some of the comments by the "specialists" on the question of selectivity:

The majority did not really want to work.

Their demands were the same as any other person who did not want to work.

They held out for jobs near home prior to exhaustion of unemployment compensation.

The older workers were less selective than the younger.

They felt they were worth more than they really were.

Their demands were completely unrealistic.

Non-Mack workers expected a fair rate of pay for their job experience; Mack workers' demands were exorbitant.

The difference between Mack and non-Mack workers was in degree of motivation or desire for work, not selectivity.

The attitude of the average Mack worker was not what he had to offer an employer, but what he felt he should receive in the way of compensation.

Mack employees with less than five years of service were more realistic than employees with higher seniority.

Mack workers asked for more pay for longer potential commuting distances; non-Mack workers made no such demand.

Most Mack workers were called in at least once by the NJSES regarding a job opening and many were called in several times. This is not to suggest that all or even most persons called in and referred would have been hired, but most Mack workers, after hearing the description of the job at the Employment Service office, simply refused to pursue the matter further.

When asked whether the Mack workers' job demands had changed over time, nineteen of the twenty-three "specialists" agreed that they had. Several commented as follows on the change in attitudes:

Their demands changed but not enough to make placement easier.

They substituted increased emphasis on security and union protection for wage demands.

They accepted lower wages and greater distances.

There was a surge of new demands when TEC (extended unemployment compensation) benefits seemed likely.

Their attitudes didn't change until their UC (unemployment compensation) claims began to run out.

By the time their attitudes changed, so had employers' attitudes.

Mack workers who had experienced some unemployment were asked in the survey if they had established a definite, standard, acceptable wage and round-trip commuting distance at the time they first started looking for a job, and what these standards were. The responses indicated that 73 percent had some minimum acceptable wage in mind, and that 51 percent had established some maximum acceptable commuting distance. A large number of respondents to these two questions said that they were willing to accept any "reasonable" wage and commute a "reasonable" distance but refused to be more specific. Among all the respondents questioned, 33 percent had wage standards in excess of $2.50 an hour. Only 31 percent of those asked were willing to commute over twenty miles daily (round trip). Since the major demand areas were over twenty miles away, this placed important restrictions on their availability. A number of respondents also indicated that they had definite standards regarding the type of work they would accept.

Those workers who were still unemployed at the time of the survey were asked whether or not they had changed their standards at all since they began looking for work. The results indicated that 70 percent of the unemployed workers had in some way altered their standards. The largest group were willing to accept lower pay, a small group were willing to accept greater distance, and a few in-

**TABLE 5. Changes in Standards of Unemployed Workers During Their Search for a Job, After Nine to Ten Months**

| Change in Standard | Number | Percent |
|---|---|---|
| No change | 26 | 30 |
| Willing to accept: | | |
| Lower pay | 26 | 30 |
| Greater distance | 12 | 14 |
| Different type of work | 15 | 17 |
| Anything I can get | 6 | 7 |
| Other | 1 | 1 |
| Total | 86 | 100 |

Source: Interviews with random sample of former Mack workers.
Note: Details may not add to totals due to rounding.

**TABLE 6.** Number of Respondents Who Admitted Refusing Jobs,
Ranked by Month First Employed After the Shutdown

| Months Prior to First Re-employment | Total Respondents | Number Who Refused One Job or More | Total Jobs Refused |
|---|---|---|---|
| 3 | 27 | 6 | 23 |
| 4 | 20 | 6 | 21 |
| 5 | 27 | 7 | 19 |
| 6 | 25 | 13 | 31 |
| 7 | 28 | 13 | 36 |
| 8 | 17 | 6 | 12 |
| 9–10 | 14 | 2 | 9 |
| Unemployed | 71 | 23 | 39 |

Source: Interviews with random sample of former Mack workers.

dicated that they would take anything they could get. Table 5 summarizes the ways in which the standards of workers unemployed at the time of the survey had changed since the shutdown.

Unpublished data from the NJSES reveal that many workers were offered one or more jobs through the NJSES which they refused. Respondents were asked if they had received any job offers on the basis of their own initiative. The answers to this question had to be treated rather skeptically, since workers may have been reluctant to admit that they had turned down several jobs. On the other hand, some might have been ashamed to admit they had no offers.[14] With these limitations in mind, it was found that many of the workers admitted that they could have been employed sooner if they had been willing to accept the conditions of the job offered to them. As Table 6 shows, of the seventy-one continuously unemployed workers, twenty-three admitted that they had turned down at least one job, and the total number of jobs admittedly turned down by this group was thirty-nine. The 132 respondents who were unemployed for at least six months admitted turning down ninety-six jobs.

*The Influence of Separation Payments*

In the argument concerning employment thus far, age, education, skill, family status, and area of residence have been discussed as the important variables affecting the employment of Mack workers.

[14] In order to insure maximum accuracy in answers to this question, the interviewer probed deeply into at least one of the offers which each respondent mentioned.

All of these were logical and perhaps even predictable variables in the employment picture. Two nonquantifiable factors—employer resistance and worker attitudes—have also been discussed.

The data have shown that as the length of time taken to find a job increased, the rate of pay in the new job declined relative to the pay at Mack. There is considerable evidence from the NJSES records and from the survey that some jobs were available, but that they were less desirable than former positions at Mack either in terms of pay or commuting distance. It could be argued, therefore, that since the younger, better educated, more skilled workers were better able to match their Mack wages and enjoyed less financial security from separation pay, they returned to work more quickly. On the other hand, since the older, less educated, less skilled workers were being offered jobs at very low rates compared with their former Mack wages, and since their separation pay and pensions gave them greater financial security, this group may have waited longer in the hope that better prospects for employment would develop.

The Employment Service "specialists" had a number of interesting comments on this question. When asked: "What importance do you attach to unemployment compensation and separation pay in the [Mack] workers' reluctance to accept jobs?" eight of twenty-eight indicated they thought them "very important"; seventeen found them "important"; and three, of "moderate importance." The comments recorded by these "specialists" include:

Separation pay and unemployment compensation permit a worker to shop for a job.

A worker will obviously not work when he receives $90 a week to sit home.

Unemployment compensation and separation pay make workers hold to unrealistic standards.

The Mack workers' attitude was: "I don't have to rush; I'll look around." There is a human reluctance to accept jobs at reduced rates of pay unless economic need compels it.

The financial condition of any job applicant is reflected in his attitude. Unemployment compensation and separation pay make people reluctant to accept jobs as soon as they should.

Unemployment compensation alone or separation pay alone is not bad, but both together curb the availability for work.

Unemployment compensation and separation pay made workers refuse to accept marginal jobs.

Unemployment compensation and separation pay prevented workers from seeing the necessity to go to work.

Workers could not afford to be as selective without unemployment compensation and separation pay.

These payments do not in themselves result in worker reluctance. They do, however, postpone economic pressure to accept unsuitable or substandard jobs. Large payments do temporarily reduce the availability for and desire to work by giving a feeling of security and independence.

Further evidence was provided by Mack workers themselves. Near the end of the interview, those Mack workers who had been continuously unemployed were asked a very direct question: "If you had not received unemployment compensation and separation pay, do you think you would have been more likely to accept a job which was undesirable in terms of pay or commuting distance from your home?" Of the seventy-one workers who were asked this question, forty-eight said "yes"; fourteen, "no"; four, "maybe"; and five, "do not know." Since the question was admittedly a leading one, the comments of the respondents are more interesting. Those who answered "yes" to the question made the following comments:

My wife was pregnant at the time; I needed money.
I would have had to take night work or a low-paying job.
I would have taken anything.
I would have been in a desperate position; I would have taken anything.
The absence of these (unemployment compensation and separation pay) would have created extreme hardship.
I would have tried a little harder to get a job or taken a low-paying one.
I wouldn't have taken an undesirable job right away, but later on I would have.
I would have found some kind of job—any kind.
I would have taken one of the jobs I refused.
When a man is desperate anything can happen.
I would never ask for welfare as long as I can walk.
I'd have grabbed the first job available.
I'd have looked for a nonskilled job.
A rat will come out of his hole when he is starving.

Those who answered "no" to the question commented:

I would have gone on relief.
It wouldn't pay—I'm used to well-paying jobs.
Nothing worthwhile paywise was available.
I would have gone to live with relatives or perhaps gotten married (a woman).
I'd have lived off my wife's salary.
I would have used my savings.
I would have made my own jobs—doing odds and ends.
Even with the big benefits I would have taken any job that came along.
My husband works.
Any job I take must pay well.
I would have expected more help from my children or gone on welfare.
I just can't see working for $1.50 an hour.
I wouldn't rush to another job regardless.
I can live with my parents. I have no financial problems.

Those who answered "maybe" to the question commented:

My husband is the breadwinner; it doesn't matter.
I just would have managed as best I could.

Those who answered "don't know" to the question commented:

I'll jump that fence when I come to it.
I didn't have any offers so it doesn't matter.


Now it must be realized that one of the purposes of unemployment compensation, and of separation pay as well, is to give a worker who is laid off time to find a new job and to insure that he will not be forced to take substandard employment. The $50 a week which most Mack workers received in unemployment compensation represented on the average only about 35 to 40 percent of their gross weekly wage, though a somewhat higher percentage of their net wage, since unemployment compensation benefits are not taxable. Certainly they could not have maintained their previous standards of living on this amount.

Few would claim that $50 a week for twenty-six weeks could have a long-run retarding influence on the search for a job, but with the addition of rather substantial severance payments and pension benefits, one could argue that the frictional period may well have been lengthened. Yet if the frictional period was lengthened by

**TABLE 7. Separation Payments: Mean, Standard Deviation, and Range**

| Age Group | Mean | Standard Deviation | Range | Number of Observations |
|---|---|---|---|---|
| 35–44 | $1,172 | $1,497 | $0–6,100 | 107 |
| 45–57 | 2,493 | 1,935 | 0–8,720 | 91 |
| All | 1,338 | 1,690 | 0–8,720 | 310 |

Source: Interviews with random sample of former Mack workers.

such payments, this fact should be demonstrable by extending the multiple regression model previously developed to include separation pay. The mean separation payment received by the 310 sample workers was $1,338; the standard deviation was $1,690; and the range was from $0 to $8,720. Since most of the workers were eligible for the maximum unemployment compensation payment, this factor was treated as constant.

While the evidence from this analysis is not conclusive, due to multicollinearity between age and separation pay, it appears that separation pay was not an important variable in the job search.

The addition of separation pay to the regression model[15] discussed in a previous section contributed virtually nothing to the explained variation in the length of the frictional period and resulted in a regression coefficient of $-0.0000$ with a standard error of $0.0001$. The major problem was the high correlation between age and the amount of separation pay.

I attempted to eliminate the multicollinearity problem by fitting a regression line across an age group, thereby constraining the influence of age as a variable. As Table 7 shows, in the group between ages forty-five and fifty-seven there was still a high correlation between age and separation pay. The thirty-five to forty-four age group presented a different picture, however. While the correlation between age and separation pay was eliminated, separation pay did not appear to be related to the length of the frictional adjustment period.

Since the total separation pay received by a worker was apparently unrelated to the length of his frictional adjustment period, it was felt that perhaps the importance of this payment varied with the family size. That is, it would seem that a family with five children should have reacted differently from a single man or a married

[15] Thus creating a new variable, $X_{14}$, the amount of separation pay in dollars received by each worker.

man with no children. Separation pay was thus deflated by family size by determining the amount of separation pay per family member, and this new variable was introduced in the regression model. This was tried using the forty-five to fifty-four age group where the simple correlation between separation pay and the length of the frictional period was positive but insignificant. The simple correlation between separation pay per family member and the length of the frictional period was only 0.0088, the regression coefficient was positive, and the $F$ ratio very insignificant (0.01).

Another possibility was that the influence of separation pay varied with the skill status of the worker. It seemed possible that workers with different skills had different job aspirations. This hypothesis was tested for semiskilled workers in the thirty-five to forty-four age group, but the correlation was also insignificant.

Still another possibility and perhaps the most logical was that the entire financial position of a worker was the important variable. It could have been that separation pay and unemployment compensation were important only when considered along with the size of a worker's savings, number of other family members employed, real estate holdings, outstanding debt, and other financial considerations. Unfortunately, no data were available to extend the analysis in this way.

The conclusion is uncertain. Comments by NJSES "specialists" presented earlier indicated that separation pay was important, but the regression model did not verify this. The "specialists" may have been influenced by the general frustration created by the Employment Service's special Mack project. It was necessary to blame the repeated refusal of jobs by Mack workers on something. The separation payments received by the workers were widely publicized and a few unrepresentative cases where Mack workers had admittedly refused jobs because of their financial security became a topic of discussion in Employment Service offices throughout the state. It became generally accepted among Employment Service personnel that the reason for the difficulty in placing Mack workers in new jobs was the extraordinary combination of unemployment compensation and separation pay.

On the other hand, the regression model was hampered by multicollinearity problems, and the results were not convincing.[16]

[16] In the case of a plant shutdown in 1929 studied by Clague and Cooper,

What effects, if any, can then be attributed to the series of payments which Mack workers received? Earlier it was pointed out that a number of workers had retired prematurely from the labor force. Although many of them would have had difficulty finding a job due to their age, no doubt many would have remained in the labor force if they had not received double early retirement payments. Moreover, among the unemployed workers there were a number of women whose husbands were employed and who collected unemployment compensation for twenty-six weeks. It is very possible, since ten of the fifteen women in the sample fell into this category, that they were really out of the job market during this period, although this cannot be proved. On the other hand, a few of the workers used their severance pay to set up businesses of their own and as a result may have gone back to work before they could have had they faced the normal processes of the labor market.

Throughout the interviews, the workers expressed several ideas over and over again. One was that a man needs to work and is unhappy unless he is working. A second was that separation pay is no substitute for the benefits of seniority which are lost when a worker is forced to change jobs after many years of service with the same company. I believe personally that most people wanted to work and that separation payments were viewed by workers as partial though inadequate compensation for the losses incurred as a result of having to start over again in some other job.

It would appear that no case of much substance can be made against separation pay and unemployment compensation in the readjustment of the workers.

## The Financial Adjustment of Mack Workers During Unemployment

In order to find out what financial adjustments Mack workers made to unemployment, a subsample was selected for an extended interview. During this extended interview the workers were asked to

---

dismissal wages ranging from $137 to $2,088 with a median of $402 and an average of $514 were paid to only about one-seventh the total workers. The authors compared, as a group, the workers who received payments with those who did not and found their employment experience to be similar. Ewan Clague, Walter J. Cooper, and E. Wight Bakke, *After the Shutdown* (Yale University Press, 1934), pp. 36-39.

recall their income and expenditures during their last month of employment, the last month during which they collected unemployment compensation, and the month prior to the interview, providing they had not returned to work.[17]

*Kinds of Financial Adjustment*

The Mack workers made many kinds of financial adjustment to unemployment. Among these were:

(1)  Cutting expenditures on some kinds of items;
(2)  Making fewer installment purchases;
(3)  Borrowing less;
(4)  Postponing the payment of bills;
(5)  Postponing the planned purchase of some items;
(6)  Canceling life insurance;
(7)  Dissaving;
(8)  Selling assets;
(9)  Moving in with relatives or bringing relatives into the household.

Seventy-seven of the one hundred respondents indicated that they had cut some expenses during their period of unemployment. The number of respondents who mentioned cuts in various categories of expenditure was as follows:

| Category of Cut in Expenditure | Number of Respondents |
|---|---|
| Food | 39 |
| Clothing | 47 |
| Furniture and appliances | 31 |
| Recreation | 67 |
| Travel and vacations | 58 |
| Medical and dental | 18 |

Sixty of the one hundred respondents in the subsample indicated that during the previous three years of employment they sometimes had purchased items on the installment plan. The most frequently mentioned items were cars (thirty-three), large appliances (thirty-two), and furniture (twenty-nine). Clothing (four)

[17] For a complete discussion of the methodology of this part of the study see Appendix C.

and small appliances (three) were also listed. During the period of unemployment, only eleven respondents made installment purchases. The distribution of items purchased by this group was as follows:

| Category of Installment Purchase | Number of Respondents |
|---|---|
| Car or truck | 2 |
| Clothing | 4 |
| Large appliance | 2 |
| Small appliance | 3 |
| Furniture | 2 |
| Other | 3 |

Forty-nine respondents indicated that unemployment had forced them to postpone purchasing some items which they had definitely planned to buy. As shown below, nineteen of the respondents postponed purchasing automobiles, and seventeen postponed purchasing large appliances (costing over $50).

| Item Postponed | Number of Respondents |
|---|---|
| Car | 19 |
| Clothing | 4 |
| Large appliances | 17 |
| Small appliances | 3 |
| Furniture | 12 |
| Home repairs | 8 |
| House | 5 |

Eighty-nine of the respondents already owned automobiles. Twenty-one stated that they had borrowed money at some time during their last three years of employment. Only thirteen borrowed during the period of unemployment.

Eight respondents admitted that they had sometimes postponed paying bills during their last three years of employment. Twenty admitted postponing the payment of bills during the months of unemployment.

At the time of the shutdown, ninety-three of the one hundred respondents had some life insurance. During the unemployed period, thirty-six either canceled or lost part or all of it. Many had purchased life insurance policies through the Mack Company and decided to discontinue their policies when the plant closed.

Mack workers in general were very thrifty. All but five of the respondents in the subsample indicated that they had some savings at the time of the shutdown and before separation payments were made. Eighty-three families were forced to use some savings for expenses during the unemployed period. As shown below, only seventeen had exhausted their savings by the time of the survey, while forty-three had used up 50 percent or less.

| Amount of Savings Spent | Number of Respondents |
|---|---|
| Less than half | 28 |
| More than half | 20 |
| All | 17 |
| Just half | 15 |
| Do not know | 3 |
| None | 12 |
| Had no savings | 5 |
| Total | 100 |

No attempt was made during the interviews to secure information on the total savings or assets of each respondent since these were items of a very personal nature. However, one respondent volunteered the information that his savings account was $6,000 at the time of the shutdown, and another respondent stated that his was $4,000. Although over 3,000 workers were affected by the shutdown, only a few were reported on the welfare rolls in the area.

A few respondents indicated that they had postponed going to a doctor or a dentist while unemployed, but they also admitted that they had often postponed these visits when employed.

Nine respondents reported selling some belonging, aside from trade-ins. Two sold their automobiles, while others sold rugs, paintings, and a camera.

Three families had moved since the shutdown. Two had moved in with relatives in order to cut expenses, and two families had taken in relatives for the same reason.

Thus the most important kinds of financial adjustment appeared to be curtailment or postponement of purchases of major items, especially those normally bought on the installment plan. Expenditures for automobiles, houses, large appliances, and furniture, as well as expenditures for home repairs, were curtailed or postponed according to many respondents. A large percentage of respondents also indicated they had cut expenditures for recreation, travel and vacations, and clothing.

## Characteristics of the Workers Selected for Extended Interview

Although there were one hundred respondents in the subsample selected for the extended interview, the detailed financial data for eighteen of them were unusable. The subsample with acceptable financial data had a median age of forty-nine years. Over 50 percent of the respondents had no children under eighteen years, and 91 percent had two or fewer. About 75 percent were homeowners. Most (80 percent) were semiskilled and unskilled workers, although thirteen (16 percent) were clerical, of whom eleven were women. The subsample had a median formal education of ten years, had worked for Mack on the average (median) for sixteen years, and had received a median gross weekly wage while with Mack of $143.

During their unemployed period, fifty-nine of the eighty-two workers in the subsample received median separation pay of $1,000 each; fifteen collected social security; seventy-eight received unemployment compensation of $50 a week for twenty-six weeks, and three received lesser amounts of supplementary unemployment benefits—in most cases $30 a week for thirty-nine weeks.

## Income Loss During Unemployment[18]

As Table 8 shows, the total family income of unemployed Mack workers dropped after the plant shutdown, but in the sixth month of unemployment was still about 60 percent of income in the employed month for the median family.[19] However, for the group still unemployed after eight to nine months, median family income dropped to 35 percent of what it had been during the selected month of employment.

Families in which the respondent was not the head of the

[18] The method of analysis used in this section is elaborated in Appendix C. The method is simply to compare family income with expenditures in three months—the last month of employment, the last month of unemployment in which the respondent collected unemployment compensation (the sixth month), and the month of unemployment prior to the interview (the eighth or ninth month).

[19] Total family income includes take-home wages and salaries of all family members who pool their income plus income from all other sources including unemployment compensation and supplementary unemployment benefits.

**TABLE 8. Total Family Income of Mack Workers from All Sources During Months of Employment and Unemployment**[a]

| Monthly Income Range | Number of Mack Families in Income Range in Employed Month | | Number of Mack Families in Income Range in: | |
|---|---|---|---|---|
| | | | Sixth Unemployed Month | Ninth Unemployed Month |
| $0 | 0 | (0) | 1    (0) | (5) |
| 1–200 | 0 | (0) | 20   (7) | (16) |
| 201–300 | 1 | (0) | 12   (5) | (8) |
| 301–400 | 4 | (1) | 17   (11) | (8) |
| 401–500 | 16 | (9) | 13   (8) | (2) |
| 501–600 | 23 | (9) | 9    (6) | (6) |
| 601–700 | 14 | (9) | 6    (6) | (1) |
| 701–800 | 9 | (8) | 3    (3) | (0) |
| 801–900 | 5 | (3) | 1    (0) | (0) |
| 901+ | 10 | (7) | 0    (0) | (0) |
| All Ranges | 82 | (46) | 82   (46) | (46) |

Source: Interviews with random sample of former Mack workers.
[a] Figures in parentheses represent the forty-six respondents who were unemployed for the full nine-to-ten-month period from the shutdown to the time of the survey. Figures not in parentheses represent the eighty-two workers in the subsample for whom valid data were available. See Appendix C for the exact months included.

household experienced the least decline in family income and the highest median income at all stages. Among this group of families, median income dropped from $775 in the employed month to $633 in the sixth month after the shutdown. Among families in this group whose former Mack worker was unemployed for the entire period, median income dropped from $800 in the employed month to $667 in the sixth month, and to $500 in the eighth or ninth month.

Among the several classifications of family income, take-home pay from wages and salaries showed the greatest decline during the unemployed period. In the two surveyed months of unemployment —the sixth and ninth—58 percent and 50 percent, respectively, of the families had no income from wages and salaries.

As shown in Table 9, family income from other work, odd jobs, or profits from business showed a minor increase during the unemployed months among those families which received such income. Naturally, income from unemployment compensation and supplementary benefits increased substantially in the unemployed months. Most families received $200 during April from unemployment compensation and some received additional help from supplementary unemployment benefits. In July, 76 percent of the unemployed

**TABLE 9. Family Income of Mack Workers from Nonwage and Nonbenefit Sources During Months of Employment and Unemployment**[a]

| Monthly Income Range | Number of Families in Income Range in Employed Month | Number of Families in Income Range in: | |
|---|---|---|---|
| | | Sixth Unemployed Month | Ninth Unemployed Month |
| $0 | 74 (40) | 62 (31) | (29) |
| 1–50 | 4 (4) | 4 (3) | (2) |
| 51–100 | 1 (0) | 2 (1) | (3) |
| 101–150 | 1 (1) | 4 (3) | (2) |
| 151–200 | 2 (1) | 8 (6) | (8) |
| 201–250 | 0 (0) | 1 (1) | (1) |
| 251–300 | 0 (0) | 0 (0) | (0) |
| 301–350 | 0 (0) | 0 (0) | (0) |
| 351+ | 0 (0) | 1 (1) | (1) |
| All Ranges | 82 (46) | 82 (46) | (46) |

Source: Interviews with random sample of former Mack workers.
[a] See note to Table 8 for explanation of numbers within and without parentheses.

no longer received unemployment compensation or supplementary unemployment benefits, and of those still collecting, most were receiving income only from the latter source. Family income from cash gifts, pensions, social security, rent, and other nonwage and nonbenefit sources also increased during the unemployed period. During the month of employment, 90 percent of the families had no income from these sources, while during the sixth month of unemployment only 76 percent had no such income. Among workers for whom complete data were available for the three-month comparison, the percentages were 87 percent in the employed month, 67 percent in the sixth month of unemployment, and 63 percent in the ninth month of unemployment.

Many of the families in the survey included several working members. During September, before the shutdown, 40 percent of the families had some income which was contributed by a family member other than the respondent. This proportion rose to 50 percent during April. Of course, part or all of this change may have been due to seasonal factors.

Since family income declined as the period of unemployment lengthened, living expenses had to be met from other sources, mainly from savings. During the survey month of employment, 77 percent of the families were able to add something to their savings.

The median family addition to savings during this month was $54; only 6 percent of the families dissaved. During the months of unemployment over 70 percent of the families used up some of their accumulated savings.

### Expenditure Change During Unemployment

Mack workers made a downward adjustment in family expenditures which increased as the period of unemployment grew longer. Table 10 shows the change in total family expenditures during the three survey months. The median total family expenditure for all eighty-two workers for whom acceptable financial data were available declined from $307 in the employed month to $297 in the sixth month of unemployment. The decline was much less than might have been expected. For the forty-six workers who were eligible for the three-month study, median total family expenditures declined from $317 in the employed month to $304 in the sixth month of unemployment and to $277 in the eighth or ninth month of unemployment. This amounted to a total cut for the median family of $40 a month. The greatest decline in expenditures came after the exhaustion of unemployment compensation benefits.

Both for purposes of the interviews and for analysis, it was convenient to divide family expenditures into two classes—recurrent and unusual. Recurrent expenditures were those which generally occurred regularly every month, including rent or mortgage payments, utilities, medical and dental care, food, payments on items bought before the beginning of the month and on money borrowed, and payments for the support of people not living with the respondent. Unusual expenditures were defined as those made for items

**TABLE 10. Median Total Monthly Expenditures by Family Status[a]**

| Family Status | Month of Employment | Month of Unemployment | |
|---|---|---|---|
| | | Sixth | Ninth |
| All Families | $307 ($317) | $297 ($304) | ($277) |
| Married: | | | |
|     Headed by Worker | $300 ($289) | $283 ($283) | ($262) |
|     Not Headed by Worker | $398 ($417) | $397 ($406) | ($262) |
| Single | Too few observations to compute median | | |

Source: Interviews with random sample of former Mack workers.
[a] See note to Table 8 for explanation of numbers within and without parentheses.

**TABLE 11. Total Recurrent Family Expenditures During Months of Employment and Unemployment**[a]

| Expenditure Range | Number of Families in Income Range in Employed Month | | Number of Families in Income Range in: | | |
|---|---|---|---|---|---|
| | | | Sixth Unemployed Month | | Ninth Unemployed Month |
| $0–100 | 2 | (2) | 2 | (2) | (2) |
| 101–150 | 4 | (2) | 4 | (3) | (4) |
| 151–200 | 7 | (5) | 11 | (7) | (9) |
| 201–250 | 11 | (4) | 20 | (10) | (8) |
| 251–300 | 26 | (12) | 22 | (9) | (8) |
| 301–350 | 14 | (10) | 12 | (8) | (8) |
| 351–400 | 4 | (2) | 6 | (5) | (2) |
| 401–450 | 4 | (1) | 4 | (2) | (3) |
| 451+ | 10 | (8) | 1 | (0) | (2) |
| All Ranges | 82 | (46) | 82 | (46) | (46) |
| Median[b] | $277 ($276) | | $256 ($256) | | ($248) |

Source: Interviews with random sample of former Mack workers.
[a] See note to Table 8 for explanation of numbers within and without parentheses.
[b] Medians computed from ungrouped data.

like insurance, taxes, repairs, and major appliances bought for cash —all of which occur only infrequently. It is important to recognize that no attempt was made to account for every dollar spent by the respondent. For example, travel, recreation, clothing (unless over $50 per month), laundry, personal items like haircuts, cosmetics, and so forth, and contributions to charitable organizations or churches, were omitted. Therefore, total expenditures were considerably understated for each month. But it is known from the experience of previous expenditure surveys that respondents have difficulty remembering dollar amounts for these omitted items, and hence information about them was not solicited.[20] I did, however, ask respondents whether they spent more, less, or the same amount for these items after they became unemployed than they had before. Other studies have shown that between 60 and 65 percent of family expenditures normally are allocated for the items for which dollar amounts were secured in my survey.

Table 11 shows the distribution of total recurrent expenditures during the three survey months. For the two-month survey the

[20] See, for example, Bureau of Labor Statistics, *Survey of Consumer Expenditures in 1950.*

median fell from $277 in the month of employment to $256 in the month of unemployment; and for the three-month study the median declined from $276 in the employed month to $256 and $248 in the sixth and ninth months of unemployment, respectively.

As expected, expenditures for rent, mortgage payments, and utilities changed very little. Family expenditures for medical and dental care actually showed an increase during the unemployed months, suggesting that these items were not responsive to fluctuations in income. Payments for support of persons not living with the family, payments on installment purchases made before the beginning of the month, and payments on money borrowed all showed a small decline in the months of unemployment.

Family expenditures for food showed a moderate decline in the sixth month of unemployment. The median family expenditure for food to be consumed at home declined from $138 in the employed month to $126 in the sixth month of unemployment. However, in the three-month comparison, expenditures on food for consumption at home showed little decline from the sixth month of unemployment to the eighth and ninth months. Similarly, expenditures for meals and snacks eaten away from home showed rather substantial declines in the sixth month of unemployment but little additional decline in the eighth and ninth months.

Unusual expenditures, shown in Table 12, seemed to be less closely related to unemployment than were recurrent expenditures. During the sixth month of unemployment, total unusual expenditures among all families were actually larger than they had been in the employed month, although more than half of the respondents in each case had no unusual expenditures. The distribution of respondents for the three-month study also showed an increase in unusual expenditures during the sixth month of unemployment; however, these expenditures declined during the eighth and ninth months.

There were several reasons for the continued high level of expenditures during the sixth month of unemployment. For most workers, this happened to be the month of April, the deadline for paying federal income taxes and also the month when real estate taxes in many New Jersey communities are paid. Fourteen families paid taxes during April, while only four did so in September. There were also more insurance payments which fell due in April than in September, more autos were in need of repair, and more wedding

**TABLE 12. Total Unusual Family Expenditures During
Months of Employment and Unemployment[a]**

| Expenditure Range | Number of Families in Expenditure Range in Employed Month | Number of Families in Expenditure Range in: | |
|---|---|---|---|
| | | Sixth Unemployed Month | Ninth Unemployed Month |
| $0 | 58 (32) | 43 (20) | (29) |
| 1–25 | 5 (3) | 2 (0) | (5) |
| 26–50 | 5 (1) | 9 (6) | (6) |
| 51–75 | 2 (2) | 9 (7) | (3) |
| 76–100 | 2 (2) | 6 (5) | (0) |
| 101–150 | 3 (2) | 3 (1) | (2) |
| 151–200 | 1 (0) | 3 (1) | (0) |
| 201–250 | 0 (0) | 0 (0) | (0) |
| 251–500 | 2 (1) | 4 (3) | (1) |
| 501+ | 4 (3) | 3 (3) | (0) |
| All Ranges | 82 (46) | 82 (46) | (46) |

Source: Interviews with random sample of former Mack workers.
[a] See note to Table 8 for explanation of numbers within and without parentheses.

gifts were purchased. Thus, unusual expenditures and hence total expenditures were maintained at a high level during April, largely for seasonal reasons. Had it not been for these seasonal factors, median total expenditures would have shown a greater decline. During the eighth and ninth months of unemployment, unusual expenditures declined, and so did total expenditures. Yet even in these months (June and July), a large number of wedding and graduation gifts were purchased, a fact which also helped to maintain total expenditures.

Thus, among the items for which dollar amounts were secured in the survey, most of the decline in expenditures in the first survey month of unemployment was in recurrent expenditures, and primarily in food. On the other hand, in the eighth and ninth months of unemployment, the decline was largely in nonrecurrent, or unusual expenditures.

Among those expenditure items for which no dollar amounts were secured, shown in Table 13, the respondents indicated that clothing, furniture and appliances, and recreational and educational activities were the categories on which less was spent during months of unemployment than during the month of employment. Many re-

**TABLE 13. Changes During Unemployment in Levels of Family Expenditure for Items Not Priced in the Survey**

| Item | Spent Less | Spent at Same Rate | Spent More | Never Bought Item |
|---|---|---|---|---|
| | | Number of Respondents Who: | | |
| Clothing | 63 | 33 | 4 | 1 |
| Furniture and appliances | 58 | 28 | 3 | 13 |
| Recreational and educational expenses (for example, books, movies, magazines) | 56 | 30 | 1 | 13 |
| Transportation (for respondent) | 53 | 17 | 29 | 3 |
| Transportation (for other family members) | 21 | 64 | 2 | 13 |
| Laundry and dry cleaning | 30 | 69 | 0 | 1 |
| Contributions to charities and churches | 40 | 60 | 0 | 2 |
| Items for personal care (for example, haircuts, cosmetics) | 23 | 78 | 0 | 1 |

Source: Interviews with random sample of former Mack workers.

spondents also indicated that they spent less for transportation, but a substantial number said they spent more—probably while looking for jobs. Most respondents indicated that there was no change in their expenditures for the other items listed.

*Income and Expenditures*

Table 14 combines median monthly income and median monthly expenditures. What is striking about the table is the very large gap between expenditures and income for the median family in the month of employment. Of course, part of the explanation lies in the high rate of savings of Mack workers and in the omitted expenditure items. Savings for the median family in the employed month were $54. How much the median family spent for clothing, transportation, recreation, tobacco, alcohol, personal items, small appliances, and so forth, is a question which cannot be answered. However, it does not seem reasonable that the entire gap between income and expenditure could be explained by these items. Another explanation may be the faulty memory of the respondents. Since, of the three months surveyed, the employed month was farthest in the past, the respondent's recollection of what he spent in that month may be the least reliable of the statements of expenditures. Whereas income data could often be verified by records, expenditure data

**TABLE 14. Comparison of Median Monthly Income With Expenditures by Family Status During Months of Employment and Unemployment**[a]

| Month and Budget Item | Dollar Amounts by Family Status | | |
| --- | --- | --- | --- |
| | | Married Families | |
| | All Families | Headed by Worker | Not Headed by Worker |
| **Employed Month:** | | | |
| Median Income | $587 (644) | $576 (612) | $775 (800) |
| Median Expenditures | 307 (317) | 300 (289) | 398 (417) |
| Excess Income | 280 (327) | 276 (323) | 377 (383) |
| **Sixth Unemployed Month:** | | | |
| Median Income | 347 (400) | 338 (382) | 633 (667) |
| Median Expenditures | 297 (304) | 283 (283) | 397 (406) |
| Excess Income | 50 (96) | 55 (99) | 236 (261) |
| **Eighth or Ninth Unemployed Month:** | | | |
| Median Income | (225) | (187) | (500) |
| Median Expenditures | (277) | (262) | (342) |
| Excess Income | (−52) | (−75) | (158) |

Source: Interviews with random sample of former Mack workers.
[a] See note to Table 8 for explanation of figures within and without parentheses.

generally could not. If this hypothesis is correct, expenditure data for the unemployed month are understated, and the gap was not really as wide as it appears in the table. This could also help to explain the relatively small decline in expenditures from the employed month to the sixth month of unemployment.

By the sixth month of unemployment the gap between median income and median expenditures had narrowed substantially, but income still exceeded expenditures among all types of respondents. During the eighth or ninth month of unemployment, median expenditures exceeded median income for all classes of respondents except nonheads of households.

Another way of viewing this financial adjustment is in terms of expenditures as a percentage of take-home income. As Table 15 shows, both recurrent and total expenditures rose substantially as a percentage of take-home income (for all categories of respondents) as the period of unemployment increased. The percentages rose substantially more for heads of households than for nonheads.

**TABLE 15. Family Expenditures as a Percentage of Take-Home Income**[a]

| Type of Expenditure and Family Status | Percent of Income in Employed Month | Percent of Income in: | |
|---|---|---|---|
| | | Sixth Unemployed Month | Ninth Unemployed Month |
| **Total Expenditures for:** | | | |
| All Families | 51  (50) | 78  (71) | (111) |
| Married Famlies: | | | |
| Headed by Worker | 48  (50) | 85  (77) | (130) |
| Not Headed by Worker | 54  (54) | 59  (59) | (75) |
| **Recurrent Expenditures for:** | | | |
| All Families | 48  (45) | 69  (57) | (130) |
| Married Families: | | | |
| Headed by Worker | 48  (45) | 71  (62) | (119) |
| Not Headed by Worker | 48  (48) | 54  (54) | (71) |

Source: Interviews with random sample of former Mack workers.
[a] See note to Table 8 for explanation of figures within and without parentheses.

These rising percentages were more a reflection of declining income than of declining expenditures.

Thus as the period of unemployment lengthened the propensity of Mack workers to consume increased, primarily because they attempted to hold to their previous consumption patterns as their income declined. This is an example of the kind of adjustment described by Duesenberry's "rachet effect."[21] Duesenberry argued that consumers adjust their consumption not only to current income but also to previous peak income. Thus, during their period of unemployment, Mack workers tried to protect the consumption standards acquired while they were working for Mack. As income fell they reduced consumption as little as possible (thus sharply reducing saving).

### The Role of Unemployment Compensation

Unemployment compensation was very helpful to all classes of respondents. Table 16 shows weekly unemployment insurance payments as a percentage of weekly recurrent expenditures. For all classes of respondents unemployment compensation seemed to provide substantial protection. Even though it was insufficient to meet

[21] See James S. Duesenberry, *Income, Saving, and the Theory of Consumer Behavior* (Harvard University Press, 1949).

**TABLE 16. Unemployment Compensation as a Percentage of Family Expenditures, Sixth Month of Unemployment**

| Family Status | Unemployment Compensation as a Median Percentage of: | |
| --- | --- | --- |
| | Total Weekly Expenditures | Recurrent Weekly Expenditures |
| All Families | 67 | 81 |
| Married Families: | | |
|   Headed by Worker | 68 | 83 |
|   Not Headed by Worker | 56 | 75 |

Source: Interviews with random sample of former Mack workers.

total expenditures, it was still adequate to provide for well over half of measured family outlays.

## Summary and Major Conclusions

This study was concerned with the following three general questions associated with the decision of the Mack Company to move its Plainfield, New Jersey, plant to Hagerstown, Maryland: (1) interplant transfers of workers; (2) the re-employment experience and problems of workers who did not transfer; and (3) the financial adjustment of the workers to unemployment.

### Interplant Transfers

The Mack Company wanted to discourage production workers from transferring to the new plant and thus directed company policy toward this end. Although the implementation of this policy varied from time to time, it is clear that the company was in general vague when it described conditions at the new plant but quite specific in describing conditions of severance. Separation payments were increased several times in an effort to discourage workers from transferring to the new plant.

One of the interesting questions which emerged from this situation was the identification of the important factors which guided workers' decisions to transfer or not to transfer. Did the large separation payments strongly influence workers to remain in New Jersey or were other factors more important? Interviews with a random sample of workers indicated that separation benefits combined with unemployment compensation did reduce workers' fears about the loss of income they would face during a potential period of unemployment but that this compensation was not the most important influence on their decision.

The determining influences in fact varied with the workers' occupational-skill status. Professional employees received very favorable terms of transfer and possessed strong company loyalty. The company encouraged their transfer by offering salaries equal to or higher than the ones they were currently receiving and by paying all relocation expenses. In addition, professional employees had, for the most part, lived in their area of New Jersey for shorter periods of time than had nonprofessional workers and they showed less reluctance to leave. The result was that a large proportion of them transferred with the company.

Production workers seemed largely motivated by two sets of factors. Those workers who had been with Mack for a long time felt attached to the company. They liked their jobs and did not want to lose the advantages of long seniority which they could carry with them. Some of them were older workers who feared that they would have difficulty finding another job if they stayed in New Jersey. On the other hand, most workers felt a strong geographic attachment to their area. They owned their homes; they had children in school or grown children who had settled nearby; they had friends and relatives in the area and were active in civic affairs. When area attachment was combined with the prospect of a substantial wage cut at the new plant in Maryland and the financial security which the company offered them in the form of separation or retirement benefits, most of them decided not to transfer. Among those who did transfer, job attachment outweighed area attachment in importance.

## Re-employment Experience and Problems

Since most of the production and clerical workers did not transfer to the new plant, there were suddenly nearly 3,000 unemployed workers in the Mack-affected area of New Jersey. About one-third were living in the vicinity of Plainfield, with other large concentrations in Highland Park, Somerville, and Perth Amboy. The rest were scattered over the state. Most of the affected area was at that time experiencing moderate unemployment (3.0 to 5.9 percent).

A random sample of workers interviewed nine to ten months after the shutdown revealed that at that time about 64 percent were employed, 23 percent were unemployed, 10 percent had withdrawn from the labor force, and 3 percent were still awaiting transfer to the new plant. Those workers who withdrew from the labor force were for the most part older people, some of whom would have withdrawn in a few years even if the plant had not moved, although a substantial portion would have continued to work for more than five years. Offsetting the loss to the labor force was the movement into the labor force of a number of wives who had previously been keeping house, but who, because of family financial need, went to work after the shutdown.

Workers who had found new jobs after the shutdown were in general earning much less than they had received at Mack. They were also working longer hours, but usually closer to their homes. Many of them were dissatisfied with their new jobs and were still searching for other employment. Most found their new jobs through their own initiative or through the help of a friend. Despite the intensive effort of the New Jersey State Employment Service (NJSES), only about 8 percent of the employed workers in the sample found jobs through this source.

The local union at Mack was strong and had pushed wages to a high level. Moreover, since Mack had operated under a quota-incentive system, most workers were able to earn a day's wages with less than eight hours of work. In general, Mack workers were semi-skilled experts who had mastered the technique of operating one machine rapidly and efficiently. Many of them could not read blueprints and use precision instruments, and most of them could not operate a variety of machines, but they were generally superbly skilled at running their own particular machine. In their own minds, they were skilled workers. When they approached a prospective employer, it was frequently with this attitude.

Within a few months after the layoff, rumors had spread throughout the state about the "ridiculous demands" which former Mack workers were making. In addition, several employers who hired Mack workers had unfortunate experiences with them. Some workers became dissatisfied with the lower pay and/or longer commuting distances in their new jobs, and quit. Others were found agitating among the regular employees of their new company for a stronger union. Still others proved unsatisfactory and were dismissed. The experience of some employers with Mack workers became a topic of conversation whenever employers met and, as a result, some of them informed the NJSES that under no circumstances would they hire former Mack employees. Other employers were willing to hire one or several, but not very many. Yet by the tenth month after the shutdown, about 70 percent of those still in the labor force were employed.

The success of the workers in finding new jobs depended on a variety of factors. Since the median age of Mack workers was forty-three years, age was naturally an important factor. Younger workers were considerably more successful in finding jobs than older workers and they found them more quickly. Education was also an important factor; a worker's chances for employment and the speed with which he was employed increased as his formal education increased. In addition, those workers who occupied positions as breadwinners in their families went back to work more quickly than others. Married males were considerably more successful in finding jobs than married females, perhaps because the financial needs of their families were greater.

The re-employment of a worker was affected by the area of New Jersey in which he lived. Since Mack workers had been accustomed to high wages, many were reluctant to accept jobs at lower rates of pay which involved relatively long commuting distances. Some consistently asked higher pay for jobs which required longer commutation. As a result, the impact of the shutdown tended to be more heavily concentrated in those areas where the workers lived than it would have been if the workers had been willing to commute to job-demand areas. Thus, those workers who lived in the areas of New Jersey which were most affected by the shutdown were at a distinct disadvantage by comparison with workers who lived in other areas.

Skill was another important factor in re-employment. As suggested above, many of the specialized skills Mack workers possessed were not transferable to other industries in the area, and were not useful in small machine shops which demanded workers who possessed a variety of machine skills. There was, of course, a

small nucleus of genuinely highly skilled workers and some unskilled workers. The skilled workers experienced little difficulty in
finding new jobs and by the tenth month all of them in the sample
were working. Of the three groups—skilled, semiskilled, and unskilled—the semiskilled workers were least successful in their job
search. Perhaps the reason for this is that, more than any other
group, they tended to overrate their own skills and thus clung longest to unrealistic job demands. Unskilled workers, realizing that
they had little to offer a prospective employer, were more willing to
accept prevailing rates of pay than semiskilled workers, many of
whom were forced eventually to accept unskilled jobs because of
lack of demand for their specialized skills.

Thus, it was among the semiskilled workers that the need for
retraining was most vital. Unfortunately, the Mack-affected area
did not qualify for federal aid at the time, so retraining was limited
to the few workers who could be accommodated by county vocational
schools and to those who were willing to accept jobs as trainees at
low rates of pay.

Among five variables tested for their relationship to re-employment—age, skill, sex and family status, education, and area of residence—age was quantitatively the most important as an explanation of the length of workers' frictional adjustment period. Employer hostility and worker attitudes were important factors which could
not be expressed quantitatively.

On the other hand, one aspect of worker attitudes about which
some quantitative statements could be made was the extent to which
separation payments influenced the search for a job. A great deal of
evidence exists that Mack workers were particular about the kind of
jobs they would accept. Many had established definite standards—
of pay, commuting distance, and type of work—which severely limited their availability. Hundreds of job referrals by the NJSES were
refused by Mack workers because the jobs did not measure up to
their demands. Many of the Employment Service interviewers who
were "specialists" in Mack placements expressed the opinion on a
mail questionnaire and through personal interviews that the combination of separation payments and unemployment compensation
was largely responsible for the Mack workers' reluctance to accept
jobs. These "specialists" argued that the financial position of a

worker was reflected in his attitude toward re-employment. Some of the workers themselves admitted that if it had not been for the large separation payments they would have been willing to accept substandard jobs.

The sample of Mack workers interviewed collected separation payments ranging from zero to about $9,000. Almost all of them were eligible for the state's maximum unemployment compensation payment of $50 a week for twenty-six weeks. Since most workers were eligible for the maximum payment, this factor could be treated as a constant and the relationship between the amount of separation pay and the length of the frictional period could be tested.

An examination of the relationship between the amount of separation pay and the length of the frictional adjustment period using the multiple regression technique revealed no correlation between these variables. Since there was some multicollinearity between separation pay and age through seniority, regressions were examined across age groups, but these also were found insignificant. Moreover, separation payments deflated for family size were not correlated with the length of the frictional period.

Yet to demonstrate the absence of a relationship between separation pay and the frictional period in this way is not conclusive proof that it did not influence workers' attitudes. Separation pay may have influenced attitudes in a more complex manner through its relationship to the workers' entire asset position. Perhaps total assets, rather than separation pay alone, was the influential variable. Unfortunately, no data were available with which to test this possibility.

### The Financial Adjustment of Workers to Unemployment

About 30 percent of the sample of Mack workers was unemployed for longer than six months, and about 20 percent was still unemployed at the time of the interviews, nine to ten months after the shutdown. Those workers who were willing to submit to an extended interview and who had been unemployed for at least six months were asked a series of questions about their financial adjustment during unemployment.

The most important kinds of financial adjustment were: cutting expenditures on such items as food, clothing, recreation, travel and vacations; postponing the purchase of items—especially automobiles—which the family was definitely planning to buy; curbing installment buying; cancelling insurance policies; and dissaving instead of saving. Before the shutdown most Mack families were able to save part of their monthly pay check; afterward, most families became dissavers.

A detailed analysis of consumer spending in three months—the last month of employment, the last month of unemployment in which the respondent collected unemployment benefits, and the most recent month of unemployment after the exhaustion of unemployment compensation benefits—indicated that consumers adjusted some categories of expenditures downward in response to falling income, but that the decline in consumer spending was substantially less than the decline in income. Expenditures for food especially declined, but most other categories of recurrent expenditures, such as rent, mortgage payments, and medical care, were little changed. In general, there was a substantial core of expenditures over which the workers had little control: rent, mortgage payments, taxes, insurance, medical care, and items purchased on the installment plan before the layoff. Expenditures on most other types of items were cut, but the evidence indicates that workers made every effort to cling to previously established standards of consumption.

The expenditure decline accelerated after unemployment compensation was exhausted. In general, unemployment benefits covered recurrent or ordinary expenditures for most families and by this standard they could be considered to have been adequate.

## APPENDIX A

# Tables of Detailed Survey Results

The tables in this Appendix show the principal findings of a survey of workers who remained in New Jersey when the Mack plant moved to Maryland. The survey was conducted during the ninth and tenth months after the shutdown of the plant. See Appendix B for a description of the procedure followed in the survey.

## TABLE A-1. Distribution of Employed Workers by Industry, Summer 1962

| Industry | Number of Workers | Percent |
|---|---|---|
| Aircraft and auto manufacturing | 22 | 9 |
| Other manufacturing | 126 | 51 |
| Trades | 23 | 9 |
| Services | 56 | 22 |
| Construction | 13 | 5 |
| Sales | 1 | —ᵃ |
| Transportation | 7 | 3 |
| Other | 1 | —ᵃ |
| Total | 249 | 100 |

Source: Interviews with random sample of former Mack workers.
Note: Details may not add to totals due to rounding.
ᵃ Less than 0.5 percent.


## TABLE A-2. Comparison of Mack Wages with Wages of Employed Workers in New Jobs, Summer 1962

| Gross Weekly Wage Range (In Dollars) | All Workers in Sample | | Re-employed Workers in Sample | |
|---|---|---|---|---|
| | Number | Percent | Number | Percent |
| Under $75 | 0 | 0 | 36 | 15 |
| 75–100 | 47 | 13 | 96 | 40 |
| 101–115 | 45 | 12 | 40 | 17 |
| 116–125 | 35 | 10 | 21 | 9 |
| 126–140 | 72 | 20 | 23 | 10 |
| 141–155 | 74 | 20 | 10 | 4 |
| 156–175 | 62 | 17 | 8 | 3 |
| 176–200 | 26 | 7 | 5 | 2 |
| Over 200 | 4 | 1 | 1 | —ᵃ |
| Not availableᵇ | 2 | — | 9 | — |
| Total | 367 | 100 | 249 | 100 |

Source: Interviews with random sample of former Mack workers.
Note: Details may not add to totals due to rounding.
ᵃ Less than 0.5 percent.
ᵇ Excluded from the percentage calculations

### TABLE A-3. Weekly Hours of Employed Workers in New Jobs, Summer 1962

| Weekly Hours of Work | Re-employed Workers in Sample | Percent |
|---|---|---|
| Less than 20 | 5 | 2 |
| 21–30 | 3 | 1 |
| 31–34 | 3 | 1 |
| 35–40 | 158 | 67 |
| Over 40 | 66 | 28 |
| Varied[a] | 14 | — |
| Total | 249 | 100 |

Source: Interviews with random sample of former Mack workers.
Note: Details may not add to totals due to rounding.
[a] Excluded from the percentage calculations.


### TABLE A-4. Former Gross Weekly Mack Wages of Workers Who Remained in the Labor Force After the Shutdown, Summer 1962

| Gross Weekly Wage Range (In Dollars) | Re-employed Workers in Sample | | Unemployed Workers in Sample | | Total Workers in Sample | |
|---|---|---|---|---|---|---|
| | Number | Percent | Number | Percent | Number | Percent |
| Under $75 | 0 | 0 | 0 | 0 | 0 | 0 |
| $75–100 | 29 | 12 | 10 | 14 | 39 | 13 |
| 101–115 | 26 | 11 | 12 | 17 | 38 | 12 |
| 116–125 | 24 | 10 | 8 | 11 | 32 | 10 |
| 126–140 | 55 | 23 | 9 | 13 | 64 | 21 |
| 141–155 | 44 | 18 | 17 | 24 | 61 | 20 |
| 156–175 | 40 | 17 | 10 | 14 | 50 | 16 |
| 176–200 | 18 | 7 | 4 | 6 | 22 | 7 |
| Over 200 | 3 | 1 | 1 | 1 | 4 | 1 |
| Not available | 2 | 1 | 0 | 0 | 2 | 1 |
| Total | 241 | 100 | 71 | 100 | 312 | 100 |

Source: Interviews with random sample of former Mack workers.
Note: Details may not add to totals due to rounding.

236

## TABLE A-5. Comparison of Distances Commuted to Work by All Employees at Mack and by Respondents with New Jobs, Summer 1962

| Round-trip Mileage Between Home and Work | All Mack Workers | | Re-employed Workers | |
|---|---|---|---|---|
| | Number | Percent | Number | Percent |
| 5 or less | 101 | 28 | 79 | 34 |
| 6–10 | 37 | 10 | 30 | 13 |
| 11–15 | 31 | 8 | 24 | 10 |
| 16–20 | 64 | 17 | 33 | 14 |
| 21–30 | 87 | 24 | 32 | 14 |
| 31–40 | 23 | 6 | 10 | 4 |
| 41–50 | 13 | 4 | 3 | 1 |
| Over 50 | 11 | 3 | 24 | 10 |
| Not available[a] | — | — | 14 | — |
| Total | 367 | 100 | 249 | 100 |

Source: Interviews with random sample of former Mack workers.
Note: Details may not add to totals due to rounding.
[a] Excluded from the percentage calculations.


## TABLE A-6. Sources of Jobs Held by Re-employed Workers at Time of Survey, Summer 1962

| Source of New Job | Number of Re-employed Workers | Percent |
|---|---|---|
| State Employment Service | 20 | 8 |
| Friend | 28 | 11 |
| Relative | 55 | 22 |
| Newspaper advertisement | 6 | 2 |
| Own initiative | 89 | 36 |
| Had worked at new job before Mack employment | 19 | 8 |
| Private placement agency | 12 | 5 |
| Other | 20 | 8 |
| Total | 249 | 100 |

Source: Interviews with random sample of former Mack workers.
Note: Details may not add to totals due to rounding.

## TABLE A-7. Workers' Attitudes Toward Permanency of New Jobs, Summer 1962

| Worker's Attitude Toward New Job | Number of Re-employed Workers | Percent |
|---|---|---|
| Viewed job as permanent | 135 | 54 |
| Viewed job as temporary; looking elsewhere | 92 | 37 |
| Did not know whether job was temporary or permanent | 22 | 9 |
| Total | 249 | 100 |

Source: Interviews with random sample of former Mack workers.
Note: Details may not add to totals due to rounding.

## TABLE A-8. Workers' General Opinion of New Jobs as Compared With Old, Summer 1962

| Worker Felt New Job Was: | Number of Re-employed Workers | Percent |
|---|---|---|
| Better than Mack position | 60 | 24 |
| Worse than Mack position | 139 | 56 |
| Equal to Mack position | 50 | 20 |
| Total | 249 | 100 |

Source: Interviews with random sample of former Mack workers.
Note: Details may not add to totals due to rounding.

238

## TABLE A-9. Workers' Reasons for Withdrawing from the Labor Force After the Shutdown, Summer 1962

| Withdrawn Worker's Expressed Reason | Number of Withdrawn Workers | Percent |
|---|---|---|
| Advanced age | 31 | 84 |
| Pregnancy | 4 | 11 |
| Illness | 1 | 3 |
| Lack of training | 1 | 3 |
| Total | 37 | 100 |

Source: Interviews with random sample of former Mack workers.
Note: Details may not add to totals due to rounding.


## TABLE A-10. Number of Years Respondents Had Planned to Remain in the Labor Force If the Plant Had Not Closed, Summer 1962

| Years Worker Had Planned to Remain in the Labor Force | Number of Workers Withdrawn from Labor Force | Percent |
|---|---|---|
| Less than 1 year | 11 | 30 |
| 1–2 | 7 | 19 |
| 3–4 | 9 | 24 |
| 5–6 | 5 | 14 |
| 7–8 | 4 | 11 |
| 9–10 | 1 | 3 |
| Total | 37 | 100 |

Source: Interviews with random sample of former Mack workers.
Note: Details may not add to totals due to rounding.

## TABLE A-11. Minimum Wage Acceptable to Respondents Who Had Experienced Some Unemployment After the Shutdown, Summer 1962

| Minimum Acceptable Hourly Wage Range (In Dollars) | All Workers Unemployed at Some Time | | Workers Who Specified Precise Minimum Standards | |
|---|---|---|---|---|
| | Number | Percent | Number | Percent |
| Any reasonable wage | 88 | 27 | — | — |
| $1.50–2.00 | 33 | 10 | 33 | 14 |
| 2.01–2.50 | 93 | 29 | 93 | 40 |
| 2.51–2.75 | 69 | 21 | 69 | 30 |
| 2.76–3.00 | 8 | 2 | 8 | 3 |
| 3.01–3.25 | 21 | 7 | 21 | 9 |
| 3.26–3.50 | 4 | 1 | 4 | 2 |
| 3.51–4.00 | 1 | —ª | 1 | —ª |
| 4.01–4.50 | 2 | 1 | 2 | 1 |
| Over 4.50 | 3 | 1 | 3 | 1 |
| Total | 322 | 100 | 234 | 100 |

Source: Interviews with random sample of former Mack workers.
Note: Details may not add to totals due to rounding.
ª Less than 0.5 percent.

## TABLE A-12. Maximum Round-Trip Commutation Acceptable to Respondents Who Had Experienced Some Unemployment After the Shutdown, Summer 1962

| Maximum Acceptable Round-Trip Commutation (In Miles) | All | | Workers Who Specified Precise Minimum Standards | |
|---|---|---|---|---|
| | Number | Percent | Number | Percent |
| Any reasonable distance | 158 | 49 | — | — |
| Under 6 | 15 | 5 | 15 | 9 |
| 6–10 | 10 | 3 | 10 | 6 |
| 11–15 | 9 | 3 | 9 | 5 |
| 16–20 | 31 | 10 | 31 | 19 |
| 21–30 | 39 | 12 | 39 | 24 |
| 31–40 | 47 | 15 | 47 | 29 |
| 41–50 | 6 | 2 | 6 | 4 |
| Over 50 | 7 | 2 | 7 | 4 |
| Total | 322 | 100 | 164 | 100 |

Source: Interviews with random sample of former Mack workers.
Note: Details may not add to totals due to rounding.

APPENDIX B

# Sampling Procedures in
# New Jersey and Maryland

No complete and fully accurate list of Mack workers affected by the layoff was available from any source. The company turned over a list of its workers to the NJSES, but this list provided no information except the names and addresses of workers and, moreover, it was found to be inaccurate since some workers who were not with the company at the time of the layoff were included on the list, and others, especially some of the salaried, had been omitted. According to the company, plant employment figures on October 31, 1961—the day of the shutdown—were as follows:

| Class of Employee | Number |
|---|---|
| Supervisory and administrative | 238 |
| Hourly | 2,448 |
| Salaried | 505 |
| Total plant employment | 3,191 |

*The New Jersey Sample*

The NJSES had decided to make the Mack case a special project and had ordered each of its local offices to separate their files on Mack workers from the rest of their employment and claims services. Many Mack workers were registered *en masse* at the union hall in Plainfield while others came to the local offices in the usual way. In any event, each of the local offices in the Mack-affected area had a Mack file which contained, in addition to the name and address of each registered worker, his age, employment status, and much additional information. A check of the local office files revealed that over 2,800 of the Mack workers had been registered by NJSES. I decided to use the NJSES local office records as the master list and then add to it other names by cross-checking against the Mack layoff list. The NJSES list was found to contain its share of normal clerical mistakes, but in general it was highly accurate. Since the NJSES list was incomplete, however, supplementary information from another source was required.

In late May, 1961, a team of six NJSES employees went out to the local offices and copied data from the local office records onto special forms. Forms were prepared for each Mack worker who had registered in the local offices or filed a claim in the local offices. The job was completed in mid-June and the forms were returned to the central office in Trenton. Since some workers were registered in more than one local office, the forms were arranged by social security number, and all duplicates were removed. IBM machines were used to prepare lists of workers who had not contacted the local offices, but who did appear on the Mack layoff list. These lists were then double-checked against the local office forms to make sure no duplicates were present. It was found that there were 2,863 Mack workers with local office records. Seventy-nine of these had interstate claims or out-of-state addresses and were dropped from the sampling population, since no funds were available for interviews outside of New Jersey. The IBM machines uncovered an additional 236 Mack workers with no local office records. Nineteen of these had out-of-state addresses and were removed from the sampling population. These two sources together accounted for 3,099 Mack employees out of a total of 3,196 on the Mack payroll on October 31. A check revealed that most of the missing employees were supervisory and administrative personnel who transferred immediately to Hagerstown with the company, and as a result were not laid off. They therefore did not contact the Employment Service and did not appear on the Mack layoff list. In any event, after elimination and cross-checking, the sample population consisted of 3,001 Mack employees.

The local office forms and additional population cards were then sorted by local office areas. Local offices were grouped into five geographic areas—Plainfield, Highland Park, East and Southeastern Jersey, North and Northeastern Jersey, West and Central Jersey. The sample was divided among the geographic areas in the same proportion as their relative weights in the population. A sampling proportion of 15 percent (450 workers) was selected largely on the basis of financial constraints. Selection of a sample by geographic areas was convenient since the NJSES files were arranged by local offices. The sample was selected by the procedure shown in Table B-1. A proportionate stratified random sample was then selected from each geographic area by age and employment status at the time of the local office survey. (Employment status was determined by whether the worker was or was not actively seeking work through the NJSES.)

**TABLE B-1. Geographic Allocation of the New Jersey Sample**

| Area | Proportion of State Population in Area | | Total Sample of Workers | | Subsample of Workers |
|---|---|---|---|---|---|
| Plainfield | .39420 | × | 450 | = | 178 |
| Highland Park | .29623 | × | 450 | = | 134 |
| West and Central Jersey | .14562 | × | 450 | = | 65 |
| North and Northeastern Jersey | .08064 | × | 450 | = | 36 |
| East and Southeastern Jersey | .08331 | × | 450 | = | 37 |

Source: Interviews with random sample of former Mack workers.

Once the sample was determined by strata, the survey director and several personnel of the NJSES selected the sample at random from their files and from the supplementary lists compiled for that purpose. Names, addresses, and other relevant information were transcribed from the files and lists onto assignment cards, each person in the sample was assigned a number, and the sample was allocated geographically among the interviewing staff.

Interviewers were recruited during May and June through two sources—the local offices of the NJSES and the Sociology Department at Rutgers University. Initially, there were seven interviewers—four with previous interviewing experience. One of the inexperienced interviewers proved ineffective and was replaced almost immediately. Two other members of the original staff resigned for personal reasons before the survey was completed. Later, during the second month of the survey, three experienced interviewers and one inexperienced interviewer were added to the staff in order to insure completion of the survey on schedule.

Interviewers were trained at special sessions by the survey director on the techniques of interviewing as well as on the use of the survey form. In addition, the survey director visited each interviewer every week and phoned each of them frequently.

During his weekly visits with the interviewing staff, the survey director picked up the completed interview forms. He then edited and coded the forms for IBM processing. If there were any errors, the interviewer was contacted immediately in order to preclude repetition of the mistake.

The survey ended on September 1, 1962. Classification of workers surveyed as of that date is shown in Table B-2.

The extent to which workers refused to be interviewed was minimized by sending out a different interviewer in cases in which respondents refused to talk to the first interviewer assigned. The group of workers who moved out of New Jersey could not be contacted since no

**TABLE B-2. Classification of Status of Workers Contacted in the New Jersey Survey, September 1, 1962**

| Survey Status of Worker | Number of Workers | Percent |
|---|---|---|
| Survey completed | 367 | 82 |
| Moved out of state | 14 | 3 |
| Moved to Hagerstown | 22 | 5 |
| Not eligible for survey | 11 | 2 |
| Deceased | 3 | 1 |
| In armed services | 1 | —ᵃ |
| In college | 1 | —ᵃ |
| Refused interview | 8 | 2 |
| Could not be contacted | 23 | 5 |
| Total | 450 | 100 |

Source: Interviews with random sample of former Mack workers.
ᵃ Less than 0.5 percent.

funds were available for distant interviews. More than twenty—or nearly one-third—of the nonrespondents had moved with the company to its new plant in Hagerstown, Maryland.

An analysis of the nonrespondents by stratification criteria to determine how nonrespondents differed from the sample population indicated that, by such standards and with a few exceptions, they were very similar.

### The Hagerstown Sample

The Mack Company provided names and addresses of 301 employees who transferred with the company to its new plant. At the time the list was drawn up, a number of these employees had not yet moved to Maryland. They were not included in the Hagerstown sample. Many of the top executives were also excluded.

Since no other information was available, a simple random sample of seventy employees in Hagerstown was selected. Forty-nine interviews were completed. Many of the addresses on the company list proved to be only temporary and no forwarding addresses could be found in many cases. Only two people refused to be interviewed.

The interviews were conducted by a professional interviewer from the Maryland State Employment Service who worked on the survey after regular working hours. The interviews in Hagerstown were completed about the same time as those in New Jersey.

# Methodology of the Expenditure Study

From 1954 through 1958, seven budget studies were conducted in six states to determine the adequacy of state unemployment benefits. Studies were made in the following labor markets: Pittsburgh, Pennsylvania (August, 1954); Tampa-St. Petersburg, Florida (October, 1956); Anderson-Greenville-Spartanburg, South Carolina (March, 1957); Albany-Schenectady-Troy, New York (April, 1957); Portland, Oregon (March, 1958); St. Louis, Missouri (April, 1958); and Utica, New York (October, 1958). In each of the first six cases, a sample of about 300 unemployment compensation claimants was selected from the files of the state office of employment security for intensive interviewing. The interviews (which averaged about three hours in length) gathered expenditure and income data for the twelve months prior to the survey.

The study in Utica, New York, used a much larger sample (about 800) than the others and confined its attention to two months: the last full month of employment and the most recent month of unemployment. The advantage of this procedure was that costs of research were held to a minimum and analysis of a much larger sample was feasible. An excellent summary and analysis of these seven studies has already been published by Father Joseph M. Becker.[1]

The questionnaire completed by former Mack workers for this study was a revised version of the one used in Utica, New York, by the Bureau of Applied Social Research at Columbia University for the New York State Department of Labor.[2]

Only workers who had been unemployed for at least six months and who were still in the labor force were considered eligible for the budget

[1] Joseph M. Becker, *The Adequacy of the Benefit Amount in Unemployment Insurance* (Michigan State University, 1961).

[2] For a complete discussion of the methodology used in the Utica study, see *Unemployment Insurance Beneficiaries in Utica, A Procedural Report of the Columbia University Bureau of Applied Social Research* (The Bureau, June 1959).

study. There were several reasons for limiting the sample in this way: (1) Funds were not available for an intensive, extended interview of all workers in the original sample. (2) Experience had shown that workers who are unemployed currently or who have recently been unemployed for an extended period are more willing to submit to an extended, intensive interview than other workers. (3) It was felt that workers who had been unemployed for at least six months were more likely than workers unemployed for lesser periods to have made conscious changes in their family expenditures and that they therefore would be better prepared to report these changes to interviewers.

For workers who were continuously unemployed from the plant shutdown to the time of the interviews, three months were chosen for comparison—the last normal month of employment (September 1961, in most cases), the last month during which the respondent collected unemployment compensation for the entire month (April 1962, in most cases), and the most recent complete month before the interview (June or July, 1962). In this way it was possible to compare the family budget during three distinct stages: employment, unemployment with unemployment compensation, and unemployment after unemployment compensation had been exhausted. For workers who had returned to work before the interview, of course, only the first two stages listed above could be analyzed.

The budget study was an extension of the regular interviews on which earlier parts of this study were based and took an average of forty-five additional minutes of interview time. In brief, the procedure consisted of asking the respondent how much he and his family spent for selected classes of recurrent expenditures—for food and rent, for example—during the selected months. The categories are specified and discussed in the text. In some cases, it was found that families had kept records; in others, workers had to rely on memory. The listing of recurrent expenditure items was supplemented by a listing of unusual expenses for items such as repairs, gifts, and taxes. No attempt was made to account for every dollar of unusual expenditure during any survey month. Income data were also collected for each family member, and, in addition, each worker was asked to specify amounts saved and borrowed in each month.

After each interview, the questionnaires were carefully audited. The interview included a number of cross-check questions to test the accuracy of respondents' answers. Before actually securing any financial data from him, the interviewer asked each worker a number of questions about his spending habits. If these answers were clearly inconsistent with the financial data secured later in the interview, the validity of the interview was questioned, and in most such cases the questionnaire was discarded. The financial data were also closely audited. As a test for accuracy, a ratio was developed, with total family expenditures as the numerator and total expendable family income as the denominator. To determine expendable family income, take-home income was increased by amounts borrowed during the month, by money paid back to the family from loans, by savings expended, and decreased by amounts added to savings. All questionnaires which passed the tests of internal consistency mentioned above and whose ratios fell within the range of 50 to 80 percent were accepted as valid. This range was the same one used in the New York study, for which it seemed to work very well. If data for one or more of the months did not fall within the acceptable range, the respondent was recalled. In cases where minor errors appeared, the recall was made by phone; in other more serious cases the respondent was reinterviewed at his home. Of 100 interviews conducted for the expenditure study, sixty-eight recalls were required, and the financial data on eighteen of the questionnaires were considered to be unusable after attempts were made to obtain more valid information. In most cases it was found that the errors which were made involved savings. The concept of savings used in the study was a broad one which included money held as cash in the household. In considering his savings for the month, a respondent often ignored cash held around the house. His positive savings were frequently understated by his failure to consider this cash to be savings and thus the amount of savings he spent was often understated for the same reason.

The major difficulty in conducting the expenditure study was that interviewers had to rely largely on the respondents' memory. As a partial means of overcoming this problem, interviewers asked that married workers' wives be present since their memories about financial matters proved much more reliable than their husbands'. It is significant that six of the seven interviews held with unmarried men proved to be unusable because of inconsistent data—a much higher percentage of rejection than for any other category in the sample. Even with audits and cross-checks, however, the data had to be accepted as an approximation and not much significance could be attached to small changes. Thus large changes over time and the direction of change were the major factors of interest.

Dollar figures for income were viewed as much more reliable than those for expenditures since in many cases records of income were available, and also because the sources of income in most cases were few and easily remembered. Expenditure data for rent, mortgage payments, utilities, repayment of loans, and very unusual items, such as a daughter's wedding, were also viewed as reliable since, in the case of the first three items, records were generally available and, in the case of the last two items, they occurred so infrequently that they were unlikely to have been forgotten. Other expenditure figures, such as those for food, seemed less reliable except in the few cases where records of detailed family budgeting were available. However, it appeared that many families did make a conscious attempt to reduce family expenditures on food as the period of unemployment increased, and although the dollar magnitude of expenditures may not have been reported precisely, the directions of change indicated were certainly valid.

# Index

Aaron, Henry, 5, 6, 61$n$
Abramovitz, Moses, 89$n$
Actuarially justified annuities: calculation of, 63-65; comparison with Social Security benefits, 65-69
Advisory Council on Public Assistance, 110$n$
Advisory Council on Social Security, 55, 58$n$, 59
Age: and re-employment, 187, 196, 198, 199, 211, 212, 213, 229, 230, 231; of welfare programs (*see also* Maturity of social insurance systems), 5, 15-17, 21, 24, 25-27, 28, 29, 30-31, 32-33, 36, 37, 39, 41, 42, 44
Age of population: and prevalence of blindness, 137; and public assistance expenditures, 112, 113-14, 137-39, 156, 157, 158, 159; and welfare expenditures, 21, 28$n$, 32-33, 34, 36-39
Aid to the Blind, 9, 97, 100, 104, 105, 106$n$, 107, 135-45, 160, 169, 171, 172
Aid to Families with Dependent Children, 9, 10, 97, 100, 104, 105, 106$n$, 107, 108, 119, 123-35, 139, 140, 159, 163, 169, 170, 171, 172
Aid to the Permanently and Totally Disabled, 9, 97, 100, 104, 105, 106$n$, 107, 108, 145-56, 169, 172
Alling, Elizabeth, 129$n$
Altmeyer, Arthur, 76, 79
Apparel industry, Massachusetts, 86, 87, 88$n$, 89, 90, 91, 92, 93
Area attachment, effect on worker transfer, 11, 183-84, 185, 186, 228
Australia, 20$n$
Austria, 17, 20$n$, 29

Automatic pension adjustment, 6, 50-52, 60
Automatic stabilization, 77-78

Bakke, E. Wight, 212-13$n$
Becker, Joseph, 79$n$
Belgium, 6, 20$n$, 41, 51
Bell, Winifred, 110$n$
Benefits. *See under* specific program heading.
Berolzheimer, Jozef, 98$n$
Blank, Theodore, 52$n$
Blindness, prevalence of, 135-37, 141, 171
Boles, Donald E., 98$n$
Brehm, C. T., 98$n$
Brown, Douglas, 79$n$
Brumberg, R. E., 18$n$
Bureau of Labor Statistics (U.S. Department of Labor), 221$n$

Canada, 20$n$
Cartwright, P. W., 89$n$
Catholic countries, family allowances in, 41
Children, proportion in population, 156, 157-59
Childhood dependency, prevalence of, 124-25, 171
Chile, 6, 17, 27$n$, 29, 41, 51
Clague, Ewan, 212-13$n$
Collins, Lora S., 8, 9, 10
Committee on Economic Security, 75
Commons, John R., 75
Commuting distance, and re-employment, 12, 189$n$, 190, 196, 204, 206, 230
Construction industry, Massachusetts, 85, 86, 87, 88, 89-92, 93

249